Quantitative Methods in Risk Analysis

A Practitioner's Guide

World Scientific Series in Finance

(ISSN: 2010-1082)

Published:*

Vol. 22 *Quantitative Methods in Risk Analysis: A Practitioner's Guide*
by Michael Foster (Dalhousie University, Canada) &
Leonard MacLean (Dalhousie University, Canada)

Vol. 21 *Selected Works of William T. Ziemba: A Memorial Volume*
edited by Leonard MacLean (Dalhousie University, Canada) &
Sébastien Lleo (NEOMA Business School, France)

Vol. 20 *Essays on Trading Strategy*
by Graham L. Giller (Giller Investments, USA)

Vol. 19 *Adventures in Financial Data Science: The Empirical Properties of Financial and Economic Data*
Second Edition
by Graham L. Giller (Giller Investments, USA)

Vol. 18 *Sports Analytics*
by Leonard C. Maclean (Dalhousie University, Canada) &
William T. Ziemba (University of British Columbia, Canada)

*To view the complete list of the published volumes in the series, please visit:
www.worldscientific.com/series/wssf

World Scientific Series in FINANCE vol. 22

Quantitative Methods in Risk Analysis

A Practitioner's Guide

Michael Foster
Dalhousie University, Canada

Leonard MacLean
Dalhousie University, Canada

World Scientific

NEW JERSEY • LONDON • SINGAPORE • BEIJING • SHANGHAI • HONG KONG • TAIPEI • CHENNAI • TOKYO

Published by

World Scientific Publishing Co. Pte. Ltd.
5 Toh Tuck Link, Singapore 596224
USA office: 27 Warren Street, Suite 401-402, Hackensack, NJ 07601
UK office: 57 Shelton Street, Covent Garden, London WC2H 9HE

Library of Congress Cataloging-in-Publication Data
Names: Foster, Michael, 1946– author | MacLean, L. C. (Leonard C.) author
Title: Quantitative methods in risk analysis : a practitioner's guide / Michael Foster, Dalhousie University, Canada, Leonard MacLean, Dalhousie University, Canada.
Description: Singapore ; Hackensack, NJ : World Scientific Publishing Co. Pte. Ltd, [2026] | Series: World scientific series in finance, 2010-1082 ; vol. 22 | Includes bibliographical references and index.
Identifiers: LCCN 2025041965 | ISBN 9789814327091 hardcover | ISBN 9789819824489 paperback | ISBN 9789814329996 ebook | ISBN 9789819824472 ebook other
Subjects: LCSH: Risk assessment | Quantitative research
Classification: LCC HD61 .F68 2026 | DDC 658.15/5--dc23/eng/20260120
LC record available at https://lccn.loc.gov/2025041965

British Library Cataloguing-in-Publication Data
A catalogue record for this book is available from the British Library.

For any available supplementary material, please visit
https://www.worldscientific.com/worldscibooks/10.1142/7957#t=suppl

Desk Editors: Nambirajan Karuppiah/Pui Yee Lum

Typeset by Stallion Press
Email: enquiries@stallionpress.com

Preface

The world we inhabit is structured by systems which transform states between time points. The state of a transformation is typically random, with many possible outcomes. So, the system outcome is a stochastic, dynamic process. Part of the variation in outcome is the result of characteristics of the system. The characteristics can be endogenous design features or exogenous environmental factors in which the system operates. As well, there is idiosyncratic variation. This general structure applies to biological, social, health, and economic systems.

A significant contributor to system transformation is human decisions. That is, systems trajectories are partly controlled by use and maintenance interventions. The record of past trajectories and maintenance decisions provides valuable information about the state transformation process and the impact of decisions. The consequence of decisions is revealed in the data.

In practice, there are system outcomes which are undesirable, and reaching such states constitutes a system failure. Assuming there is a threshold for failure, the history of system outcomes can be analyzed for the rate and consequence of failures. Traditionally, the failure doublet (rate, average failure size) is considered the essence of risk.

With the potential for controlling risk in decision-making, the decisions which satisfy a specified risk condition define a feasibility set. Within the feasibility set, the decision-dependent outcomes can be compared and possibly ordered. The ordering implies a preference relation, and there should be consensus on the relation and its properties.

There are distributions over outcomes which have the same risk profile. However, the ordering of distributions will introduce other features, such as the expectation. In many systems, there is a trade-off between expectation and risk. The objective with decisions is to anticipate positive outcomes while maintaining a low risk of failure.

The chapters in this volume develop the methodology for selecting decisions which control risk and optimize returns from a stochastic dynamic system. The methods are based on models for the operation of a system. It is understood that real-world systems do not operate according to equations defining a model for the system, but techniques for calibrating the model to actual system outcomes are available. The error in the calibration is an important part of the performance of decisions based on models.

In Chapter 1, we have an overview of the foundations of risk analysis. The systems framework is defined, and elements of the system structure which are detailed in subsequent chapters are introduced. The emphasis is on exogenous factors which impact endogenous system components and maintenance decisions which reflect the importance placed on the state of components.

The core concept of risk is developed in Chapter 2. The outcome from system operation is uncertain which is modeled with a probability distribution. With the probability assignment to real values of a random variable, the percentiles and quantiles (inverse percentiles) are important quantities in risk. With a specified percentile and an associated threshold quantile, the outcome distribution quantile from the system is compared with the threshold quantile to define failure. Failure size is calculated by averaging the quantiles below the threshold quantile. The chance and size of failure are the risk measures which are emphasized. They can be determined from an empirical distribution or a theoretical distribution. A standard theoretical distribution is the Gaussian or normal. An advantage of the normal distribution is the formulas for risk measures. The formulas are determined by the mean and variance so that the variance is the measure of risk for a given mean.

In Chapter 3, we consider exogenous factors which can affect system operation. The factors condition the operating environment of the system, in effect generating factor-dependent systems. Part of the variability of system outcomes is attributable to the variation of factors and is therefore systemic. The mechanism for assessing the effects of factors is the linear factor model. Of course, this is a first-order approximation to the possible relationship between system component status and factor levels. The linear model has many analytic advantages. It separates the variability of outcomes into a systemic part explained by factors and an unexplained idiosyncratic part. That separation also carries over to the risk measures so that the systemic risk is explained. Also, the linear factor model equations are amenable to the estimation of equation coefficients from observations on system outcomes and factor levels.

There are important assumptions built into the linear model, and some alternative models which relax these assumptions are considered in Chapter 4. A logistic model focuses on the downside risk of failure, so it is attractive for risk calculations. It does have some similarity to the linear factor model. A nonparametric model which works with the empirical distribution is introduced with quantile regression. The empirical distribution for outcomes is linked to risk factors, and tests on the factor effects are analyzed in much the same manner as with the linear model. The quantile approach is less powerful than the linear model approach if the assumptions are satisfied. It is often the case with time series that there is a cyclical pattern. Some cycles are deterministic and can be incorporated into the linear model. However, the length of business cycles is random and is another source of random variation. An alternating regimes approach uses the same model (linear or quantile) within a regime but a different model between regimes. The regime model is described with the linear factor model within a regime and a regime switching which follows a Markov process.

Systems models and statistical techniques for estimating model parameters are methods for understanding the dynamics of the system outcomes. In particular, identifying the impact of past decisions on the performance of a system is a basis for determining best practice. However, the objective with decisions is forward-looking, with the anticipation that today's decisions will produce desirable outcomes in the future. In Chapter 5, we consider the future outcomes from decisions, with the intention of determining the best decisions to control the uncertain future outcome from a stochastic dynamic system. Efficient decisions are not dominated, and efficient risk–return decisions are considered for the theoretical models proposed as an approximation to the operation of a stochastic system. Of course, the decisions are determined by estimated parameters, and the estimation error can be a major contributor to the performance of decisions.

A feature of the models proposed for the variation in system outcomes is that the idiosyncratic volatility is the same, independent of the state, although that is only applied within a regime in the hidden Markov model. As noted, improved decisions follow from improved estimates/forecasts of outcome distributions. In Chapter 6, the issue of state-dependent volatility is developed a bit more. The chapter is really an addendum, intended to continue the discussion of the variation of outcomes.

Included in the content of each chapter are real-world cases. The data from actual operating systems is analyzed with the methods presented in the chapter. The results of the analysis are generated with computational software. The theory leading up to the cases provides the background for the software algorithms. It is important to have a general understanding of the workings of the algorithms. So, familiarity with relevant software routines is assumed. Risk analysis is data and software-driven. Interpretation of the output from computer software will require an understanding of the system generating outcomes, the data on outcomes, and the computations producing tabulations. There are many software packages available to perform the computations. There is a brief introduction in the Appendices to the EViews software.

This book is not a compendium of quantitative methods in risk analysis. The intention is to introduce quantitative risk analysis and illustrate methods with cases. There is an extensive literature on risk, and each chapter has references which supplement the material covered. Some background is required to read the text, so the Appendices provide the basics of matrix algebra and probability.

About the Authors

Michael Foster is President of Canmac Economics Ltd. He has over 35 years of experience in economic analysis, modeling, and forecasting. Dr. Foster has conducted numerous program evaluations, economic impacts, strategic plans, market analysis, and general economic studies. He currently maintains a database of thousands of economic variables of the Atlantic Canadian, Provincial, and National economies supported by years of experience in data collection, including a thorough knowledge of Statistics Canada and other sources of economic data. Recent model-building projects include a Self-sufficiency Model of Atlantic Canada BDC, Input/Output Models of the Nova Scotia and Prince Edward Island economies, and Economic Benefits (investment impact) Models for the Nova Scotia and Prince Edward Island economies.

Dr. Foster has taught statistics and economics at Dalhousie University, St. Mary's University, and Cape Breton University, where he was Associate Chair, Management of Technological Change.

Leonard C. MacLean is Professor Emeritus in the Rowe School of Business at Dalhousie University in Halifax, Canada. Dr. MacLean has held visiting appointments at Cambridge University, University of Zimbabwe, and University of Indonesia. From 1989 to 1995, he served as Director of the School of Business Administration at Dalhousie University. He is the finance books editor for World Scientific Press and has held editorial positions with several journals. Professor MacLean's research focuses on stochastic models in finance, systems reliability in transportation, and sports analytics. He has published more than 100 articles, with papers appearing in journals such as *Journal of Economic Theory*, *Management Science*, *Quantitative Finance*, *Transportation Research*, *Safety Science*, *Journal of Banking and Finance*, and *Journal of Economic Dynamics and Control*. Professor MacLean has also co-authored eight books. This work has been funded by grants from the Natural Sciences and Engineering Council of Canada and the Herbert Lamb Trust. Dr. MacLean teaches in the areas of statistics and operations management.

Contents

Chapter 1

Foundations of Risk Analysis

1.1 Introduction

People and the environment in which they operate are subject to laws, both natural and human. The laws or rules and the operating environment characterize a system for transforming inputs into outputs. The output from a particular system is variable, depending on process factors. A scenario is an outcome or set of outcomes that are characterized by process factors.

When a system is engaged, the possible outcomes are anticipated. Some outcomes are undesirable and may be hazardous. Risk is a term associated with the occurrence of undesirable outcomes. To analyze risk, it is necessary to do the following:

(1) identify the possible system outcomes,
(2) determine the likelihood or chance of occurrence of outcomes,
(3) assess the consequences or impact of outcomes,
(4) specify the preferences, either individual or societal, for various outcomes,
(5) find a set of decisions that control the risk of undesirable consequences.

Figure 1.1 organizes the aspects of risk that comprise risk analysis.

This chapter will provide an overview of the dimensions of risk analysis associated with the outcomes of an operating system. We are considering stochastic dynamic systems, where the system outcome is stochastic (uncertain) and changes over time.

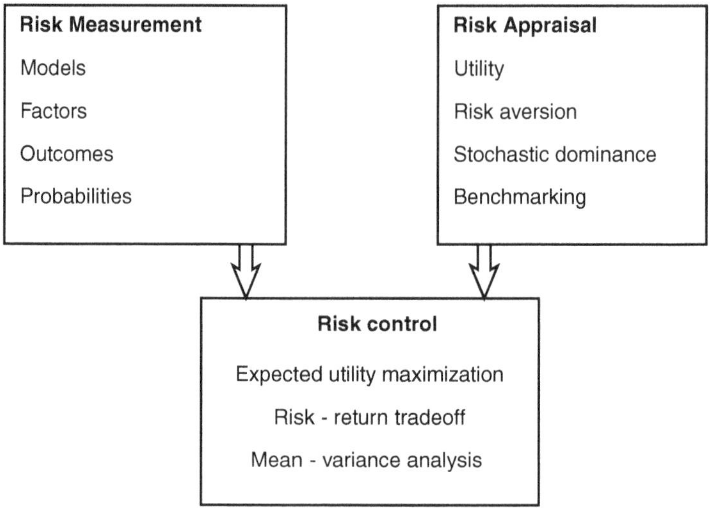

Figure 1.1. Dimensions of risk analysis.

1.2 Stochastic Systems

A system is an integrated set of interconnected components working to process inputs in a prescribed operating environment with specified outcomes and probabilities. In general, inputs are fed into a system that processes the inputs and produces an output. The system should add value to the input in producing an output. We are considering stochastic dynamic systems, where the input is the state from the most recent time and the system transforms or updates the status. For example, in a financial system determined by investment decisions, the status is current, wealth which is revised over time based on market dynamics and the investment decisions. In a mechanical operating system, such as aircraft, the status is the operating worthiness (airworthiness), which depends on the operating environment and decisions on use/maintenance over time. For a health system, the outcome is population health status, which is transformed with system capability and practice decisions.

In Figure 1.2, the attributes of a system which include contributory factors required for specifying, designing, and developing a system are presented.

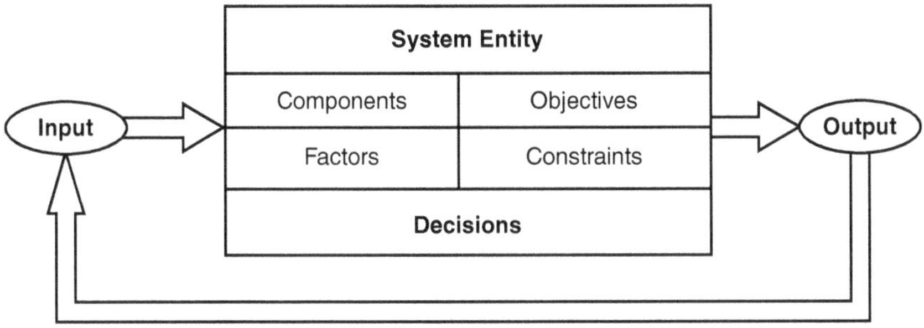

Figure 1.2. Analytical system entity construct.

The identified attributes are as follows:

1. **Components:** Discrete, identifiable internal building blocks within a larger system.
2. **Factors:** Broad external forces and conditions that influence system operation.
3. **Objectives:** Goals established for system performance.
4. **Constraints:** The restrictions on system operation.
5. **Decisions:** Investment in the functionality of system components.

At any given time, a dynamical system has a state given by a set of real numbers, which can be represented by a point in an appropriate state space. The evolution rule of the dynamical system describes the future states following from the current state. The rule is deterministic if, for a given time interval, only one future state follows from the current state. The rule is stochastic if a transition to multiple states is possible, with specified probabilities. Because of the uncertainty over transitions, stochastic systems involve the risk of undesirable states occurring. To quantify risk we will define the dynamic system with equations relating outputs to control decisions and internal characteristics of the system. We understand that real operating systems do not have dynamics which exactly follow laws defined by equations. The attempt is to approximate the dynamics for selected performance measures with equations.

1.2.1 *System equations*

In a dynamic system, the output is given in terms of a combination of the current system state and the current system control through the output equation. We will present equations in discrete time, so the input at time $t-h$ is transformed to the output at time t. Time points will be taken as $t = 1, \ldots, T$. The discretization is reasonable since the transformation takes an interval of time, and more importantly, observations on system status are recorded at discrete time points.

When modeling a system with equations, we first need to define types of variables: control variables, input/output variables, internal system component variables, and exogenous factors. We denote the control variables with X, the input/output variables with Y, and the internal system variables with R, and the exogenous factors with F. A generic definition and examples of the system variables are provided in Table 1.1. The term health status is used for the condition of a service system, but it includes operational concepts such as airworthiness of aircraft, functionality of machines, and the wealth output of an economic system.

The equations relating variables in the system will have systematic and idiosyncratic parts. We are concerned with the risk resulting from the uncertain or random outputs. The uncertainty in the systematic part is controlled, but there is randomness in the system that is independent of systematic factors.

The output equation is formulated as follows:

$$Y(t) = Y(t-1) + f(R(t), F(t), X(t)) + \varepsilon. \tag{1.1}$$

Table 1.1. System variables.

Variable	Notation	Example
System state	$Y(t)$	• Accumulated wealth at time t • System health status at time t
Component state	$R'(t) = (R_1(t), \ldots, R_n(t))$	• Return on assets at time t • Health status of components at time t
System factors	$F'(t) = (F_1(t), \ldots, F_m(t))$	• Macroeconomic variables at time t • Operating conditions at time t
Control variables	$X'(t) = (X_1(t), \ldots, X_n(t))$	• Fractions of capital invested in assets • Resources allocated to service dimensions, frequency of repairs

So, the expected change from time $t-1$ to time t is $f(R(t), F(t), X(t))$, given component states $R(t)$ and factors $F(t)$, decisions $X(t)$, and random error ε. This additive form is advantageous for analysis and sufficiently flexible to enable modelling in applications. In practice, the function $f(R, F, X)$ will be specified, and the form of random error ε is typically Gaussian.

We consider that the endogenous variables $R(t)$ and exogenous variables $F(t)$ are independent of the control variables $X(t)$. Furthermore, the exogenous variables affect the system through the endogenous variables:

$$R(t) = g(F(t)) + \epsilon. \tag{1.2}$$

The system defined by equations (1.1) and (1.2) is general, with decisions focused on the status of components. We will consider examples where the defining functions are specific.

Example 1: Financial System

In finance, the system is the process that allows the transfer of money between savers and borrowers. It comprises a set of complex and closely interconnected financial institutions, markets, instruments, services, practices, and transactions. We can consider the components of the system as a set of financial assets. In the financial market, assets are bought and sold by investors, with the return on investment in assets (buying/selling) determined from price changes for those assets. The input to the dynamic system at time t is the wealth of an investor $W(t-1)$ at time $(t-1)$. The anticipated return between investment decision points is the basis of portfolio planning and risk control. The output of the financial system is $W(t)$, the updated wealth at time t, which becomes the input to the next decision period.

A critical feature of the system is anticipated returns on investment. The information on asset prices to date is used to forecast the future prices with error. Consider that there are n assets, with prices at time t being $\{P_i(t), i = 1, \ldots, n\}$. Between decision points $(t-1, t)$, we have prices on asset i: $P_i(t) = P_i(t-1) \times [P_i(t)/P_i(t-1)]$. The return from the price change is $[P_i(t)/P_i(t-1)] = [1 + R_i(t)]$.

So the rate of return is defined as $R_i(t) \cong \ln[1 + R_i(t)] = \ln(P_i(t)) - \ln(P_i(t-1))$. The rates of return are the focus of decisions to generate wealth and control the risk of losses.

The price in the next period is uncertain, as is the rate of return. To predict the rate of return, the usual approach is to link returns to exogenous market factors. If the vector of factors is $F(t)$, it will be composed of some observable factors $F_o(t)$ and some hidden or unobservable factors $F_u(t)$, giving the factor space $F(t) = \binom{F_o(t)}{F_u(t)}$. One approach is to consider that the unobservable factors create zones in multidimensional space, with the zones being discrete classes. Consider the class indicators $I(t) = \{I_1(t), \ldots, I_{K-1}(t)\}$ for K classes. Of course, the classes are still unobservable.

For illustration, assume there are two classes, and there is an indicator with $I = 0$ for class 1 and $I = 1$ for class 2. A factor model relating returns to factors by class is defined by the following equation:

$$R_i(t) = A(t) + B(t)I(t) + C(t)F_o(t) + D(t)(F_o(t) \times I(t)) + E(t)\varepsilon(t).$$

There are equations for both classes $I = 0$ and $I = 1$:

$$R_{i0}(t) = A_0(t) + B_0(t)F_o(t) + E_0(t)\varepsilon(t).$$
$$R_{i1}(t) = A_1(t) + B_1(t)F_o(t) + E_1(t)\varepsilon(t).$$

From the equations, we have factor models for each of the classes/regimes. The equations define distributions for the returns in distinct regimes. An understanding of the prevailing class/regime is important for decisions on risk and return. Even the simplified case of two regimes could be a classification into expansion and contraction markets, and decisions would differ in those classes.

The regimes are hidden, so the regime-dependent equations are hypothetical. However, there are econometric methods for assigning probabilities (estimating) for the hidden classes/regimes using the observations on the observed factors F_o. We will consider those econometric methods in subsequent chapters.

Given the distributions for the unit rates of return on assets, a decision is made at the discrete time points, with the decision denoted by $X(t) = (x_0(t), x_1(t), \ldots, x_n(t))$. We have $x_i(t) =$ the fraction of capital invested in asset i, and $\sum_{i=0}^{n} x_i = 1$. Asset "0" is risk free with a rate $r \geq 0$. The wealth accumulation process is multiplicative, so $W(t) = W(t-1)[(1+R(t))'X(t)]$. It is standard to transform wealth to $Y(t) = \ln(W(t))$, obtaining an arithmetic process for the system output:

$$Y(t) = Y(t-1) + \ln[(1+R(t))'X(t)].$$

This equation is a special case of (1.1). The increment $\ln(1 + \sum R_i(t)x_i(t)) \approx \sum R_i(t)x_i(t)$ depends on the factors $F(t)$ through the linear equation for $R_i(t)$, which is the sum of a systemic part and an error part. That is,

$$\ln\left(1 + \sum R_i(t)x_i(t)\right) = f(R(t), F(t), X(t)) + \varepsilon(X(t)),$$

where $f(R(t), F(t), X(t))$ is the systemic part. We have $Y(t) = Y(t-1) + f(R(t), F(t), X(t)) + \varepsilon(X(t))$. Both the systemic and error parts are controlled by the decision $X(t)$.

The objective of financial decisions is to manage the trajectory of wealth flowing from the financial system. The key characteristics of the wealth trajectory are the growth and significant/unsustainable losses. In terms of losses, we will define a threshold b, with $Y(t) < b$ being a significant loss. So, at each decision period, there is a growth function $G(Y(t))$ and a loss function $L(Y(t))$ associated with the change in wealth, where the loss function is of particular interest since risk is our focus.

In the financial system, period-by-period investment decisions can be determined using estimated parameters in the model. As an illustration, consider the Select Sector SPDR ETFs, with the proportion of wealth invested in each ETF being the decisions. With an objective of maximizing the growth rate of wealth and a risk constraint that wealth exceeds the threshold b with probability $(1-\alpha) = 0.95$, we have wealth output from weekly decisions illustrated in Figure 1.3. Note that wealth W is geometric and $\ln(W) = Y$ is arithmetic.

The intention in this illustration is to emphasize the exponential trajectory for wealth accumulation and the importance of tailoring investment decisions to the factors and the anticipated economic regime. We will have details on the estimation of returns distributions, the measures of return and risk, and the trade-offs in later chapters.

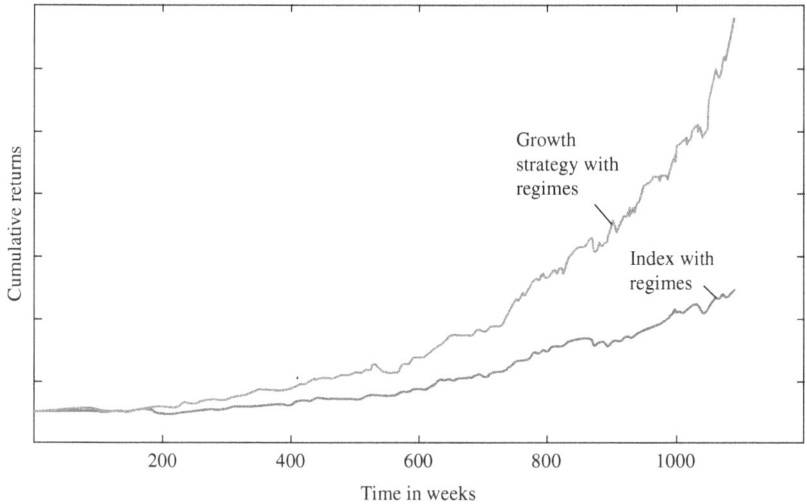

Figure 1.3. Wealth output from growth investment.

Example 2: Repairable System

Life is supported by many mechanical, biological, and social systems that operate over time. The output of such systems can be viewed from the perspective of the ability to perform, i.e., produce acceptable outputs. The performance function at time t is defined as the health status $Y(t)$. The input to the system at a time t is the health status, $Y(t-1)$, which gets transformed by the system to the updated status $Y(t)$. The transformation function depends on characteristics of the system, defined by component rates of change $R(t)$, factors $F(t)$, and decisions on system maintenance defined by $X(t)$. The output is random, with systemic variation from the factors $F(t)$ and idiosyncratic variation from error $\varepsilon(t)$. If the health status is on a logarithmic scale, then the output equation is

$$Y(t) = Y(t-1) + f(R(t), F(t), X(t)) + \varepsilon(X(t)),$$

where $f(R(t), F(t), X(t))$ is the systemic change in health status. We will define the systemic rate as $R(X(t)) = f(R(t), F(t), X(t))$ to emphasize the dependence on decisions. It is implied that the rate also depends on components and factors. So, $R(X(t))$ is the rate of change in health status with age/time. The rate is random, with effects from factors and decisions. Factors include design features and the operating environment; decisions include the frequency of repairs/maintenance interventions. It is assumed that $E(R(X(t))) < 0$, and the system degrades with time.

Systems are complex with numerous interrelated components. If system components/parts degrade with use/time, there will be an age (accumulated use) at which a component fails in the sense that it no longer performs its function. Depending on the component, the consequences of failure vary. For example, with complex machines (aircraft), there is a minimum list of components for which component failure does not cause an immediate machine failure or flight stoppage. Such components can be replaced when it is convenient. There is scheduled maintenance after a specified time of use, and these major repairs are planned to renew the system and avoid or delay failure.

A depiction of health status degradation with age is presented in Figure 1.4. Failure occurs when the health status falls below the critical state, where the system is no longer able to perform/operate.

The trajectory of health status is a random variable, and the objective of maintenance decisions is to control the trajectory. The key characteristics of the trajectory are the expected degradation rate $E(R(X(t)))$ and the loss from failures during the transition of status from time $t-1$ to time t.

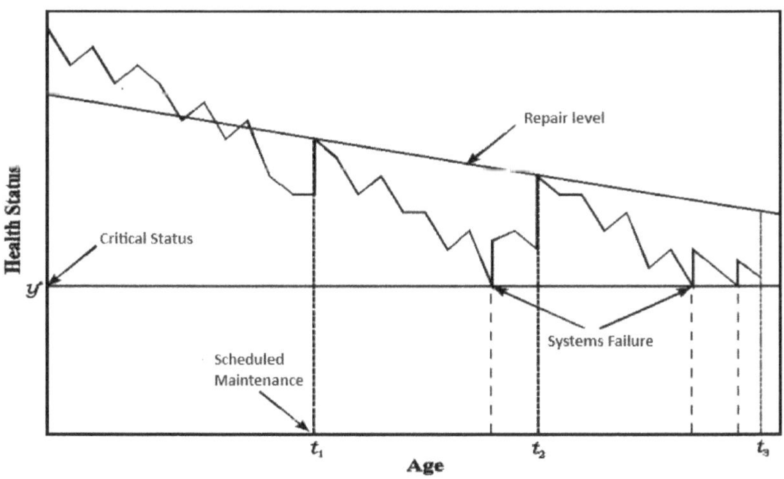

Figure 1.4. System degradation.

The repairable system model is conceptual. In later chapters, we will develop the degradation model with data from aircraft operations.

The key variable in the system dynamics is the rate of change, which we have defined by $R(X(t))$ to focus on decisions. In the financial example, it is anticipated that $E(R(X(t))) > 0$, that is, there is expected growth. In the degradation case, $E(R(X(t))) < 0$, and there is expected decay. In either case, the rate is controlled by the decision $X(t)$.

The system as presented is a design for transforming input $Y(t-1)$ to output $Y(t)$. The processing time of the system is left arbitrary so that it can accommodate many systems, which have defined factors $F(t)$ and decisions $X(t)$ during the transformation. When analyzing a financial system, a time interval is selected, e.g., a week. Then, weekly changes in wealth with factors $F(t)$ and decisions $X(t)$ are observed. With a mechanical/biological system, the transformation in health status $Y(t)$ would be considered over a period related to the operation. For example, for the airworthiness/health status of aircraft, the natural time interval is a flight cycle – time between takeoff and landing. The factors include the model of aircraft, age of aircraft, and the operator. The decisions are inspection and maintenance efforts before takeoff.

The examples provided are considered because of their relevance to human activity. In the modern market economy, the growth of wealth through investment is fundamental. Likewise, the degradation of biological, environmental, and societal systems is a dominant issue in modern life. These examples for stochastic dynamic systems highlight a contrast in objectives. The financial system emphasizes growth, with a requirement that the chance of failure/bankruptcy is rare. The biological/mechanical/social system emphasizes failures, with a requirement that the cost of failure avoidance through maintenance is constrained. In either approach, risk is a core concept, and we need to consider the definition and measurement of risk.

The foundation of risk is the variability or unpredictability in system output, and a goal of decisions is to control variation. To quantify risk, it is required that for system status $Y(t)$, there is a loss function $L(Y(t))$ defined on the output $Y(t)$. The loss is defined relative to a target, b, and departures from the target $(y < b)$ are increasingly penalized. In a financial system, falling below the threshold

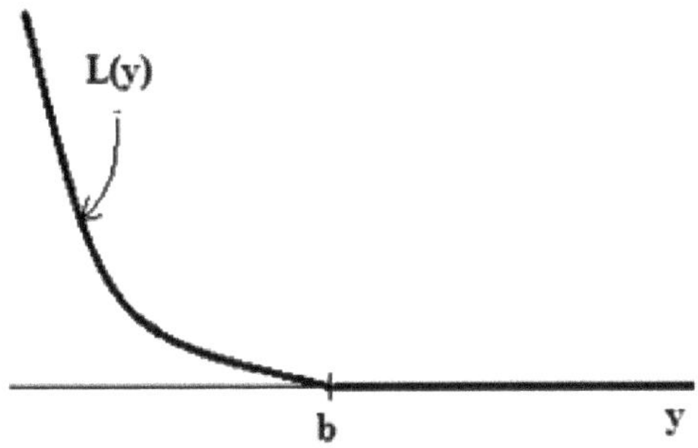

Figure 1.5. Loss function.

would entail consequences such as margin calls. In operating systems, falling below the threshold would result in an interruption of operations for maintenance, with costs for service delays and repairs. A hypothetical depiction of a loss function is presented in Figure 1.5.

The loss function is zero above the threshold b and positive and non-increasing below the threshold:

$$L(Y(t)) > 0, \quad \frac{d}{dy}L \leq 0 \quad \text{if } Y(t) < b.$$
$$L(Y(y)) = 0 \quad \text{if } Y(t) \geq b.$$

The risk approach puts the emphasis on downside loss. The loss is a random variable, and the quantification of the risk from losses is required to assess decisions on systems operation. Clearly, decisions have consequences, and measurement of the consequences is a key part of risk control.

1.3 Risk Definition

In the context of the systems model, the observable output is uncertain or variable. Some of that variation is attributable to inherent aspects of the system, such as design, and exogenous factors that impact performance. Also, there is idiosyncratic variation or randomness. In an analysis of a system defined by parameters and equations, the statistical methods for estimating parameters add another layer of error and uncertainty.

The uncertainty in system output can be viewed as the basis of risk, but the terms uncertainty and risk need clear definitions:

1. **Uncertainty:** A situation of having limited knowledge of an existing state or future outcome, where more than one outcome is possible. In system equations, probabilities are assigned to each possible state or outcome.
2. **Risk:** A state of uncertainty where some possible outcomes have an undesired effect or significant loss. The chance of losses and the magnitude of losses are measurable aspects of the risk of a system.

We are concerned with decision-making under uncertainty, where possible outcomes involve significant loss. If decisions are made so that the risk of loss is controlled, then it is necessary to have a measure of risk that is suited to analysis. There are functional requirements of a measure if we expect decisions based on the measure to be valid. We will consider principles of risk measurement in this section.

1.3.1 *Risk measurement*

Consider $Y(t)$, the system output at time t, where $Y(t)$ is a stochastic dynamic process. With a loss function, $L(Y(t))$, associated with output $Y(t)$, define the *risk process* as the accumulated losses to time t: $\wp(t) = \sum_{=1}^{t} L(Y(s))$. The risk process is a stochastic dynamic process, with trajectories $\{\wp(t), t = 1, 2, \ldots\}$. *The risk function* is the expected value of the risk process:

$$\varrho(t) = E(\wp(t)) = \sum_{s=1}^{t} E(L(Y(s))) = \sum_{s=1}^{t} \rho(s). \tag{1.3}$$

We are concerned with system operation between input and output times, and in particular with the increments $\rho(t)$ in the risk function, which is controlled by the decisions at times $t = 1, 2, \ldots$.

The choice of a loss function $L(Y(t))$ is an important part of the analysis of risk. We will consider some loss functions that lead to common risk measures:

(1) In financial systems, a standard benchmark is the expected value of output in transition time $(t-1, t)$: $\mu(t)$. Then, risk is defined

as the variability or volatility of asset/portfolio returns relative to $\mu(t)$, and thus includes both potential worse-than-expected as well as better-than-expected returns. Although risk is usually concerned with loss from a worse-than-expected return, a measure of variability will incorporate such loss, and for symmetric distributions, variability is directly related to losses. In this case, the loss function is squared error, and hence the risk process is the total squared error. The risk function is the total expected squared error:

$$\varrho(t) = \sum_{s=1}^{t} E[(Y(s) - \mu(s))^2] = \sum_{s=1}^{t} \sigma^2(s).$$

The risk measure for the transition between times $t-1$ and t is the variance of output $Y(t)$:

$$\sigma^2(t) = E[(Y(t) - \mu(t))^2].$$

If with decision $X(t)$, growth is the mean $\mu(X(t))$, risk is $\sigma(X(t))$, and the risk-free return is r, then a standard measure combining growth and risk is the *Sharpe Ratio*:

$$\varphi(X(t)) = \frac{\mu(X(t)) - r}{\sigma(X(t))}. \tag{1.4}$$

In the context of mean variance analysis, the Sharpe ratio measures the trade-off between risk and return.

(2) It is possible to focus on the downside directly in the definition of risk. Consider $G_t(y)$, the distribution function for the random variable $Y(t)$ = the output at time t. The increment in the risk function at time t is $E(L(Y(t))) = \int_{-\infty}^{b} L(y)dG_t(y)$. Let the loss function be a binary classification:

$$L(Y(t)) = 1, \quad \text{if } Y(t) < b.$$
$$L(Y(t)) = 0, \quad \text{if } Y(t) \geq b.$$

Then, $E(L(Y(t))) = \int_{-\infty}^{b} dG_t(y) = G_t(b) = \alpha_b$ or equivalently

$$\mathrm{VaR}_{\alpha_b} = b.$$

Keep in mind that output is $Y(R(t), F(t), X(t))$, that is, the output depends on the decision $X(t)$. So, $\alpha_b(X(t))$ is a measure of the risk of falling short of b, with the decision $X(t)$. If $\alpha_b(X(t)) < \alpha$ for decision $X(t)$, then the risk is acceptable. Alternatively, if $G_t^{-1}(\alpha|X(t)) = \text{VaR}_\alpha(X(t)) > b$, then the risk is acceptable. So, acceptable decisions satisfy the constraint $\text{VaR}_\alpha(X(t)) > b$. In this formulation, the risk measure for decision $X(t)$ given α is

$$\text{VaR}_\alpha(X(t)). \tag{1.5}$$

(3) When outcomes below a threshold b are increasingly undesirable, the loss function is zero above the threshold and positive and non-decreasing below the threshold, i.e., $L(Y(t)) > 0$, $\frac{d}{dy}L \leq 0$, if $Y(t) < b$.

Specifically, we can define $L(Y(t)) = b - Y(t)$ for $Y(t) < b$, $L(Y(t)) = 0$ for $Y(t) > b$. Then consider

$$E(L(Y(t))) = b - \frac{1}{\alpha_b}\int_{-\infty}^{b} ydG(y).$$

So $E(L(Y(t)))$ is the average shortfall with the decision $X(t)$. If $b = \text{VaR}_\alpha(X(t))$, then $E(L(Y(t))) = b - \frac{1}{\alpha}\int_{-\infty}^{\text{VaR}_\alpha(X(t))} ydG(y)$. The expected loss is determined by

$$\text{CVaR}_\alpha(X(t)) = \frac{1}{\alpha}\int_{-\infty}^{\text{VaR}_\alpha(X(t))} ydG(y),$$

Another measure of risk for the decision $X(t)$ given α is

$$\text{CVaR}_\alpha(X(t)).$$

(4) Considering threshold b is the critical output value, so that falling short of b is a failure, it is reasonable to measure both $\alpha_b(X(t))$ and $\text{CVaR}_{\alpha_b}(X(t))$, the probability of a shortfall and the average size of the shortfall, respectively. The pair $(\alpha_b, \text{CVaR}_{\alpha_b})$ is a common measure of risk. We can combine the risk measures in the *risk priority number*

$$\psi(X(t)) = \alpha_b(X(t)) \times \text{CVaR}_{\alpha_b}(X(t)). \tag{1.6}$$

In systems safety analysis, the RPI balances the chance of failure and the expected consequence of failure.

The loss functions and risk measures being considered are presented in Table 1.2.

Table 1.2. Risk measures for decision $X(t)$.

Loss function	Measure	Description
$L(Y(t)) = [(Y(t) - \mu)^2]$	$\sigma^2(X(t))$	Variance of $Y(X(t))$
$L(Y(t)) = 1, \quad \text{if } Y(t) < b$	$\text{VaR}_\alpha(X(t))$	αth percentile of $Y(X(t))$
$L(Y(t)) = 0, \quad \text{if } Y(t) \geq b$		
$L(Y(T)) = b - Y(t), \quad \text{if } Y(t) < b$	$\text{CVaR}_{\alpha_b}(X(t))$	Mean value of $Y(X(t))$ below threshold b
$L(Y(t)) = 0, \quad \text{if } Y(t) \geq b$		

1.4 Risk Axioms

As a functional defined on real-valued random variables, there exist mathematical properties which may reasonably be expected to be satisfied by a risk measure ρ. The properties apply to systems output Y_1 and Y_2 with distributions G_1 and G_2, respectively. It is assumed that the same time point applies to each process and will not be displayed.

(A1) Law invariance: $G_1(y) = G_2(y), \ \forall y \Rightarrow \rho_1 = \rho_2$.
(A2) Monotonicity: $G_1(y) \geq G_2(y), \ \forall y \Rightarrow \rho_1 \geq \rho_2$.
(A3) Translation invariance: $\rho(Y + m) = \rho(Y) - m, m \in \mathbb{R}$.
(A4) Sub-additivity: $\rho(Y_1 + Y_2) \leq \rho(Y_1) + \rho(Y_2)$.
(A5) Positive homogeneity: $\rho(\lambda Y) = \lambda p(Y), \lambda > 0$.
(A6) Consistency: Y_1 second order dominates $Y_2 \Rightarrow \rho(Y_1) \geq \rho(Y_2)$.

The properties do not constitute a definition of a risk measure, and they are not sufficient to build a risk measure. For a proposed risk measure, these properties can be verified. Law invariance is clear. Monotonicity requires that the risk measure is ordered as implied by the distribution; that is, if one distribution is above another, it implies greater risk. Translation invariance states that adding cash to a financial position reduces the risk by the same amount.

The sub-additivity property is significant since it implies that diversification typically reduces risk. However, there are times when correlated processes Y_1 and Y_2 are such that the risk of $Y_1 + Y_2$ is more than the risk of Y_1 plus the risk of Y_2.

As a set of properties, A2–A5 have been used by Artzner *et al.* (1999) to characterize the class of *coherent risk measures*.

Positive homogeneity and sub-additivity together imply convexity:

$$\rho(\lambda Y_1 + (1-\lambda)Y_2) \leq \lambda\rho(Y_1) + (1-\lambda)\rho(Y_2).$$

Convexity does not imply that both positive homogeneity and sub-additivity hold. Since convexity is a desired property, it can replace sub-additivity and homogeneity. The resulting class of *convex risk measures* is considered in Föllmer and Knispel (2013). Convexity of the risk measure ρ is important for decision problems where the risk measure is used to formulate constraints. The resulting set of feasible decisions is convex, with the property that a linear combination of feasible decisions is feasible.

We have progressed from system output to a risk process and a risk measure. Although we have not included the system components and factors as arguments in the risk process and measure, it is intended that the factors affect the system components, which are combined by decisions in the system output. Given the factors and components, the risk measure is a function controlled by the decision X.

1.5 Risk and Utility: Decision Choice

If performance is partly controlled by decisions, it is required that individual decision-makers know their preferences among alternative outcomes. For individuals, considering alternative outcomes $Y(X_1)$ and $Y(X_2)$, if they prefer $Y(X_1)$ to $Y(X_2)$ or are indifferent between the two, the relation is stated as $Y(X_1) \gg Y(X_2)$. An essential characteristic of a system involving risk is uncertainty about outcomes. Suppose the system outcome is defined by a real-valued function, such as total loss in a time/use interval. Then, the outcome is a random variable, and the alternatives are different distributions over the outcome measure. When evaluating decision alternatives X_1 and X_2, using outcome $Y(X)$, the distributions G_1 and G_2 over $Y(X)$ for alternatives X_1 and X_2 are the basis for preference.

To put the preference relation for an individual into a theory of utility, the following axioms were proposed by Von Neumann and Morgenstern (1944) and Savage (1954). Let S be the set (possibly infinite) of alternatives for a system, where the alternatives are distributions over a performance measure.

Preference axioms:

(P1) Completeness: For any two alternatives $Y(X_1)$ and $Y(X_2)$ in S, either $Y(X_1) \gg Y(X_2)$, or $Y(X_2) \gg Y(X_1)$, or both.
(P2) Transitivity: For alternatives $Y(X_1)$, $Y(X_2)$ and $Y(X_3)$ in S, if $Y(X_1) \gg Y(X_2)$ and $Y(X_2) \gg Y(X_3)$, then $Y(X_1) \gg Y(X_3)$.
(P3) Continuity: If $Y(X_1) \gg Y(X_2) \gg Y(X_3)$, then there exists some $\pi \in [0,1]$ such that $Y(X_2)$ is indifferent to $\pi Y(X_1) + (1-\pi)Y(X_3)$.
(P4) Independence: For any two alternatives $Y(X_1)$ and (X_2), $Y(X_1) \gg Y(X_2)$ if and only if $\pi Y(X_1) + (1-\pi)Y(X_3) \gg \pi Y(X_2) + (1-\pi)Y(X_3)$, for all $Y(X_3)$ and $\pi \in [0,1]$.

These axioms have been the basis of rational decision-making.

Example 3

To illustrate the axioms, consider a simple outcome with 0/1 values and the alternative distributions:

Y	X_1	X_2	X_3
0	$1-p_1$	$1-p_2$	$1-p_3$
1	p_1	p_2	p_3

Consider that $Y = 0$ for the system not working, and $Y = 1$ for the system that is working. So, $Y(X_1) \gg Y(X_2)$ if and only if $p_1 \geq p_2$. It can easily be seen that completeness and transitivity are satisfied. If $p_1 \geq p_2 \geq p_3$, then with $\pi = \frac{p_3-p_2}{p_3-p_1}$, we have $\pi p_1 + (1-\pi)p_3 = p_2$, and $Y(X_2)$ is indifferent to $\pi Y(X_1) + (1-\pi)Y(X_3)$. So, continuity is satisfied. Since adding the same amount to p_1 and p_2 retains the ordering, then independence is satisfied.

If the four preference axioms are satisfied, then the relationship can be expressed in terms of a utility function $u(Y)$.

Expected Utility Theorem

If the preference relation $\gg$ *over random outcomes* $Y(X_1)$ *and* $Y(X_2)$ *satisfies the completeness, transitivity, continuity, and independence axioms, then* $Y(X_1) \gg Y(X_2)$ *if and only if there exists a utility function* u *such that* $Eu(Y(X_1)) > Eu(Y(X_2))$.

Obviously, u is a utility function that reflects a preference relation. In fact, any monotone transformation of u will also reflect the preference, so the utility is not unique. The fact that preferences can be defined by a utility function is very useful for the analysis of preferences and the decision problem of choosing the best alternative. In following this approach, it is important to keep in mind that it is assumed that decision-makers satisfy the axioms in stating their preferences. This is referred to as rational decision-making (Savage, 1954). There are examples of choice problems where preferences do not satisfy the axioms. The Allias paradox (Allais, 1953) and the Ellsberg paradox (Ellsberg, 1961) provide well-known contradictions to the expected utility theorem. There is also an effect from extreme values where there is a trade-off between the probability of large losses and the sensitivity to extremely large losses with very low probability (Ditlevsen, 2003). This contrast between percentiles and tail means has played an important part in financial risk management (Artzner *et al.*, 1999).

Assuming the axioms are satisfied and therefore preferences can be expressed by a utility function, there are aspects of preference that are reflected in properties of the utility. The focus here is on the aversion to risk. It is natural to associate risk with randomness and uncertainty. If the choice is between a sure thing and a random alternative with the same expectation, then an aversion to risk would say take the sure thing. More generally, if $Y(X_1)$ is a random outcome and $Y(X_2)$ is a random outcome with a distribution equal to that of $Y(X_1) + \varepsilon$, where ε is uncorrelated noise, then $Y(X_1)$ is preferred to $Y(X_2)$ by any risk averter. To make this more explicit, consider the distribution functions G_1 and G_2 with the inverse cumulative distributions G_1^{-1} and G_2^{-1}, respectively. Let $T(\alpha) = \int_0^\alpha [G_1^{-1}(p) - G_2^{-1}(p)]dp$ be the area between the distributions in the α-tail. With the construction $Y(X_2) = Y(X_1) + \varepsilon$, then $T(\alpha) > 0$, $0 \leq \alpha \leq 1$. This area between the cumulative distributions' result follows from the greater variability of $Y(X_2)$ around the same mean as $Y(X_1)$.

So, there is a class of decision-makers who are averse to risk as characterized by greater uncertainty. Going back to the expected utility theorem, this class has a particular type of utility function. A utility function U for which $\{T(\alpha) > 0, 0 \leq \alpha \leq 1\} \Longrightarrow Eu(Y(X_1)) \geq Eu(Y(X_2))$ is concave (Rothschild and Stiglitz, 1970). So, the risk averter has a concave utility, and risk aversion and concavity have the same underlying principle.

1.6 Risk Management

The output from the stochastic dynamic system is the focus of system control. The system producing outputs is composed of features such as endogenous components, exogenous risk factors, random variation, estimation error, and control decisions. The system is dynamic, so (1) characterizing the past outputs and (2) controlling uncertain future outputs are both problems for consideration in risk management.

1.6.1 *Summarizing system output*

At the current time, a record of the past performance of the system is available for analysis. The record includes system outputs as well as the values of component status, risk factors, and maintenance decisions. The approach to description is to locate the system trajectory of a single user in the population of trajectories. The factors are conditioning variables, so that the conditional population is an appropriate baseline. We will display two descriptions: expected values and extreme values.

Expected values: Conditional (mean, variance)

Consider a record of system output for times $t = 1, \ldots, T$ for a population of N users: $\{y_{nt}, n = 1, \ldots, N, t = 1, \ldots, T\}$. The mean and standard deviation are $\{(\mu_t, \sigma_t), t = 1, \ldots, T\}$. Population confidence intervals are calculated as (mean $\pm z\times$ standard deviation).

In Figure 1.6, the population status is depicted, and the trajectory of a single user is plotted to illustrate unexpected values. Note that there are phases or regimes defined by risk factors.

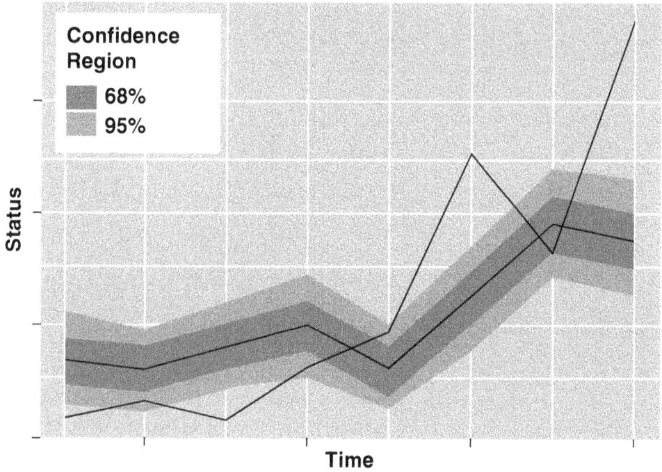

Figure 1.6. System trajectory on population distribution.

Conditional extremes (probability, shortfall)

Consider again a record of system output for times $t = 1, \ldots, T$ for a population of N users: $\{y_{nt}, n = 1, \ldots, N, t = 1, \ldots, T\}$. Assume there is a failure level (threshold) at each time. Each user has a failure rate (probability) δ_n and average failure size (loss) θ_n. The failure data $\{(\delta_n, \theta_n), n = 1, \ldots, N\}$ create a matrix template for the joint distribution.

Figure 1.7 displays the matrix template for critical outcomes (below a threshold). An extreme outcome is highlighted in red. The lines are neutral ranges of log [prob $\times$ loss] = log[prob] + log[loss]. The high-risk zone identifies users with high probability and/or high loss from failure.

The risk matrix is a popular tool in risk analysis. We will consider the matrix in quantitative analysis, with emphasis on the quantitative assessment of the failure probability and loss.

1.6.2 *Controlling future output*

The observations on past system outcomes provide information on the relative performance in comparison with alternative users. The aggregate information on all participants is the source data for

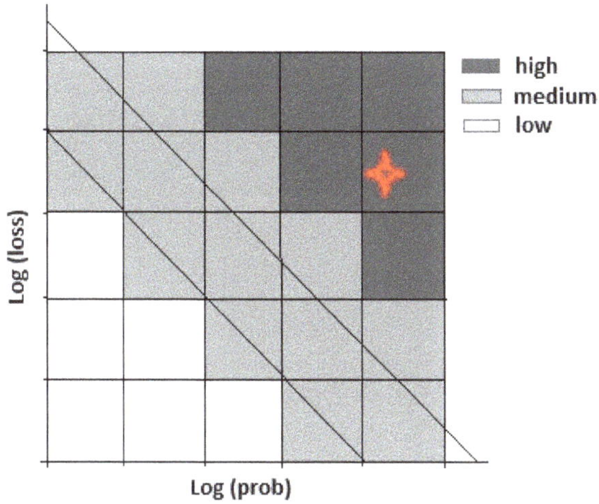

Figure 1.7. Extreme values matrix.

estimating the parameters in the equations that characterize the system. With the estimated dynamics of the system for all participants, it is possible to predict the uncertain future system outcome. Decisions on the maintenance and control of the system are an important ingredient in the variability of the trajectory. In terms of risk, there are decisions that are acceptable or feasible based on individual conditions or constraints on performance. Within the set of feasible decisions, those with the best risk profile are preferred.

The decision problem can be posed as a trade-off between risk and reward. Given a return outcome $Y(R, F, X)$ that is dependent on the component status R, factors F, decision vector X, and random element ε, the risk measure is $\rho(Y(X)) = \rho(Y(R, F, X))$ and the reward function is $\pi(Y(X)) = \pi(Y(R, F, X))$. The problem is to select the decision X that maximizes the reward while ensuring that the risk does not exceed ρ_0:

$$\max_X\{\pi(Y(X))|\rho(Y(X)) \leq \rho_0\}. \tag{1.7}$$

Alternatively, a weighted combination of risk and reward is optimized:

$$\max_X\{\pi(Y(X)) - \lambda\rho(Y(X))|\lambda \geq 0\}. \tag{1.8}$$

In this problem, λ is a risk aversion parameter. This penalty parameter may incorporate the potential effects of both model uncertainty and estimation error.

We will briefly discuss a decision model based on expected values and a decision model based on extreme values.

Expected values: Mean variance analysis

In the framework of financial decision-making, the management of risk can be viewed in the style of Markowitz's mean variance analysis. The decision is the fraction of available capital invested in each asset in an opportunity set. The risk measure is the variance of returns with the decision X, $\rho(Y(X)) = \sigma^2(Y(X))$, and the reward function is the expected return $\mu(Y(X)) = E(Y(X))$. The problem is to select the decision X that maximizes the expected return while ensuring that the variance does not exceed σ_0^2:

$$\max_X \{\mu(Y(X))\}$$
$$\text{subject to} \quad \sigma^2(Y(X)) \le \sigma_0^2.$$

Alternatively, the risk is minimized for a given target return π_0:

$$\min_X \{\sigma^2(Y(X))\}$$
$$\text{subject to} \quad \mu(Y(X)) \ge \pi_0.$$

There is substantial literature on the efficiency of mean variance optimization, and we will provide details in the chapter on risk control.

Extreme values: Minimal loss below a threshold

In risk analysis, it is natural to focus on losses. Consider that there is a threshold b such that falling below the threshold will result in a disruption/failure of the system. For the uncertain outcome in the next period, $Y(X)$, we want to control the probability and size of shortfalls below the threshold. Recall that the probability is

$$\int_{-\infty}^{b} dG(y|X) = \alpha_b(X).$$

The average shortfall size is

$$\mathrm{CVaR}_{\alpha_b}(X) = \frac{1}{\alpha_b(X)} \int_{-\infty}^{b} y dG(y|X).$$

Then, a risk control problem is

$$\min_X \{\mathrm{CVaR}_{\alpha_b}(X)\}$$
$$\text{subject to} \quad \alpha_b(X) \leq \alpha.$$

In the risk literature, $\{\alpha_b(X) \leq \alpha\}$ is a Value at Risk (VaR) constraint and $\mathrm{CVaR}_{\alpha_b}(X)$ is a Conditional Value at Risk (CVaR) function.

We will have more on these functions and the risk control with those functions in subsequent chapters.

1.7 Conclusion

In this introduction to risk, we have given an overview of a wide range of topics. The system framework, which is built on endogenous components, exogenous factors, and decisions, is well suited to modelling actual operations. Real systems do not operate from rules set down by equations. However, there is sufficient flexibility in our equations model to be confident that the model is a close approximation to operations. The advantage of quantifying the system and the outputs is the potential to define quantitative measures which can be evaluated. The impact of exogenous factors and operational decisions on outcomes measures of risk and return provides a setting for determining the best decisions.

Clearly, the risk of adverse outcomes is a major concern in real-world problems. If there is a theme in our presentation, it is that "*decisions have consequences.*" Understanding the consequences is a prerequisite for decision-making.

The quantitative approach to risk analysis is the focus, but it is acknowledged that qualitative risk analysis is another approach.

A standard qualitative risk tool is the risk matrix. Risk matrices or tables mapping "frequency" and "severity" ratings to corresponding risk priority levels are popular in applications as diverse as terrorism risk analysis, highway construction project management, office building risk analysis, climate change risk management, and enterprise risk management (ERM). National and international standards (e.g., Military Standard 882C and AS/NZS 4360:1999) have stimulated the adoption of risk matrices by many organizations and risk consultants. However, little research rigorously validates their performance in actually improving risk management decisions. Research on qualitative risk matrices (Cox, 2004) shows that they have the following limitations:

(a) **Poor Resolution:** Typical risk matrices can correctly and unambiguously compare only a small fraction (e.g., less than 10%) of randomly selected pairs of hazards. They can assign identical ratings to quantitatively very different risks ("range compression").
(b) **Errors:** Risk matrices can mistakenly assign higher qualitative ratings to quantitatively smaller risks. For risks with negatively correlated frequencies and severities, they can be "worse than useless," leading to worse-than-random decisions.
(c) **Suboptimal Resource Allocation:** Effective allocation of resources to risk-reducing countermeasures cannot be based on the categories provided by risk matrices.
(d) **Ambiguous Inputs and Outputs:** Categorizations of severity cannot be made objectively for uncertain consequences. Inputs to risk matrices (e.g., frequency and severity categorizations) and the resulting outputs (i.e., risk ratings) require subjective interpretation, and different users may obtain opposite ratings of the same quantitative risks.

These limitations suggest that qualitative risk matrices should be used with caution and only with careful explanations of embedded judgments.

We will develop details of the quantitative approach to risk analysis in subsequent chapters. In addition to some theory for quantitative techniques, we will present cases that apply the techniques to the outcomes from actual systems in finance and operations.

Bibliography*

Ale, B., Burnap, P., and Slater, D. (2015). On the origin of PCDS – (Probability consequence diagrams). *Safety Science*, 72, 229–239.

Allais, M. (1953). Le comportement de l'homme rationnel devant le risque: Critique des postulats et axiomes de l'école Américaine. *Econometrica*, 21(4), 503–546.

Ang, A. and Bekaert, G. (2002). International asset allocation with regime shifts. *Review of Financial Studies*, 15(4), 1137–1187.

Artzner, P., Delbaen, F., Eber, J., and Heath, D. (1999). Coherent measures of risk. *Mathematical Finance*, 9, 203–228.

Aven, T. and Jensen, U. (1999). *Stochastic Models in Reliability.* Springer Verlag, New York, USA.

Basak, S. and Shapiro, A. (2001). Value at risk based risk management: Optimal policies and asset prices. *Review of Financial Studies*, 14, 371–405.

Bedford, T. and Cooke, R. (2001). *Probabilistic Risk Analysis: Foundations and Methods.* Cambridge University Press, Cambridge, UK.

Bowles, J. (2003). An assessment of RPN prioritization in failure modes effects and criticality analysis. In *Proceedings of the Annual Reliability and Maintenance Symposium*, Tampa, January, 2003.

Buhlmann, H. (1970). *Mathematical Methods in Risk Theory.* Springer, Berlin.

Chopra, V.K. and Ziemba, W.T. (1993). The effect of errors in means, variances and covariances on optimal portfolio choice. *Journal of Portfolio Management*, 19, 6–11.

Clemens, P.L., Pfitzer, T., Simmons, R., Dwyer, S., Frost, J., and Olsen, E. (2005). The RAC matrix: A universal tool, or a toolkit. *Journal of Systems Safety*, 4(2), 14–20.

Cox, L.A. (2008). What's wrong with risk matrices? *Risk Analysis*, 28(2), 497–512.

Cuoco, D., He, H., and Issaenko, S. (2008). Optimal dynamic trading strategies with risk limits. *Operations Research*, 47, 1209–1227.

Ditlevsen, O. (2003). Decision modeling and acceptance criteria. *Structural Safety*, 25, 165–191.

Duijm, N.J. (2015). Recommendations on the use and design of risk matrices. *Safety Science*, 76, 21–31.

*The literature on risk analysis is extensive and diverse. A list of relevant publications on the topic is provided here.

Ellsberg, D. (1961). Risk, ambiguity, and the savage axioms. *Quarterly Journal of Economics*, 75(4), 643–669.

Fama, E.F. and French, K.R. (1993). Common risk factors in the returns on stocks and bonds. *Journal of Financial Economics*, 33(1), 3–56.

Föllmer, H. and Knispel, T. (2013). Convex risk measures: Basic facts, law-invariance and beyond, asymptotics for large portfolios, in: MacLean, L. and Ziemba, W. (Eds.), *Handbook of the Fundamentals of Financial Decision Making*. World Scientific, pp. 507–554.

French, K.R., Schwert, G.W., and Stambaugh, R.F. (1987). Expected stock returns and volatility. *Journal of Financial Economics*, 19(1), 3–29.

Hanoch, G. and Levy, H. (1969). Efficiency analysis of choices involving risk. *Review of Economic Studies*, 36, 335–346.

Jorion, P. (1986). Bayes-Stein estimation for portfolio analysis. *Journal of Financial and Quantitative Analysis*, 21, 279–329.

Kahneman, D. and Tversky, A. (1979). Prospect theory: An analysis of decision making under risk. *Econometrica*, 47(2), 263–291.

Kaplan, S. and Garrick, B. (1981). On the quantitative definition of risk. *Risk Analysis*, 1, 11–27.

Klein, R.W. and Bawa, V.S. (1976). The effect of estimation risk on portfolio choice. *Journal of Financial Economics*, 3, 215–231.

Levine, E.S. (2012). Improving risk matrices: The advantage of logarithmically scaled axes. *Journal of Risk Research*, 15(2), 209–222.

Levy, H. (1998). *Stochastic Dominance*. Kluwer Academic Publishers. Norwell, MA.

Loffler, G. (2003). The effects of estimation error on measures of portfolio credit risk. *Journal of Banking and Finance*, 27(8), 1427–1453.

Ma, Y., MacLean, L., Xu, K., and Zhao, Y. (2011). A portfolio optimization model with regime-switching risk factors for sector exchange traded funds. *Pacific Journal of Optimization*, 7(2), 281–296.

MacLean, L., Richman, A., Richman, V., and Larsson, S. (2005). The dynamics of aircraft degradation and mechanical failure. *Journal of Transportation and Statistics*, 8(1), 1–11.

Maes, M.A. and Faber, M.H. (2008). Utility, preferences, and risk perception in engineering decision making. Document # 6. Joint Committee of Structural Safety.

Markowitz, H. (1952). Portfolio selection. *Journal of Finance*, 7(1), 77–91.

Moubray, J. (2001). *Reliability Centered Maintenance*. Industrial Press, Inc., Norwalk, Connecticut, USA.

Rogers, L.C.G. (2000). The relaxed investor and parameter uncertainty. *Finance and Stochastics*, 5, 131–154.

Rothschild, M. and Stiglitz, J.E. (1970). Increasing risk: I. A definition. *Journal of Economic Theory*, 2, 225–243.

Savage, L.J. (1954). *The Foundations of Statistics.* John Wiley & Sons, Inc., New York, USA.

Sharpe, W.F. (1964). Capital asset prices: A theory of market equilibrium under conditions of risk. *The Journal of Finance*, 19(3), 425–442.

Sortino, F.A. and Satchell, S. (2001). *Managing Downside Risk in Financial Markets.* Butterworth-Heinemann, Oxford.

Von Neumann, J. and Mortenstern, O. (1944). *Theory of Games and Economic Behavior.* Princeton University Press, Princeton, New Jersey, USA.

Virling, J.K., van Hengel W., and Houben, R.J. (1998). Acceptable risk as a basis for design. *Reliability Engineering and System Safety*, 59, 141–150.

Chapter 2

Risk Assessment

2.1 Introduction

We are considering stochastic dynamic systems where the output from the system is a random variable. A number of applications for stochastic systems were described in Chapter 1. The variation in system output creates a chance that an observed result falls short of critical benchmarks. Our concern is with risk, which is defined by the chance and size of shortfalls. If we are to assess the risk inherent in stochastic systems, we need to (1) determine the likelihood or chance of occurrence of unfavorable outcomes and (2) specify the consequences or impact of unfavorable outcomes. This chapter considers methods for the assessment of risk in systems outcomes. The approach is quantitative, so techniques for dealing with random variables and their distributions are fundamental to analysis. The quantification of risk involves observations of the output from systems, and the data accumulated require statistical techniques. The chapter provides some systems applications and introduces the E-Views software for statistical analysis.

Initially, we deal with the system outcome as a univariate random variable. In subsequent chapters, we will consider aspects of the system such as factors and decisions, which affect the system outcome and therefore are part of the risk assessment.

2.2 A Review of Statistical Concepts

The stochastic dynamic system transforms the output between times: $Y(t-1) \Rightarrow System \Rightarrow Y(t)$. The output is a random variable, and risk is a characteristic of the distribution for $Y(t)$. If we are to assess risk, it is essential to understand the concept of the distribution of a random variable. We will frame the distribution in general terms initially, and then consider empirical distributions based on observations of the output from a stochastic system. The emphasis is on the output, denote by Y, with the time argument dropped for now.

Our review discusses the important normal distribution in this section. Appendix D provides a review of several additional distributions that are used in statistical analysis.

2.2.1 *Probability*

Consider a random variable Y whose outcomes are real numbers. Let S be the set of all possible outcomes. For each realization of $Y, Y = y \in \mathcal{R}$, a number is assigned to indicate the chance of occurrence: $y \to g(y)$. An important concept in probability is a subset set of outcomes $A, A \subset S$, and the corresponding probability $P(A)$, A fundamental probability law states that *the probability of an event is the accumulation of the probabilities of the distinct outcomes in the event.*

From this basic law, we have that the probability of an event, $P(A)$, is a real-valued function[1] and has these properties:

1. $0 \leq P(A) \leq 1$ for every $A \subset S$.
2. If $A, B, C, \ldots$ constitute an exhaustive set of events, then $P(A \cup B \cup C \cup \cdots) = P(S) = 1$,where $A \cup B \cup C$ means A or B or C, and so forth.
3. If $A, B, C, \ldots$ are mutually exclusive events, then

$$P(A \cup B \cup C \cup \cdots) = P(A) + P(B) + P(C) + \cdots .$$

[1]A function whose domain and range are subsets of real numbers is commonly referred to as a real-valued function. For details, see Alpha C. Chiang, *Fundamental Methods of Mathematical Economics*, 3d ed., McGraw-Hill, 1984, Chapter 2.

4. If A, B are events and $A \cap B$ is elements in both, then

$$P(A \cap B) = P(A) \times P(B|A),$$

where $P(B|A)$ is the conditional probability of B given A.

5. If A, B are independent events, then

$$P(B|A) = P(B).$$

Our interest in these probability laws is focused on independence and conditional probability. The distribution for random outcomes will be affected by conditioning factors and we will explore the relationship between outcomes and conditioning factors in later chapters.

2.2.2 *Random variables*

A random variable (rv) may be either discrete or continuous. A discrete rv takes on only a finite (or countably infinite) number of values. For example, in throwing a die, with faces numbered 1 to 6, if we define the random Y as the number showing on the top face, then Y will take, with equal probability, one of these values: $\{1, 2, 3, 4, 5, 6\}$. Hence, it is a discrete random variable. A continuous rv, on the other hand, is one that can take on any value in some interval of values on the real line. Thus, the height of a randomly selected individual is a continuous variable.

Understanding random variables is essential to the assessment of risk. A random variable is defined by its distribution, or specifically the function assigning probabilities to values: $y \to g(y)$. The function g is called the density function (PDF).

(1) **Discrete random variable**

Let Y be a discrete rv taking distinct values $\{y_1, \ldots, y_n\}$. Then, the density function g is

$$\begin{aligned} g(y_i) &= Pr[Y = y_i] > 0, \quad i = 1, \ldots, n \\ g(y) &= 0, \quad y \neq y_i, \quad i = 1, \ldots, n. \end{aligned} \tag{2.1}$$

An equivalent representation of probability which is important for sets of values (events) is the cumulative distribution (CDF) – $G(y)$, where

$$G(y_i) = Pr[Y \leq y_i] = \sum_{j=1}^{i} g(y_j), \quad i = 1, \ldots, n. \tag{2.2}$$

We have used the following law: *The probability of an event is the accumulation of the probabilities of the distinct outcomes in the event.*

(2) **Continuous random variable**

Let Y be a continuous random variable defined on an interval $[a, b] \subseteq R$. Then, the density function g satisfies

$$\begin{aligned} g(y) &\geq 0, \quad y \in [a, b] \\ g(y) &= 0, \quad y \notin [a, b]. \end{aligned} \tag{2.3}$$

The cumulative distribution function is

$$G(y) = \int_a^y g(y)dy. \tag{2.4}$$

The accumulation of probability is continuous, so the integral (continuous sum) is used. Of course, it is equivalent to the discrete sum. The increment $g(y)dy$ is known as the probability element (the probability associated with a small interval of a continuous variable).

For an interval $[c, d] \subset [a.b]$, the probability that Y lies in the interval $[c, d]$ is $G(d) - G(c)$, with $G(b) - G(a) = 1$.

Geometrically, we have the density and cumulative distribution for a continuous random variable in Figure 2.1.

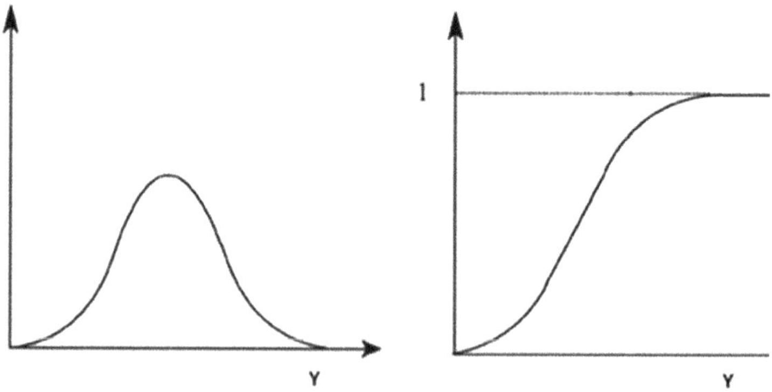

Figure 2.1. Density (left) and cumulative (right) for random variable Y.

Characteristics of probability distributions

The distribution of a random variable has complete information, informing one of what can happen and the chances. If we have the functions $g(y)$ and $G(y)$, then determining $G(y) = Pr[Y \leq y]$ is possible. However, Figure 2.1 is an abstract depiction of the distribution. In practice, the functional form of the distribution needs to be specified, either through simulation of many output trials of a system or with an equation for $g(y)$.

A useful approach to defining a pdf is to connect it to the moments of the distribution. The moments are expected values of powers of a random variable. Usually, moments are centered on the first moment, so they are powers of the difference from the first moment. The first moment is the mean and the second moment around the mean is the variance. We will emphasize distributions which are fully characterized by the first two moments. In general distributions cannot be fully characterized by moments. We will consider the important moments and their connection to the probability distribution function (pdf).

1st Moment: Mean

The mean is the expected value of rv Y, denoted by $\mu = E(Y)$, and is defined as follows:

$$\mu = \sum_{y} y \cdot g(y) \quad \text{(discrete rv)}, \tag{2.5}$$

$$\mu = \int_{-\infty}^{\infty} y \cdot g(y) dy \quad \text{(continuous rv)}. \tag{2.6}$$

2nd Central moment: Variance

Let Y be a random variable with mean $\mu = E(Y)$. Then the variance is the second moment around the mean:

$$\sigma^2 = E(Y - \mu)^2 = \sum_{y} (y - \mu)^2 \cdot g(y) \quad \text{(discrete rv)}, \tag{2.7}$$

$$\sigma^2 = E(Y - \mu)^2 = \int_{-\infty}^{\infty} (y - \mu)^2 \cdot g(y) dy \quad \text{(continuous rv)}. \tag{2.8}$$

The positive square root of variance, σ, is the standard deviation of Y. The variance or standard deviation gives an indication of how closely or widely the individual Y values are spread around their mean value.

Properties of moments

The moments are expected values, and the expectation operation has important properties, particularly for the sum of random variables. Recall that the stochastic systems we are considering are dynamic, and the change from one time to the next in output is generated by a random rate of change. Furthermore, the change is state dependent, that is, the change $Y_{t-1} \to Y_t$ depends on Y_{t-1}. The process is $Y_t = Y_{t-1} + \Delta Y_t = Y_{t-1} + Y_t - Y_{t-1} = Y_{t-1}\left(1 + \frac{Y_t - Y_{t-1}}{Y_{t-1}}\right)$, which is determined by the rate $\frac{Y_t - Y_{t-1}}{Y_{t-1}}$. Then, $Y_{t-2} \to Y_t$ becomes $Y_{t-2}\left(1 + \frac{Y_{t-1} - Y_{t-2}}{Y_{t-2}}\right)\left(1 + \frac{Y_t - Y_{t-1}}{Y_{t-1}}\right)$. So, the output grows or degrades depending on the size of the rates. That geometric process is transformed to an additive process by a logarithm function. Recall that

$$\log_e(y_1^a \cdot y_2^b) = a \cdot \log_e(y_1) + b \cdot \log_e(y_2).$$

In log space, the output is expressed as a summation of rates of change, and that additive process is closely connected to the distribution of output when the system has operated for enough time.

With $Y(t) = Y(0)\left(1 + \frac{Y_1 - Y_0}{Y_0}\right) \times \cdots \times \left(1 + \frac{Y_t - Y_{t-1}}{Y_{t-1}}\right)$, we have $\ln(Y(t) = \ln(Y(0)) + \ln\left(1 + \frac{Y_1 - Y_0}{Y_0}\right) + \cdots + \ln\left(1 + \frac{Y_t - Y_{t-1}}{Y_{t-1}}\right)$. Since $\ln\left(1 + \frac{Y_t - Y_{t-1}}{Y_{t-1}}\right) \cong \frac{Y_t - Y_{t-1}}{Y_{t-1}} = R(t), \ln(Y(t)) = \sum_{s=1}^{t} R(s)$. (We have set $\ln(Y(0)) = 0$.) The logarithm of output is the sum of the rates of return.

The moments of the sum are relevant to the distribution of a sum, so we consider those moments.

Mean

1. The expected value of a constant is the constant itself. Thus, if b is a constant,

$$E(b) = b.$$

2. If a and b are constants,

$$E(aY + b) = aE(Y) + b.$$

3. If X and Y are random variables and a and b are constants, then

$$E(aY_1 + bY_2) = aE(Y_1) + bE(Y_2).$$

Variance

4. The variance of a constant is zero.
5. If a and b are constants, then

$$\mathrm{var}(aY) = a^2\mathrm{var}(Y).$$

6. If X and Y are independent rvs and a and b are constants, then

$$\mathrm{var}(aY_1 + bY_2) = a^2\mathrm{var}(Y_1) + b^2\mathrm{var}(Y_2).$$

For systems where the outcomes are accumulated, these properties support some classic distributions, most notably the normal and lognormal.

2.2.3 *Normal distribution*

The best known of all the theoretical probability distributions is the normal distribution. A (continuous) random variable Y is said to be normally distributed if its PDF has the following form:

$$g(y) = \frac{1}{\sigma\sqrt{2\pi}} e^{-\frac{(y-\mu)^2}{2\sigma^2}}, -\infty < y < \infty, \tag{2.9}$$

where μ and σ^2, known as the parameters of the distribution, are, respectively, the mean and the variance of the distribution. In the normal case, $g \Longleftrightarrow (\mu, \sigma^2)$, and the distribution is determined by the first two moments. By convention, we denote a normally distributed variable as $Y \sim N(\mu, \sigma^2)$. A graph is shown in Figure 2.2.

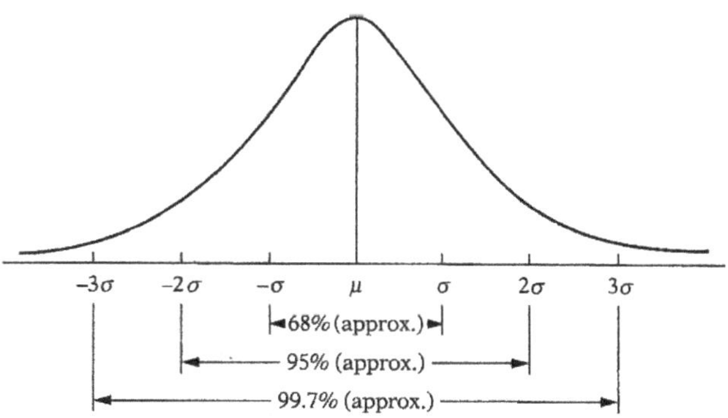

Figure 2.2. Normal distribution.

The normal is symmetrical around its mean value. One can find the probability that Y will lie within a certain interval by using the PDF of the normal distribution:

$$P[Y \leq a] = P\left[Z \leq \frac{a-\mu}{\sigma}\right] = \phi\left(\frac{a-\mu}{\sigma}\right),$$

where $Z = \frac{Y-\mu}{\sigma}$ is the standard normal $Z \sim N(0,1)$. The function $\phi(z)$ is tabulated in detail in standard software. Using an approximation (Olabiyi and Annamalai, 2012), we have the CDF for the standard normal as

$$\phi(z) \approx 1 - 0.5e^{-1.2z^{1.3}}.$$

This formula is convenient for analyzing the normal.

Let $Y_1 \sim N(\mu_1, \sigma_1^2)$ and $Y_2 \sim N(\mu_2, \sigma_2^2)$. Assume that they are independent and consider the linear combination (sum):

$$Y = aX_1 + bX_2,$$

where a and b are constants. Then, the expectation properties establish that

$$Y \sim N(a\mu_1 + b\mu_2, a^2\sigma_1^2 + b^2\sigma_2^2).$$

This result, which states that a linear combination of normally distributed variables is itself normally distributed, can be easily generalized to a linear combination of more than two normally distributed variables.

Clearly, working with normally distributed variables is advantageous. However, the normal model choice for system output needs justification, and convenience is not a justification. If risk assessment is based on an incorrect model for system output, then the assessment could be substantially in error.

The support for the normal is primarily based on the central limit theorem (CLT). Let $\{Y_1, Y_2, \ldots, Y_T\}$ denote T independent random variables, all of which have the same PDFs with mean μ and variance σ^2. Let $\bar{Y} = \frac{1}{T}\sum Y_i$ (i.e., the average). Then, as T increases indefinitely (i.e., $T \to \infty$),

$$\bar{Y} \sim N\left(\mu, \frac{\sigma^2}{T}\right).$$

Recall that $\ln(Y(t)) = \sum_{i=1}^{t} R_i$. Then, the CLT implies $\sum R_i \sim N(t\mu, t\sigma^2)$. That is, the system log(output) approaches the normal distribution. Notice that this result holds true regardless of the form of the pdf. However, it is assumed that the changes R_i are identically distributed. Under a weak regularity condition (Lyapunov condition), the convergence applies to non-identically distributed R_i. With (means, variances) as $\{(\mu_i, \sigma_i^2),\ i = 1, \ldots, t\}$, then

$$\sum R_i \sim N\left(\sum_{i=1}^{t} \mu_i, \sum_{i=1}^{t} \sigma_i^2\right).$$

There are reasons to believe that the rates of change at time points are not identically distributed. The system output at a time depends on system factors F and system decisions X, and the factors and decisions change with time.

The conclusion is that the normal distribution is a reasonable model for the logarithm of system output. In practice, the parameters need to be estimated, and that problem is addressed later in this chapter.

2.2.4 *Lognormal distribution*

The output process is considered to be multiplicative (product of rates), and the logarithm transforms the process to an additive one. The log space is appropriate for analysis, but the original units for output are important for interpretation. Following the logic in the CLT, if the rate of change of variables is independently distributed over time, then the multiplicative output has an approximate lognormal distribution.

Consider a lognormal random variable Y. If (μ, σ^2) are the (mean, variance) of $\log(Y)$, then the pdf for Y is

$$g(y) = \frac{1}{y\sigma\sqrt{2\pi}} e^{-\left(\frac{(\ln y - \mu)^2}{2\sigma^2}\right)}. \tag{2.10}$$

A picture of a lognormal pdf is given in Figure 2.3.

Although it is analytically equivalent to the normal, the lognormal presents a shape that is familiar for size distributions. For example, the return from investment in assets is known to have a skewed distribution, with a chance of extreme values. If the concern is with losses from investment and the distribution is flipped to negative

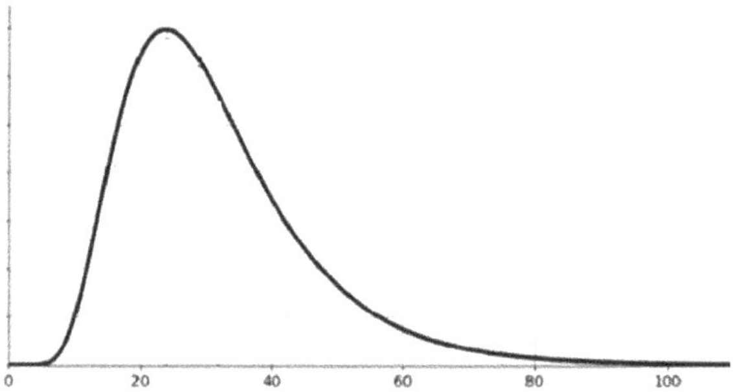

Figure 2.3. Lognormal pdf.

values, then the chance of large losses is approximated by a lognormal distribution.

2.3 Risk Measures

The distribution of output provides the probability of occurrence of various values and is the basis of the risk calculations. In this section, we examine several risk measures that are currently in use. Recall that risk is defined by the doublet (chance of a shortfall, size of a shortfall). Implicit in the definition is a threshold so that falling below the threshold (shortfall) has a low probability. In what follows, we will first define risk measures. This will be followed by techniques for evaluating the measures in practice. Any risk measure is a real-valued function of the distribution for outcomes. So, every distribution has a value for the risk measure. An important issue is the judgment on the risk measure: Does the system output have low or high risk? An assessment of risk is about the criticality of output. A benchmark(s) or threshold(s) is an essential component of risk assessment, and a comparison of the risk measure value with the benchmark(s) facilitates the classification of system risk.

2.3.1 *Variance*

Historically, variance was the usual risk measure and continues to be a preferred measure when the risk analyst undertakes optimization of stock portfolios and similar risk management activities. The variance measures the average squared distance between the realized and the expected value. Consider the random variable Y with mean μ and variance σ^2. The formula for σ^2 is

$$\sigma^2 = \sum_y (y-\mu)^2 g(y) \quad \text{if } Y \text{ is discrete,}$$

$$\sigma^2 = \int_{-\infty}^{\infty} (y-\mu)^2 g(y) dy \quad \text{if } Y \text{ is continuous.}$$

One problem with the variance as a risk measure is that it is a measure of how far output is from the mean in either a positive or negative direction. However, if the analysis of risk is based on a normal (or lognormal) distribution, the full distribution is determined by the mean and variance. In particular, the threshold $y_\alpha = \exp(\mu + z_\alpha \sigma)$ is partly determined by the variance. If the mean μ is fixed, the threshold is fully determined by variance. As a combination, (μ, σ^2) is a good basis for risk analysis when the distribution of log returns is normal. The Central Limit Theorem supports normality, and mean–variance analysis is a foundational component of risk analysis in finance.

2.3.2 *Value at risk (VaR)*

A more direct approach to risk measurement is to incorporate a lower threshold into the analysis. The focus on downside risk measures started with the development of the Lower Partial Moment (LPM) risk measure by Bawa (1975) and Fishburn (1977). This very popular risk measure was further developed by Jorion (2008). It is defined by the αth quantile of the cumulative distribution G for the outcome Y:

$$\rho(Y) = \text{VaR}_\alpha(Y) = G^{-1}(\alpha) = \inf\{y \in \mathbb{R} | G(y) \geq 1-\alpha\}. \quad (2.11)$$

In terms of losses, VaR_α is the maximum possible loss at the level of confidence level $1-\alpha$. Alternatively, we define VaR as

$$\text{VaR}_\alpha(Y) = \max\{y | G(y) \leq \alpha\}.$$

An interesting take on VaR is its application in governance for endowments, trusts, and pension plans. Worldwide adoption of the Basel II Accord established this measure as a standard. For example, $\text{VaR}^*_{0.05}$ is set by an institution, and the 5th percentile of

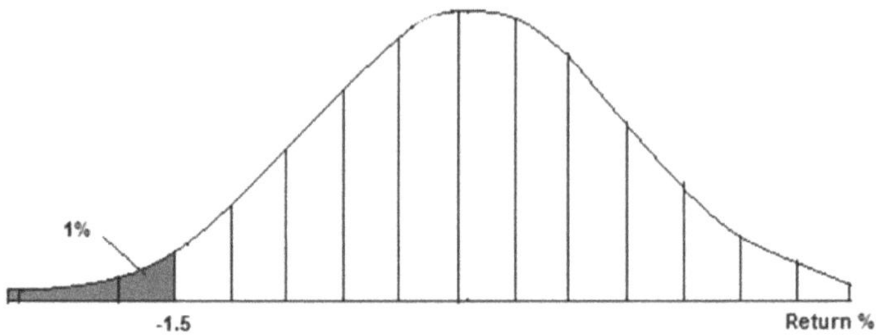

Figure 2.4. Distribution of daily rates of return (%).

the outcome at a specified time T must exceed $\text{VaR}^*_{0.05}$, that is, $\text{VaR}_{0.05}(Y(T)) \geq \text{VaR}^*_{0.05}$ is required.

Example: Calculating *VaR*

Suppose you are an investor with a $10 million portfolio, and you want to understand your potential loss from an investment. To answer the question, we need to consider the probability distribution of the returns to the stock portfolio. This involves the period under consideration (daily returns) and the probability for potential return values. Consider Figure 2.4, which shows the probability distribution for the percent portfolio return in our example.

Suppose that the investor considers a low risk to be 1% and wants to know the value at risk at that level. Our data show that 1% of the time, the daily rates of return for our portfolio are −1.5% or less, i.e., there is a .01 probability we would lose $150,000 or more on that day. At the $\alpha = .01$ level, the value at risk is $\text{VaR}_{.01} = .015$.

It is important to understand the use of VaR in risk analysis. Every return distribution has percentiles and therefore a 1% VaR. The real issue concerns the level of that VaR: Is the VaR value below a threshold specified by the analyst? Typically, there is a condition that $\text{VaR}_{0.01}(R) \geq b^*$. An equivalent condition is $\Pr[R < b^*] \leq 0.01$. This aligns with the concept of risk as the chance of falling below b^*, an unacceptable return.

2.3.3 *Conditional value at risk (CVaR)*

The VaR measure does not account for the losses below it, as all losses below the cut-off are considered the same. Figure 2.5 shows cumulative distributions with the same $\text{VaR}_{.50}$, but different percentiles for

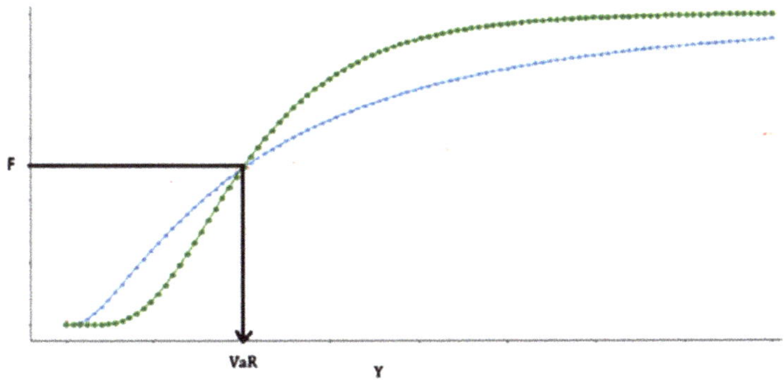

Figure 2.5. Comparing losses below VaR.

$\alpha < .50$. The blue distribution has greater probabilities for values below $\text{VaR}_{.50}$.

So, a variation of the VaR measure is to consider the average of the values at risk for $\lambda \in (0, \alpha]$

$$\rho(Y) = \text{AVaR}_\alpha(Y) = \frac{1}{\alpha}\int_0^\alpha \text{VaR}_\lambda(Y)d\lambda.$$

A related measure (Rockafeller and Uryasev, 2000) is the conditional expectation

$$\text{CVaR}_\alpha(Y) = E(Y|Y < G^{-1}(\alpha)).$$

$\text{CVaR}_\alpha(Y)$ is the conditional expectation of values below the $\text{VaR}_\alpha(Y)$ level. Obviously, $\text{CVaR}_\alpha(Y) = \text{AVaR}_\alpha(Y)$ when the distribution G for Y is continuous. However, for discontinuous distributions, the measures may differ.

VaR_α provides an estimate of the percentile given a user-specified probability and CVaR_α gives the average of the percentiles below the specified probability. Hence, $\text{CVaR}_\alpha \leq \text{VaR}_\alpha$.

The evaluation of CVaR implies a comparison with a benchmark. With the average loss being [VaR – CVaR], then we require [VaR – CVaR] less than a specified threshold.

Example: Calculating $CVaR_\alpha$

Consider the previous example of portfolio rates of return (%) and assume the distribution is normal: $R \sim N(5.5, 3.0)$. We have that $Pr[R < -1.5] = Pr\left[Z < \frac{-1.5-5.5}{3.0}\right] = Pr[Z < -2.33] = \phi(-2.33) =$

0.01. So, $\text{VaR}_{.01} = -1.5$, as indicated in Figure 2.1. To calculate the tail mean below $R = -1.5$, we have

$$\begin{aligned}\text{CVaR}_{.01} &= \frac{1}{0.01}\int_{-\infty}^{-1.5} r \times g(r)dr \\ &= \frac{1}{0.01}\int_{-\infty}^{-1.5} r \times \left(\frac{1}{\sqrt{2\pi \times 9}}e^{\frac{-(r-5.5)^2}{18}}\right) dr.\end{aligned}$$

Writing $r = 5.5 + z \times 3$, where z is standard normal, and $dr = 3dz$, we get

$$\begin{aligned}\text{CVaR}_{.01} &= \frac{1}{0.01} \times \frac{1}{\sqrt{18\pi}}\int_{-\infty}^{-2.33} (5.5 + 3z)e^{-\frac{z^2}{2}} \times 3dz \\ &= -2.4.\end{aligned}$$

So, $\text{CVaR}_{.01}$ is much smaller than $\text{VaR}_{.01}$, since it accounts for all values below $\text{VaR}_{.01}$. We have $[\text{VaR} - \text{CVaR}] = -1.5 + 2.4 = 0.9$, which is the average loss below the VaR.

2.3.4 *Properties of measures*

In the introduction, we listed properties which have been proposed for coherent risk measures. If the commonly used risk measures defined earlier are checked against the properties, the following results hold:

- Standard deviation: satisfies A1, A5, and A4 if $\text{cov}(X, Y) \geq 0$.
- VaR: satisfies A1, A2, and A3.
- AVaR/CVaR: satisfies A1, A2, A3, A4, A5, A6, and A7.

So, AVaR (or CVaR in the case of continuous distributions) has all the properties of a coherent risk measure.

2.4 Risk Priority

We have presented alternative measure doublets for risk analysis: (μ, σ^2) and $(\text{VaR}_\alpha, \text{CVaR}_\alpha)$. The measures are calculated for a system which depends on decisions. The value for the measures is an assessment of the system operating decision. Any distribution of outcomes Y has expected values, (μ, σ^2), and percentile values,

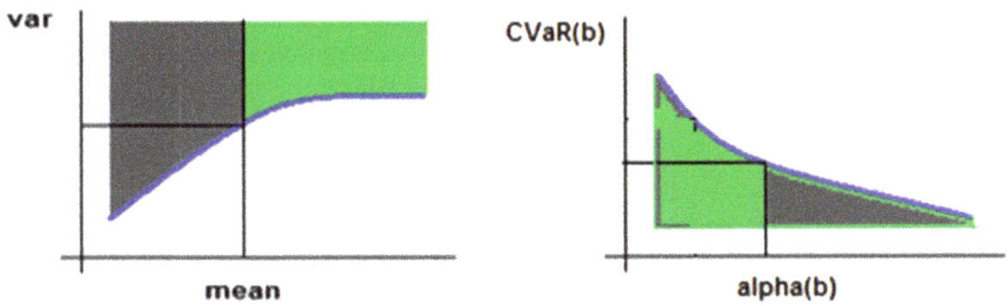

Figure 2.6. Risk: feasible regions.

$(\text{VaR}_\alpha, \text{CVaR}_\alpha)$. Those values do not necessarily capture failure, in the sense of falling short of a benchmark or threshold. For example, in a normal distribution, $\text{VaR}_\alpha = \mu + z_\alpha\sigma$ could be well above the benchmark and not indicate a shortfall.

In terms of risk, the preferred decision has the smallest variance or largest CVaR for decisions meeting the threshold. For feasible system operating decisions X, we have sets $\{(\mu(X), \sigma^2(X))|X \text{ feasible}\}$ and $\{(\text{VaR}_\alpha(X), \text{CVaR}_\alpha(X))|X \text{ feasible}\}$ as shown in Figure 2.6.

In the diagrams, a threshold for the "mean" and "risk level" is displayed on the horizontal axis. The threshold for the mean is set as μ_0 and feasibility requires $\{\mu(X) \geq \mu_0\}$. In the case of a downside threshold b, feasibility requires $\text{VaR}_\alpha(X) \leq b$. Equivalently, with α_b given by $\text{VaR}_{\alpha_b} = b$, so that $\alpha_b(X) = \text{VaR}_{\alpha_b}^{-1}(X))$, feasibility requires $\{\alpha_b(X) \leq \alpha\}$. Decisions X with measures satisfying the threshold are in green. The best decision is located on the boundary or frontier.

In terms of monitoring the risk profile of a system operating with decision X which may not be optimal, the risk measures can be plotted on a chart as in Figure 2.7. Zones are shown as red – high risk; yellow – medium risk; and green – low risk. The lines separating zones are generated by indices combining components. The indices are Sharpe ratio for (mean, variance) and Risk Priority Number for (alpha, CVaR):

$$\text{Sharpe Ratio}: \ \varphi(X) = \frac{\mu(X) - r}{\sigma(X)},$$

$$\text{Risk Priority Number}: \ \psi(X) = \alpha_b(X) \times \text{CVaR}_{\alpha_b}(X).$$

The figures have axes on a log scale. The set $\{(\ln(\mu(X)), \ln(\sigma(X)))| \ln(\mu(X)-r) - \ln(\sigma(X)) = s\}$ is an equivalence class of decisions with the same Sharpe index $\varphi(X)$, represented by

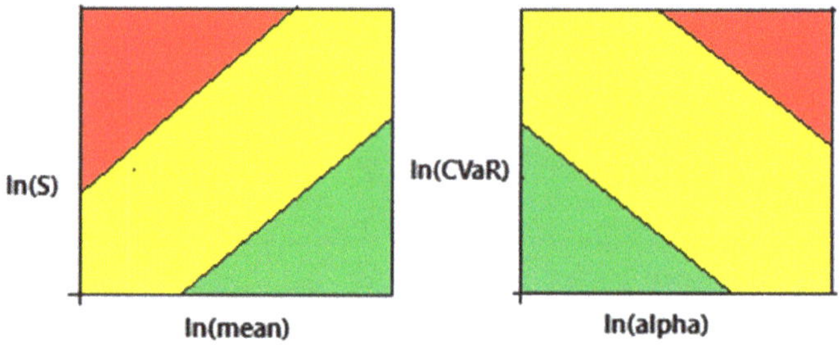

Figure 2.7. Risk control charts.

a straight line in the left graph. Upper and lower index values (s_l, s_u) create the zones.

In the same way for index $\ln(\psi(X)) = v$, the sets $\{(\ln(\alpha_b(X)), \ln(\text{CVaR}_{\alpha_b}(X))) | \ln(\alpha_b(X)) + \ln(\text{CVaR}_{\alpha_b}(X))) = v\}$ produce the control limits in the right graph.

We will be considering the use of risk measures in ordering systems and selecting the optimal control decision in Chapter 5. We initially need to consider methods for estimating parameters defining the system output distribution.

2.5 Estimation

The risk measures for a decision have been defined from a distribution for system output with that decision. The evaluation of the measures in practice requires that the distribution is specified. The approach to determining the distribution is through observations of the dynamic system in operation. In the dynamic systems, we are considering the observations over time. The variation in observed values arises from characteristics of the system (factors) as well as random variation. We are following the approach of modeling the system. We understand that a model is an abstract approximation of the system dynamics. The model has equations and parameters, and observations of system output and intrinsic system factors at each time point provide the information used to estimate parameters and relationship equations. This is a challenging task which is subject to modeling error, estimation error, and idiosyncratic error. Minimizing error is critical to good decisions. The impact of modeling and estimation error on system output is well documented. It has been reported that with a shortfall probability of $\alpha = 0.05$ in the value at risk requirement, the actual probability can be as high as 0.20 due to modeling and estimation error.

2.5.1 *Systems data*

In this section, we will consider the estimation of parameters in a distribution based on data – observations of the system at points in time. For decision X, consider the status at time $t, Y_t(X)$. Recall that output is a real-valued random variable with $Y_t(X) = Y_{t-1}(X)+ \ln(1 + R_t(X))$. The rate of change $R_s(X),\ s = 1, \ldots, t$, is the driver of the system. If we know the rates of change, we can construct the transformation of the system output for a decision. Furthermore, we are working in logspace and $\ln[1 + R_s(X)] \cong R_s(X)$.

With a focus on the rate of change $R_s(X)$, we consider the intrinsic components of the transformation system. We assume that the system is structured with n components, each with a random rate of change at time $s, \{R_{js},\ j = 1, \ldots, n\}$. The decision part of the system is the relative weight of emphasis for the components – $\{x_j.j = 1, \ldots, n\}$ and we assume that the system change is an aggregate of the component changes:

$$R_s(X) = \sum_{j=1}^{n} x_j R_{js}.$$

The distribution for $R_s(X)$ is the information needed for computing risk measures. Observations on the system at points in time are the basis of an empirical distribution, which is an approximation to the distribution for $R_s(X)$. We will consider two approaches to observation:

(1) We have observations of component rates of change $\{(R_{js}, j = 1, \ldots, n), s = 1, \ldots, T\}$. Decisions $\{x_j \cdot j = 1, \ldots, n\}$ are combined with the components' data to get the "observed" system rate of change for that decision. This is a great advantage, since the impact of decisions is directly measured. We will develop this approach with a financial system – a portfolio of investments in assets.

(2) We may only have observations of the system rates $R_s(X), s = 1, \ldots, T$. The component rates and decisions are indirectly

implied. For complex mechanical, social, or biological systems, the components and their interactions are complicated. It is not usual to have observations of the dynamic status on components. However, the operating status of the complete system is assessed, and in critical states, the components are assessed. We will consider the complete system approach with aircraft operational status.

Let's look at the trajectory of the system with rates for n components R_j and weights x_j. If we observe rates $\{r_{js}, s = 1, \ldots, T\}$, then corresponding portfolio return is $r_s(X) = \sum_{j=1}^{n} x_j r_{js}$. The trajectory of outputs (log wealth) is $y_s = y_{s-1} + \ln[1 + r_s(X)]$. The data requirement to compute the portfolio outputs for a strategy $X = \{x_j \cdot j = 1, \ldots, n\}$ is the array $D = \{r_{js}, j = 1, \ldots, n, s = 1, \ldots, T\}$. An illustration of the array is shown in Table 2.1.

Example

Suppose we have a financial system composed of m assets with observed trading prices $p_{js}, j = 1, \ldots, n, s = 1, \ldots, T$. Then, the unit rate of return values is calculated as $r_{js} = \frac{p_{js} - p_{j,-1}}{p_{j,s-1}}$. If the fractions of investment capital invested in assets at each time are X_s, then the observed rate of return for the investment portfolio at time s is $r_s(X_s) = \sum_{j=1}^{n} x_{js} \times r_{js}$. The observed trajectory of wealth is $y_s = y_{s-1} + \ln[1 + r_s(X)], s = 1, \ldots, T$. A similar calculation would produce the portfolio returns if one of the assets was risk free.

The data in Table 2.1 contain information on the dynamics of system output. However, it is an incomplete picture. The operating environment for systems affects rates of change and therefore the system output. We proposed that the operating environment is defined by factors which condition the system dynamics, and we have not included factors in our analysis. We will consider a conditional

Table 2.1. System component data.

<table>
<tr><td rowspan="5">Component</td><td colspan="4">Time</td></tr>
<tr><td></td><td>1</td><td>$\cdots$</td><td>T</td></tr>
<tr><td>1</td><td>r_{11}</td><td>$\cdots$</td><td>r_{1T}</td></tr>
<tr><td>$\vdots$</td><td>$\vdots$</td><td>$\ddots$</td><td>$\vdots$</td></tr>
<tr><td>n</td><td>r_{n1}</td><td>$\cdots$</td><td>r_{nT}</td></tr>
</table>

model in the next chapter. In the current chapter, we will assume that rates of change do not depend on factors. Equivalently, the random rates of change for the system are the same in each period. The data $\{r_{js}, s = 1, \ldots, T\}$ constitute an independent sample of observations of the rate of change for the jth component R_j, and $\{r_s(X), s = 1, \ldots, T\}$ are independent observations of the system rate of change R for the portfolio X. The data

$$\{r_s(X),\ s = 1, \ldots, T\},$$

are the basis of estimates of the risk measures for a given decision X. There are two primary approaches to evaluating risk measures and indeed any statistic: (i) empirical distribution estimates and (ii) fitted normal distribution estimates.

2.5.2 *Empirical distribution estimates of risk measures*

An empirical distribution function is the distribution function associated with the data from a sample. Let $(R_1, \ldots, R_T)$ be independent, identically distributed real random variables with the common cumulative distribution function $G(r)$, and consider observations $(r_1, \ldots, r_n)$. Then, the empirical distribution function is defined as

$$\hat{G}(r) = \frac{\text{no of observations} \leq r}{n}.$$

This cumulative distribution function is a step function that jumps up by $1/n$ at each of the n data points. Its value at any specified value of the measured variable is the fraction of observations of the measured variable that are less than or equal to the specified value. An illustration of an empirical distribution is shown in Figure 2.8.

The empirical distribution function $\hat{G}(r)$ is an estimate of the cumulative distribution function $G(r)$ that generated the points in the sample. It converges with probability 1 to that underlying distribution, according to the Glivenko–Cantelli theorem. $\hat{G}(r)$ is an unbiased estimate of $G(r)$.

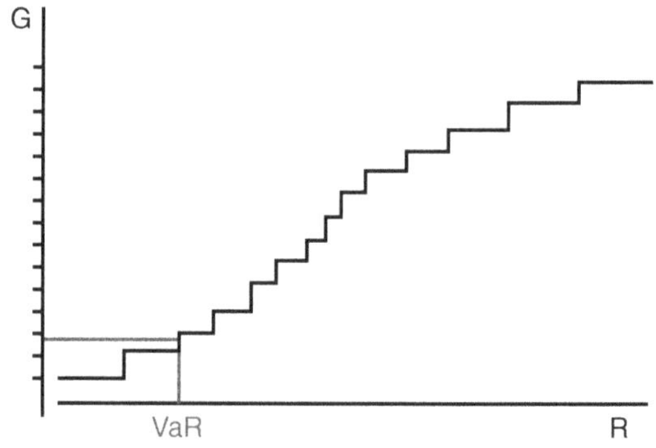

Figure 2.8. Empirical distribution.

The calculation of the risk measures from the empirical distribution is straightforward:

$$\text{Mean: } \bar{r} = \frac{\sum_{i=1}^{T} r_i}{T},$$

$$\text{Variance: } s^2 = \frac{\sum_{i=1}^{T} (r_i - \bar{r})^2}{T-1},$$

$$\text{VaR: } \text{VaR}_\alpha = \hat{G}^{-1}(\alpha),$$

$$\text{CVaR: } \text{CVaR}_\alpha = \frac{\sum r_i \le \text{VaR}_\alpha}{k}, \text{ where } k = \text{no of values} \le \text{VaR}_\alpha.$$

If there is a threshold b, then VaR_α should be greater then b. If it equals b, then $\text{CVaR}_{\alpha b} = \text{VaR}_\alpha - \text{CVaR}_\alpha$, which is the average loss below b.

These values are estimates of the corresponding measures for the unknown theoretical distribution $G(t)$. Furthermore, confidence intervals for the empirical distribution as well as the measures can be generated by bootstrapping samples from the empirical CDF.

2.5.3 *Normal distribution estimates*

Although the empirical distribution is suited to analyzing risk measures, we are going to consider subpopulations which are generated by risk factors. It is possible to have empirical distributions in subpopulations, but a preferred approach is to have population distribution parameters depending on the risk factors. To accomplish the dependence, we will consider a specific form for the population distribution. Considering the asymptotic normality of the log(outcome) we will assume that the outcome $Y_t(X)$ is lognormal and then $R_t(X)$ is normal.

If $R(X) \sim N(\mu, \sigma^2)$, and we have observations$\{r_1, r_2, \ldots, r_T\}$, then the parameters are estimated from the data. The standard estimation approach is maximum likelihood. The maximum likelihood approach begins with an assumption that the underlying probability distribution is known. Then, given a sample of observations from this distribution, the parameter values in the distribution function which yield the maximum likelihood are determined. The likelihood is the probability the observations are sampled from the distribution.

The model distribution we are emphasizing is the normal. Given a sample of observations that are drawn independently from the distribution, we proceed as follows:

1. Define the likelihood function:

$$L(r_1, r_2, \ldots, r_T\}|\mu, \sigma^2) = \frac{1}{(2\pi\sigma)^{\frac{T}{2}}} e^{-\frac{\sum_{s=1}^{T}(r_s-\mu)^2}{2\sigma^2}}.$$

2. Find the first derivatives of the log-likelihood and set these to zero:

$$\frac{\partial\{\ln L\}}{\partial\mu} = \frac{1}{\sigma^2}\sum_{s=1}^{T}(r_s - \mu) = 0,$$

$$\frac{\partial\{\ln L\}}{\partial\sigma^2} = -\frac{1}{\sigma^2}\left[\frac{T}{2} - \frac{1}{\sigma^2}\sum_{s=1}^{T}(r_s - \mu)^2\right] = 0.$$

3. Solving these, we have the estimates

$$\hat{\mu} = \frac{\sum_{s=1}^{T} r_s}{T} = \bar{r},$$

$$\hat{\sigma^2} = \frac{\sum_{s=1}^{T}(r_s - \bar{r})^2}{T}.$$

With the normal distribution, the maximum likelihood estimates are the same as the moment estimates from the empirical distribution. The usual practice is to correct the ml estimate of variance for bias, obtaining $s^2 = \frac{T}{T-1}\hat{\sigma}^2$. With the estimates, we have the estimated distribution $R_T(X) \sim N(\bar{r}, s^2)$. The risk measures can be calculated from the estimated normal distribution:

1. Mean: $\bar{r}$.
2. Variance: s^2.
3. VaR: $\text{VaR}_\alpha = \bar{r} + z_\alpha s$.
4. CVaR: $\text{CVaR}_\alpha = \bar{r} + sE_\alpha(Z)$.
5. Where $E_\alpha(Z) = -\frac{1}{\alpha\sqrt{2\pi}}e^{-\frac{z_\alpha^2}{2}}$, the CVaR_α for Z.

With $R = \mu + Z\sigma$, we get a scaling of the standard normal risk measures.[2] Maximum likelihood estimation is an attractive approach because it has been shown for larger samples that maximum likelihood estimators are most efficient.

2.6 Case Studies

This section presents several applications in risk measurement using the EViews software. The first two applications illustrate the basics of the empirical approach. Case 2.1 applies the measurement to the usual stock return data. Case 2.2 applies the measurement to growth rates for Canada's gross domestic product. This underscores the fact that VaR and CVaR are general risk measures that are useful in a

---

[2] $\text{CVaR}_\alpha = \frac{1}{\alpha}\int_{-\infty}^{\mu+z_\alpha\sigma} rf(r)dr = \frac{1}{\alpha}\int_{-\infty}^{\mu+z_\alpha\sigma} r\left[\frac{1}{\sqrt{2\pi\sigma^2}}e^{-\frac{(r-\mu)^2}{2\sigma^2}}\right]dr$. With $r = \mu + z\sigma$ and $dr = \sigma dz, rdr = \mu\sigma + \sigma^2 zdz$, $\frac{1}{\alpha}\int_{-\infty}^{z_\alpha}(\boldsymbol{\mu\sigma} + \boldsymbol{z\sigma}^2)\left[\frac{1}{\sqrt{2\pi\sigma^2}}\boldsymbol{e}^{-\frac{(\mu+z\sigma-\mu)^2}{2\sigma^2}}\right]\boldsymbol{d}z = \frac{1}{\alpha} \times \frac{1}{\sqrt{2\pi\sigma^2}}\left[\int_{-\infty}^{z_\alpha}\boldsymbol{\mu\sigma e}^{-\frac{z^2}{2}}\boldsymbol{dz} + \int_{-\infty}^{z_\alpha}\boldsymbol{\sigma}^2\boldsymbol{ze}^{-\frac{z^2}{2}}\boldsymbol{dz}\right]$. The standard normal is $\boldsymbol{f(z)} = \frac{1}{\sqrt{2\pi}}e^{-\frac{z^2}{2}}$, so $\frac{1}{\alpha}\frac{1}{\sqrt{2\pi}}\int_{-\infty}^{z_\alpha}\boldsymbol{\mu e}^{-\frac{z^2}{2}}\boldsymbol{dz} = \boldsymbol{\mu}$ **and** $\frac{1}{\alpha}\frac{1}{\sqrt{2\pi\sigma}}\int_{-\infty}^{z_\alpha}\boldsymbol{\sigma}^2\boldsymbol{ze}^{-\frac{z^2}{2}}\boldsymbol{dz} = \frac{\sigma}{\alpha}\int_{-\infty}^{z_\alpha}\boldsymbol{z}\left(\frac{1}{\sqrt{2\pi}}\boldsymbol{e}^{-\frac{z^2}{2}}\right)\boldsymbol{dz} = \boldsymbol{\sigma E_\alpha(Z)}$, where $\boldsymbol{E_\alpha(z)} = -\frac{1}{\alpha\sqrt{2\pi}}e^{-\frac{z_\alpha^2}{2}}$. So,

$$\textbf{CVaR}_\alpha = \boldsymbol{\mu} + \boldsymbol{\sigma E_\alpha(Z)}.$$

variety of applications. Case 2.3 illustrates applying the traditional approach of specifying a distribution before one calculates the risk measures. Case 2.4 provides another example that examines a risk management issue – the optimal stopping problem – and calculates risk measures for this analytical issue.

Case 2.1: VaR and CVaR estimation for the Toronto Stock Exchange Index

Consider the series of monthly returns of Standard and Poor's Toronto Stock Exchange Index from February 1985 to September 2022, which are contained in the file RetGSPTSE. The monthly returns are computed as price relatives, i.e., $\frac{p_t}{p_{t-1}} = 1 + \frac{p_t - p_{t-1}}{p_{t-1}} = 1 + r_t$. We will summarize the returns data $\{1+r_1, \ldots, 1+r_T\}$ before analyzing risk. This is done in EViews by the following:

(1) Click on the View Menu for the series.
(2) Click on Descriptive Statistics.
(3) Click on Histogram and Stats.

The results for the series are provided in Figure 2.9.

A complement of standard description statistics is displayed along with the histogram. An important use of the statistics is a decision on the approximate normality of the empirical distribution of returns:

- Mean is the average value of the series.
- Median is the middle value when the values are ordered from smallest to largest. The median is a robust measure of the center

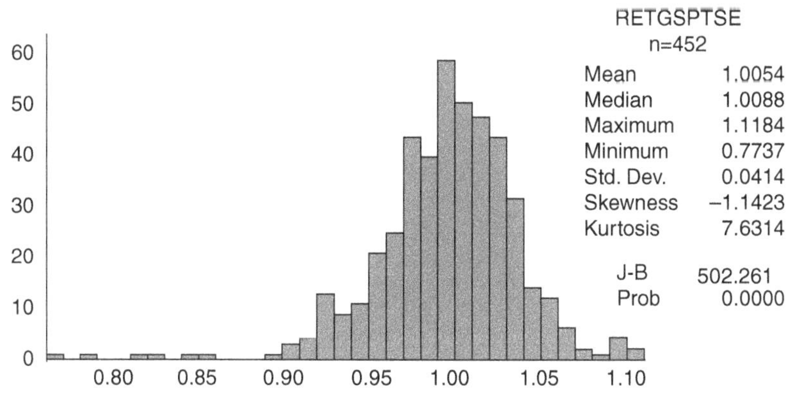

Figure 2.9. Descriptive statistics for RETGSPTSE.

of the distribution that is less sensitive to outliers than the mean.

- Max and Min are the maximum and minimum values of the series, respectively.
- Std. Dev. is $\tilde{\sigma} = \sqrt{\frac{1}{n-1}\sum_{i=1}^{n}(r_i - \bar{r})^2}$ is a measure of dispersion or spread around the mean in the series.
- Skewness is a measure of asymmetry of the distribution of the series around its mean. Skewness is computed as $S = \frac{1}{n}\sum_{i=1}^{n}\left(\frac{r_i-\bar{r}}{\hat{\sigma}}\right)^3$, where $\hat{\sigma} = \sqrt{\frac{1}{n}\sum_{i=1}^{n}(r_i - \bar{r})^2}$ is the biased ml estimator for the variance. The skewness of a symmetric distribution, such as the normal distribution, is zero. Positive skewness means that the distribution has a long right tail and negative skewness implies that the distribution has a long left tail.
- Kurtosis measures the peakedness or flatness of the distribution of the series. Kurtosis is computed as $K = \frac{1}{n}\sum_{i=1}^{n}(\frac{r_i-\bar{r}}{\hat{\sigma}})^4$. The Kurtosis of the normal distribution is 3. If the kurtosis exceeds 3, the distribution is peaked (leptokurtic) relative to the normal; if the kurtosis is less than 3, the distribution is flat (platykurtic) relative to the normal.
- Jarque–Bera is a test statistic for testing whether the series is normally distributed. The test statistic measures the difference between the skewness and kurtosis of the series and those of the normal distribution. The statistic is computed as $JB = \frac{n-k}{6}(s^2 + \frac{1}{4}(K-3)^2)$, where S is the skewness, K is the kurtosis, and k represents the number of estimated coefficients (predictor variables) used to fit the series. In this case, $k = 0$.
- Under the null hypothesis of a normal distribution, the Jarque–Bera statistic is distributed as χ^2 with 2 degrees of freedom. The reported "Prob" is the probability that a Jarque–Bera statistic exceeds (in absolute value) the observed value under the null – a small probability value leads to the rejection of the null hypothesis of a normal distribution.

The main conclusion from the description of the observations on the return $(1 + R)$ is that it does not have a normal distribution. The histogram is skewed and peaked. The estimation of risk measures for the TSX returns will proceed from the empirical distribution.

1. Empirical distribution approach

The series contains 452 observations: $\{1 + r_1, \ldots, 1 + r_{452}\}$. Suppose we want to estimate the $\text{VaR}_{0.05}$ for $(1+R)$. That is the return value such that 5% of the data lie to the left and 95% lie to the right of the data point. In EViews, we simply type the following in the command window:

$$\text{scaler var05} = @ \text{ quantile (retgsptse, .05)}.$$

The built-in EViews quantile descriptive statistics for a series is provided when the user specifies the series and quantile. Then,

$$\text{VaR}_{0.05} = .936735.$$

Calculation of CVaR for a given VaR is straightforward in EViews. We create a sorted series, determine the number of observations that are at VaR or less, and then determine the average value. More specifically, we do the following to calculate $\text{CVaR}_{.05}$, given $\text{VaR}_{.05} = 936735$. Click on Genr and make a copy of the series retgsptsecopy = retgsptse.

(1) Sort retgsptsecopy in ascending order by opening the file, click on sort, and complete the dialog box.
(2) Generate a new series retgsptsecopy by doing a copy/paste from retgsptsecopy (you must do this by copying/pasting on the sorted file to have the observations in the correct order).
(3) Generate a new series retgsptsecopy2 by using cumulative mean function ⟨GenR⟩

$$\text{Retgsptsecopy2} = @ \text{ cummean (retgsptsecopy1)}.$$

(4) This is the average value from observations 1 to 23, our required CvaR:

$$\text{CVaR}_{.05} = .900218.$$

As understood, the $\text{CVaR}_{.05}$ is less that $\text{VaR}_{0.05}$ for the monthly TSX returns. We did not introduce a lower threshold for returns. If an index investor wanted to avoid a drop greater that 10% in monthly returns, we have $\text{VaR}_{0.05} = .936735 > 0.90$ and would conclude the TSX was not risky. Also, $\text{CVaR}_{.05} = 0.900218 > 0.90$. It has been reported that 5% to 10% declines in market indices are not uncommon.

2. Theoretical distribution approach

An alternative to the empirical distribution approach to estimating VaR is to assume the data comes from a specified distribution function. The distribution most often assumed for returns $(1 + R)$ is a lognormal distribution. In that case, the log of monthly returns, $\ln(1 + R(t))$, has a normal distribution. We know that $\ln(1 + R_t) = \ln(P_t) - \ln(P_{t-1}) \cong R_t$, so the difference in log prices defines the rates of return.

Returning to the observations, we assume that the rates of return $R_s, s = 1, \ldots, T$ are mutually independent. So, the estimates for the mean and standard deviation of R are used, and we proceed with $R \sim N(\bar{r}, s^2)$. Keep in mind that the logarithm is a monotone function and probabilities from the lognormal and normal give percentiles that are linked by the log transformation. We will calculate $\bar{r} - 1.645 \times s$ for the normal rates, and get the Value at Risk for returns $\text{VaR}_{.05}(1 + R) = \exp(\bar{r} - 1.645 \times s)$. This value can be compared to the value computed from the empirical distribution.

From the descriptive statistics, we have estimates

$$\bar{r} = 0.005415,$$
$$s = 0.041385.$$

The estimate of $\text{VaR}_{0.05}$ for returns using the normal distribution is

$$\widehat{\text{VaR}}_{.05} = \exp(\bar{r} - 1.645 \times s) = \exp(-0.062663) = 0.93926.$$

The VaR values from the two approaches (empirical distribution for returns $(1+R)$ and the normal approximation for rates $\ln(1+R) \cong R$) are very close, confirming that the assumption of lognormal returns is appropriate.

We have not considered market factors in the assumption that the set of monthly returns is independently sampled from the same distribution. In subsequent chapters, we will introduce factors and consider the dependence of system output on factors at the time of observation. So, the distribution of returns will be conditional on the values of market factors. It will be part of the analysis that the rates of return given the factors are assumed to have a normal distribution. That is, the conditional distribution of log returns is considered to be normal.

Case 2.2: Canadian gross domestic product

The risk measures VaR and CVaR are commonly used in financial economics applications. Consider the Canadian economic system and the outcome Y_t = quarterly Canadian gross domestic product (CGDP).

EViews workfile RiskBK22 contains data on quarterly growth $\frac{Y_t}{Y_{t-1}} = (1 + R_t)$ for the Canadian gross domestic product (Statistics Canada Table 36-10-0104-01 Gross Domestic Product chained 2017 series, seasonally adjusted at annual rates). We have the series of growth values from 1961Q1 to 2023Q3: $\{1 + r_1, \ldots, 1 + r_{191}\}$. Figure 2.10 shows descriptive statistics for the sample: $r_t \times 100$, the rate of return in percent.

VaR and CVaR provide the analyst with useful information on the health of the Canadian macroeconomy. If we consider the Jacque–Bera test in the statistics panel in Figure 2.10, we find Prob = 0.588132. So, we do not reject the normality of the rates of return R_t, as the data support normality. We have $\bar{r} = 0.0085560$, $s = 0.00870933$, and will work with the distribution $R_t \sim N(0.0085560, 0.00870933)$.

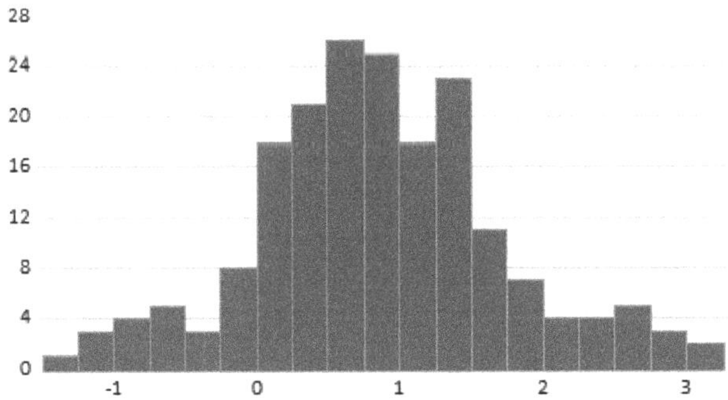

Series: CANGDPPCTSORTED	
Sample 1961Q1 2008Q4	
Observations 191	
Mean	0.855602
Median	0.820000
Maximum	3.180000
Minimum	-1.440000
Std. Dev.	0.870933
Skewness	0.126984
Kurtosis	3.262479
Jarque-Bera	1.061607
Probability	0.588132

Figure 2.10. Canadian GDP – rate of return in percent.

From the normal formulas, $\text{VaR}_{.10}(R) = 0.0085560 - 1.28 \times 0.00870933 = -0.0025919$. Then, $\text{VaR}_{.10}(1 + R) = \exp(-0.0025919) = 0.9974$. So, 10% of the time, the Canadian economy has negative growth per quarter of at least -0.0026.

A major concern in business economics is whether the economy will enter a recession. Definitions differ for when an economy is in recession. In Canada, a recession is defined as a decline in growth, $(1+R) < 1$, for two successive quarters, or the rate of growth is negative in two successive quarters. If we assume the rates are independent, then $P[R_t < 0 \text{ and } R_{t+1} < 0] = P[R < 0] \times P[R < 0] = 0.165 \times 0.165 = 0.027$. So, the probability of the economy exhibiting negative growth is found to be 16.5% and the probability of the Canadian economy going into a recession is 2.7%.

Case 2.3: Risk measures for BMO shares from the normal distribution

Shares of the Bank of Montreal trade on the Toronto Stock Exchange and the stock price returns for January 2000 to January 2005 were generated as the log ratio of prices $\left\{\ln\left(\frac{p_t}{p_{t-1}}\right) = \ln(1 + r_t),\ t = 2, \ldots, T\right\}$ in the EVIEWS workfile RiskBK23.

We begin by double-clicking lnBMO1 to open the series. Next, we

- click on View,
- then click on Descriptive Statistics and Tests,
- then click on Histogram and Stats.

Under this view, we get some basic statistics:

$$\bar{r} = 0.016462,$$

$$s = 0.055885,$$

$$\text{Jaque–Bera: Prob} = 0.3173.$$

The tail probability for the Jaque–Bera statistic calculated from the normal distribution is $P = 0.3173$. So the data supports the normal and we proceed with that distribution.

1. Estimating *VaR*

Assuming $\ln(1 + R) \sim N(\bar{r}, s)$, we can find the desired VaR value as follows. In the command window, we compute the Z value that corresponds with the desired probability as follows: Scalar $Z = @\text{q norm}(.05) = -1.645$. Then, we compute the value of our original series that corresponds with the Z score -1.645 as follows:

$$\text{VaR}_{.05} = \bar{r} - 1.645s = -.0761.$$

We can compare this with the empirical distribution approach by clicking on View, then Descriptive Statistics and Tests, and then Statistics by Classification.

In the view Statistics by Classification dialog box, check quantile and enter 0.05. Click OK. We get the estimate as $\text{VaR}_{.05} = -.075113$ for the empirical distribution version.

The $\text{VaR}_{.05}$ estimates are very close, confirming the normality of $\ln(1 + R)$.

2. Estimating *CVaR*

Calculation of CVaR is straightforward given VaR. Using the empirical distribution approach, CVaR is simply the average of the discrete values that are equal to or below the VaR value. For the normal distribution case, given $\text{VaR}_{.05}$, then $\text{CVaR}_{.05}$ is the average value in the tail from $-\infty$ to $\text{VaR}_{.05}$. From the earlier formula, $\text{CVaR}_{.05} = \hat{\mu} + \hat{\sigma}E_{.05}(Z)$, where $E_{.05}(Z) = -\frac{1}{.05}\frac{1}{\sqrt{2\pi}}e^{-\frac{z_{.05}^2}{2}} = -2.06$. Then,

$$\text{CVaR}_{.05} = 0.016462 - 2.06 \times 0.0558855 = -0.0987.$$

Again, $\text{CVaR}_\alpha < \text{VaR}_\alpha$, and the average of the rates of return below α is less than the best rate of return below α. Which risk measure is used is important when setting benchmarks for rates of return.

Another point from this example is the advantage of the normal distribution. If it is appropriate to use the normal approximation, the calculations of $(\text{VaR}_\alpha, \text{CVaR}_\alpha)$ are from formulas. Those formulas are very useful for analytic work. When we are defining problems for selecting the best decision for controlling risk, an analytic formulation is advantageous. We will consider the issue of optimal decisions in Chapter 5.

Case 2.4: Optimal stopping problem

An interesting problem in risk management with a variety of applications is the optimal stopping problem. It was originally proposed as the problem of selecting the best secretary, given n applicants for the job who arrive randomly for interviews. The manager begins to interview candidates and ranks each candidate she interviews. Once a candidate is interviewed and if not offered the job, then the applicant cannot be recalled later. The problem for the manager is to determine the optimal stopping time (number of candidates interviewed) that maximizes the probability of getting the best candidate. If she interviews a small number, then it is likely the candidate is still in the remaining population; if she interviews a large number, then it is likely she bypassed the optimal candidate.

There have been a number of applications to this problem as discussed in "*The Math of Life & Death*" by Kit Yates, 2019. Economists study the problem in the context of workers searching for work. Another special application is the parking problem. Here, the risk decision is to determine when to stop searching for a better parking spot closer to your destination, given that the closer you get, the lower the probability of finding a parking spot.

Mathematicians have derived the optimal stopping rule. It is known as the rule of 37%. The rule states that you should interview the first 37% of your candidates and then select the next candidate that scores higher than the best in the first 37%. Interestingly, it can also be shown analytically that the probability of selecting the best candidate is 0.37. This process applies to any number of candidates in the selection pool.

Suppose we consider the hiring process described here as a system with output $Y(t) = 1$ if the best candidate is hired, and $Y(t) = 0$ if the best candidate is not hired. The distribution for $Y(t)$ is as follows:

$\boldsymbol{Y(t)}$	$\boldsymbol{p(y)}$
0	0.63
1	0.37

Assume we have $n = 10$ positions to fill and used $K = \sum_{i=1}^{10} y_i =$ the number of times the best candidate is hired as a performance measure. Considering the candidates as independent, K has a binomial distribution as shown in the following:

k **Number of successes**	**Probability of k successes**	**Probability of k successes or less**
0	0.009849302919	0.009849302919
1	0.05784511238	0.06769441530
2	0.1528763684	0.2205707837
3	0.2394254236	0.4599962073
4	0.2460761298	0.7060723371
5	0.1734250819	0.8794974190
6	0.08487735492	0.9643747740
7	0.02848491730	0.9928596913
8	0.006273463929	0.9991331552
9	0.0008187589607	0.9999519142
10	0.00004808584372	1.000000000

The statistics for K are

1. Mean: $\mu_K = 3.7$,
2. Std Dev: $\sigma = 1.53$,
3. VaR: $\text{VaR}_{.05} = 0$.

The $\text{VaR}_{0.05}$ value implies that at the 5% risk level, the system will never select the best candidate.

We could consider the threshold $k = 5$, where half of the time the best candidate is selected. The downside of the system is that Pr [Best candidate was selected at least half the time] is $Pr[K \geq 5] \cong 0.30$.

Case 2.5: Kelly strategy in gambling

The Kelly strategy examines the risk issue of the optimal amount to bet in a sequence of plays of a game. It is also known as the gambler's ruin problem. Research into the optimal Kelly strategy has an extensive history. An interesting account of the use of the strategy in beating casinos is provided in "Fortune's Formula, The untold story of the scientific betting system that beat the casinos and wall street," by Poundstone, (2006). An extensive discussion on theoretical aspects of the concept is provided in "The Kelly Capital Growth Investment Criterion" by MacLean, L., Edward O Thorp, and William T. Ziemba (2010a).

1. Kelly system

Consider you have initial wealth w_0 and you play a favorable game where a fraction f of your wealth is wagered on two outcomes: win

$(1+f)$ with probability $\pi > 0.5$ or lose $(1-f)$ with probability $1-\pi$. Wealth after a play of the system is $\{W(1) = w(0)(1+R) = w(0)(1+f)\pi\}$ or $\{W(1) = w(0)(1-f)(1-\pi).\}$ After t plays with s wins and $t-s$ losses, the wealth is $W(t) = w(0)(1+f)^s(1-f)^{t-s}$. The rate of increase in wealth per play is $R = \log\left[\frac{W(t)}{W(0)}\right]^{\frac{1}{t}} = \frac{s}{t}\log(1+f) + \frac{t-s}{t}\log(1-f)$. A famous strategy is to maximize the expected growth rate in the long run:

$$\max_f G(f) = \max_f\{\pi\log(1+f) + (1-\pi)\log(1-f)\}.$$

Finding the value of f that makes this a maximum is a standard problem and leads to the solution $f = 2\pi - 1$. But since π is the chance you win and $(1-\pi)$ is the chance you lose, $\pi - (1-\pi) = 2\pi - 1$ is the size of your advantage. And that is Kelly's result: In a favorable game with even payouts, the fraction of your fortune you should bet is just the size of your advantage.

The Kelly strategy maximizes the expected growth rate, but it is considered risky. We have developed a simulation program to test the risk of the Kelly strategy in a simple game. We set the probability of a win as $\pi = .6$, hence the Kelly fraction is $f = .2$. The program simulates a random win or loss by drawing from the binomial distribution. Each game lasts 100 plays, and we simulate 500 games. The initial capital is set at \$10. A typical simulation provides the following descriptive statistics:

Statistic	**Wealth**
Mean	325.0716
Median	62.41558
Maximum	8098.193
Minimum	0.320706
Std. Dev.	867.6362
Skewness	6.124084
Kurtosis	47.82067
Jarque-Bera	44977.29
Probability	0.000000
Sum	162535.8
Sum Sq. Dev.	3.76E + 08
Observations	500

$$\text{VaR}_{.15} = 8.22,$$
$$\text{CVaR}_{.15} = 4.35.$$

The stats show that the Kelly strategy is quite volatile. The average win is \$325.07, but as shown by VaR, 15% of the time, winnings are less than the initial investment. CVaR tells us the average of the lower 15% of winnings is \$4.35.

The Kelly strategy, which optimizes the expected growth rate of returns, has important applications to stochastic dynamic systems. The gambling problem is a simple introduction. We will have more on optimal growth strategies when risk control is discussed in Chapter 5.

2.7 Conclusion

Successful risk management involves identifying and analyzing risks. The identification and the analysis of risks are collectively referred to as a risk assessment. For an organization to meet its objectives, it must be able to measure its risks so that it can take steps to improve them. Techniques commonly used by organizations to manage risk are: (i) benchmarking risks by comparison to industry averages; (ii) risk scoring by calculating a measure of the level of risk based on identified criteria.

There are basic criteria that apply to risk management: exposure, volatility, likelihood, frequency, and severity.

1. Exposure

This is a term that can mean many things depending on the context in which it is being used. Exposure provides a measure of the potential damage associated with an occurrence. The level of risk increases as the exposure increases. For example, drivers who are on the road 12 hours per day increase their exposure to having an accident significantly more than drivers who are on the road only 1 hour per day. Most risks are quantifiable, but there are many risks that are not easily quantifiable. Exposure to risk can be calculated using a simple formula:

$$\text{Risk Exposure} = \text{Probability of the Loss} \times \text{Amount in dollars of a Total Loss.}$$

We have used the terminology Risk Priority Number for the risk exposure.

2. Volatility

This is a term applied to frequent fluctuations in the price of an asset. An increase in risk is directly proportional to an increase in volatility. The volatility of the stock market, commodity prices, and retail pricing can almost always be measured or quantified.

3. Likelihood

This is the probability or frequency of an event occurring. The ability to calculate the likelihood of an event mathematically occurring is key to the ability to respond to risk in an organization. The likelihood of a risk event occurring is addressed by loss prevention techniques.

4. Consequences

This term describes the impact or severity of an event that has occurred. The consequences of an event that has occurred are addressed by loss reduction.

There is a relationship between the frequency and severity of losses. The risk response to a hazard risk that is low frequency and high severity (fire) will be different from the risk response to a hazard risk that is low frequency and low severity (minor vandalism to a building).

Bibliography

Alcover, P. and Cover, T. (1988). Asymptotic optimality and asymptotic equipartition properties of log-optimum investment. *Annals of Probability*, 16, 876–898.

Artzner, P., Delbaen, F., Eber, J., and Heath, D. (1999). Coherent measures of risk. *Mathematical Finance*, 9, 203–228.

Basak, S. and Shapiro, A. (2001). Value at risk based risk management: Optimal policies and asset prices. *Review of Financial Studies*, 14, 371–405.

Bawa, V.S. (1975). Optimal rules for ordering uncertain prospects. *Journal of Financial Economics*, 2, 95–121.

Bowles, J. (2003). An assessment of RPN prioritization in failure modes effects and criticality analysis. In *Proceedings of the Annual Reliability and Maintenance Symposium*, Tampa, January, 2003.

Broadie, M. (1993). Computing efficient frontiers using estimated parameters. *Annals of Operations Research*, 45, 21–58.

Buhlmann, H. (1970). *Mathematical Methods in Risk Theory.* Springer, Berlin.

Caputo, A.C. (2005). A new failure modes effects and criticality analysis model. In *Proceedings of the 23rd International Systems Safety Conference*, San Diego, August, 2005.

Chekhlov, A., Uryasev, S., and Zabarankin, M. (2005). A drawdown measure in portfolio optimization. *International Journal of Theoretical and Applied Finance*, 8(1), 13–58.

Duijm, N.J. (2015). Recommendations on the use and design of risk matrices. *Safety Science*, 76, 21–31.

Fishburn, P. (1977). Mean-risk analysis with risk associated with below-target returns. *American Economic Review*, 67, 116–126.

Jorion, P. (1991). Bayesian and CAPM estimators of the means: Implications for portfolio selection. *Journal of Banking and Finance*, 15(3), 717–728.

Jorion, P. (2008). Risk management for event-driven funds. *Financial Analysts Journal*, 64(1), 61–73.

Kaplan, S. and Garrick, B. (1981). On the quantitative definition of risk. *Risk Analysis*, 1, 11–27.

Kelly, J. (1956). A new interpretation of information rate. *Bell System Technology Journal*, 35, 917–926.

Klein, R.W. and Bawa, V.S. (1976). The effect of estimation risk on portfolio choice. *Journal of Financial Economics*, 3, 215–231.

Loffler, G. (2003). The effects of estimation error on measures of portfolio credit risk. *Journal of Banking and Finance*, 27(8), 1427–1453.

MacLean, L.C., Thorp, E.O., and Ziemba, W.T. (2010a). *The Kelly Capital Growth Investment Criterion: Theory and Practice.* World Scientific Publishing Co., Singapore.

MacLean, L.C., Thorp, E.O., and Ziemba, W.T. (2010b). Good and bad properties of the Kelly and fractional Kelly capital growth criterion. *Quantitative Finance*, August–September, 681–687.

MacLean, L.C., Thorp, E.O., Zhao, Y., and Ziemba, W.T. (2011). How does the Fortune's Formula – Kelly capital growth model perform? *Journal of Portfolio Management*, 37(4), 96–111.

MacLean, L., Zhao, Y., and Ziemba, W. (2016). Optimal capital growth with convex shortfall penalties. *Quantitative Finance*, 16(1), 101–117.

MacLean, L., Richman, A., Richman, V., and Larsson, S. (2005). The dynamics of aircraft degradation and mechanical failure. *Journal of Transportation and Statistics*, 8(1), 1–11.

Olabiyi, O. and Annamalai, A. (2012). Invertible exponential-type approximations for the Gaussian probability integral Q(x) with applications. *IEEE Wireless Communications Letters*, 1(5), 544–547.

Pindyck, R.S. (2002). Optimal timing problems in environmental economics. *Journal of Economic Dynamics & Control*, 26, 1677–1697.

Poundstone, W. (2006). *Fortune's Formula: The Untold Story of the Scientific Betting System That Beat the Casinos and Wall Street.* New York: Hill and Wang.

Rockafellar, R.T. and Uryasev, S. (2000). Optimization of conditional value-at-risk. *Journal of Risk*, 2, 21–42.

Rogers, L.C.G. (2000). The relaxed investor and parameter uncertainty. *Finance and Stochastics*, 5, 131–154.

Seber, G.C. (1984). *Multivariate Observations.* John Wiley, New York.

Sharpe, W.F. (1964). Capital asset prices: A theory of market equilibrium under conditions of risk. *The Journal of Finance*, 19(3), 425–442.

Sortino, F.A. and Satchell, S. (2001). *Managing Downside Risk in Financial Markets.* Butterworth-Heinemann, Oxford.

Thorp, E.O. (2006). The Kelly criterion in blackjack sports, betting and the stock market. In S.A. Zenios and W.T. Ziemba (eds), *Handbook of Asset and Liability Management*, Volume 1, 387–428. Amsterdam: North Holland.

Yates, K. (2020). *The Math of Life and Death: 7 Mathematical Principles That Shape Our Lives.* New York: Scribner.

Chapter 3

Risk Factors: Part I

3.1 Introduction

We have discussed the output from a stochastic system, with an emphasis on the risk properties of the random returns. The distribution for random returns is impacted by the design of the system and decisions undertaken to manage system operation. In this chapter, we will consider system features. The approach is to propose a model for system operation, with the system composed of interrelated components and equations for the dynamics of components. The principle in defining the equations is that exogenous factors affect the state of components, their level, and interrelationships. The structural equations in the model will be simple (linear) so that analysis of the model is feasible. We understand that stochastic dynamic systems do not behave according to linear equations. However, it will be possible to calibrate the model to actual operational data and identify any errors in the fit of models to data.

Calibration of the model equations follows from observations on the state of components and related factors over time. The estimation of parameters in model equations uses the maximum likelihood principle – parameter estimates most likely to produce the observations. Much of this chapter will be concerned with maximum likelihood estimation of parameters and the goodness of fit of the calibrated model to the observed system operation. The heavy dose of statistics is important. Our goal is not to analyze an abstract system construct. It is to learn about real-world systems, and create a setting where decisions on system maintenance result in preferred outcomes.

There is another feature in our modeling which is important. We consider that decisions do not impact the values of exogenous factors. This enables us to first analyze the factor–component relationships and then consider decisions on maintenance with knowledge of systems dynamics. So, systems maintenance and control are studied in Chapter 5, after estimating parameters in the systems equations. This approach is standard in financial systems, where it is assumed that individual portfolio decisions do not impact the market prices of financial assets. The result is that the effect of investment decisions in assets is proportional to the amount invested. So, we will assume in any system that the effect of maintenance decisions on component status is proportional.

3.2 Systems Structure: Risk Factor Model

The previous chapter defined several risk measures for the output from a stochastic dynamic system. Each of the measures is calculated from a probability distribution for system output. The uncertainty in system output is the source of risk, and it is important to understand the basis of the randomness in output. In Figure 3.1, we reproduce the abstract system structure.

The decisions are important weights (capital allocations) for system components, and output depends on those decisions. A part of the picture is the internal components and external factors that affect system operation. In the way we have structured the system, the factors impact the status of the components of the system. The effect of the factor relationship is that the distribution of random output is conditioned by the factors. Since we are concerned about

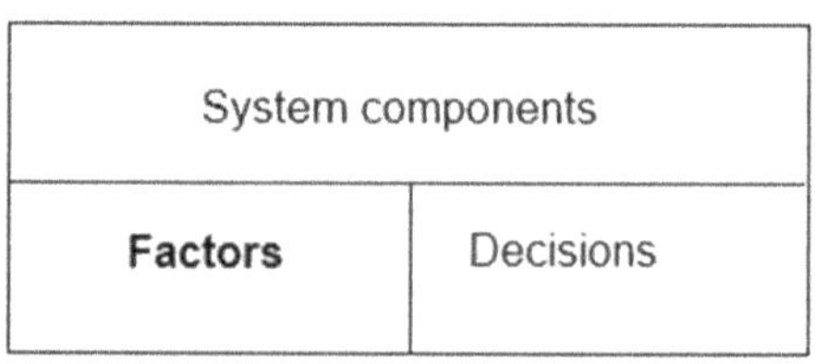

Figure 3.1. System structure.

the risk characteristics of the distribution for output, we will refer to the factors as **risk factors**.

In this chapter, we will incorporate the factors into the distribution of system output. Recall that $\ln(Y_t) = \ln(Y_{t-1}) + \ln(1+R_t(X_t))$, and we emphasize $\ln(1+R_t(X_t))$, the rate of change in output with decision X_t at time t. We have $\ln(1+R_t(X_t)) \cong R_t(X_t)$ and it is assumed that $R_t(X_t) \sim N(\mu(X_t), \sigma^2(X_t))$. Since we consider system structure, we restate that $R_t(X_t) = f(R_t, F_t, X_t)$, where $R_t =$ endogenous component rates of change and $F_t =$ exogenous factor values. We are going to assume that the factors affect the status of the components, but not the decisions directly. That is consistent with the concept that decisions are taken with an understanding of the factors affecting system components.

We consider that the system is structured with n components, each with a random rate of change at time t, $\{R_{jt}, j = 1, \ldots, n\}$. The decision part of the system is the relative weight or emphasis on the component $\{x_{jt}, j = 1, \ldots, n\}$ for system output. We assume that the system change is an aggregate of the component changes:

$$R_t(X_t) = \sum_{j=1}^{n} x_{jt} R_{jt}.$$

The structure in the above-provided equation is consequential. The component dynamics are separated from the decisions. If we have the component dynamics specified/estimated, then we can study alternative decisions with the same component dynamics. For example, with knowledge of asset price dynamics, we can make decisions on the capital to invest in assets to create wealth. Also, with knowledge of the degradation with the use of machine components, we can make decisions on component maintenance to impact the operating status of the system.

If there are exogenous system factors $F_t = (F_{t1}, \ldots, F_{tm})$, we have the rate of change for components depending on factors: $R_{jt}(F_t)$. Then, the rate of change of the system output, given the decision X, is $R_t(F_t, X_t) = \sum_{j=1}^{n} x_{jt} R_{jt}(F_t)$. Our interest is focused on risk, which we measure from the distribution for $R_t(F_t, X_t)$. We have n component rates of change depending on m risk factors. The approach to distributions is to assume normality for the component rates of change. The system's output rate is a weighted sum of component rates and therefore is also normal. We have provided support for the normality assumption in Chapter 2.

Regarding the normal distribution of component rates, we need to specify the mechanism through which the risk factors affect the parameters: (mean, variance). We will follow the standard assumption that factors affect the mean, but not the variance. In the next chapter, we will consider relaxations of that assumption.

The effect of factors on the mean rate of change in output will initially be considered as linear. That is a first-order approximation, which is reasonable if the time period for change is short. There are analytic advantages in working with a linear model, but we will ensure that the model is a valid representation of relationships. Conclusions about risk based on faulty models would be a poor basis for subsequent decisions to control risk. So, we need a comprehensive analysis of risk factors. Consider the linear equations relating the rates to the factors:

$$\begin{aligned} R_1 &= \beta_{10} + \beta_{11}F_1 + \cdots + \beta_{1m}F_m + \varepsilon_1 \\ \vdots &= \ \vdots \ + \ \vdots \ + \cdots + \ \vdots \ + \ \vdots \\ R_n &= \beta_{n0} + \beta_{n1}F_1 + \cdots + \beta_{nm}F_m + \varepsilon_n. \end{aligned}$$

It is understood that we are studying the rate of change in a period, so the time subscript t in R_{jt} is dropped. In matrix form, the equations are

$$\begin{bmatrix} R_1 \\ \vdots \\ R_n \end{bmatrix} = \begin{bmatrix} \beta_{10} & \cdots & \beta_{1m} \\ \vdots & \ddots & \vdots \\ \beta_{n0} & \cdots & \beta_{nm} \end{bmatrix} \begin{bmatrix} F_0 \\ \vdots \\ F_m \end{bmatrix} + \begin{bmatrix} \varepsilon_1 \\ \vdots \\ \varepsilon_n \end{bmatrix}, \quad \text{or} \quad R = BF + \varepsilon,$$

where $F_0 = 1$. The error term $\varepsilon' = (\varepsilon_1, \ldots, \varepsilon_n)$ is multivariate normal: $\varepsilon \sim MN(0, \Sigma)$.

The system rate change is an aggregate of the component rate change: $R(X) = X'R = \sum_{j=1}^{n} x_j R_j$. We are considering the impact of factors on risk and will take the decision weights as given. The system outcome for a given decision X and factor F is

$$\begin{aligned} R(X,F) &= \sum_{i=1}^{n} x_i \left[\sum_{j=0}^{m} \beta_{ij} F_j + \varepsilon_i \right] \\ &= \sum_{j=0}^{m} \left(\sum_{i=1}^{n} x_i \beta_{ij} \right) F_j + \left(\sum_{i=1}^{n} x_i \varepsilon_i \right) \\ &= (X'B)F + X'\varepsilon. \end{aligned}$$

The impact of the factors on the rate of change in the system outcome is written as

$$\tilde{R} = R(F) = \sum_{j=0}^{m} \tilde{\beta}_j F_j + \tilde{\varepsilon} = \tilde{B}F + \tilde{\varepsilon},$$

where $\tilde{B} = X'B, \tilde{\varepsilon} = X'\varepsilon$. So, $\tilde{R} \sim N(\mu_{\tilde{R}}, \sigma^2_{\tilde{R}})$, with parameters

$$\begin{aligned} \mu_{\tilde{R}} &= E(\tilde{R}) = \tilde{B}\mu_F, \\ \sigma^2_{\tilde{R}} &= \check{B}\Omega\check{B}' + \tilde{\sigma}^2, \end{aligned}$$

with $\mu_F = E(F)$, and $\Omega = E[(\check{F} - \mu_{\check{F}})(\check{F} - \mu_{\check{F}})']$. We use $\check{F} = \begin{pmatrix} F_1 \\ \vdots \\ F_m \end{pmatrix}$ as the vector of factors.

The equation for $\sigma^2_{\tilde{R}}$ provides a decomposition of the variance of outcome rates $\tilde{R}$ into a part defined by the factors and an error component. It is understood that the components $\tilde{B}\Omega\tilde{B}' = X'B\Omega B'X$ and $\tilde{\sigma}^2 = X'\varepsilon$ depend on the decisions $X' = (x_1, \ldots, x_p)$. However, the decomposition provides a basis for evaluating the risk associated with a decision. With the knowledge of the risk for decisions, we can analyze decisions in later chapters.

The distribution for $\tilde{R}$ is dependent on the factors, therefore the risk measures for $\tilde{R}$ are factor dependent. In the model $\tilde{R}$ is normal, and the normal formulas apply. We have in Table 3.1 the formulas for the featured risk measures, assuming the normal distribution for rates of change in output.

Table 3.1. Risk measures for linear factor model.

Measure	Formula
Mean	$\mu_{\tilde{R}} = E(\tilde{R}) = \tilde{B}\mu_F$
Variance	$\sigma^2_{\tilde{R}} = \tilde{B}\Omega\tilde{B}' + \tilde{\sigma}^2$
VaR	$\text{VaR}_\alpha(\tilde{R}) = \mu_{\tilde{R}} + z_\alpha\sigma_{\tilde{R}}$
CVaR	$\text{CVaR}_\alpha = \mu_{\tilde{R}} + \sigma_{\tilde{R}}E_\alpha(Z)$

There are some notable differences in Table 3.1 from the risk formulas which are only based on the distribution for the rate of change for output in Chapter 2. The factor parameters (μ_F, Ω) are involved through the linear relationship parameters $\tilde{B}$. There are important results implied by the linear factor model:

1. The mean rate of change in system outcome is a linear function of the mean factor values. This is very convenient for analyzing factor effects, and differential effects are the basis of risk interpretations of factors.
2. The variance in rates is the sum of a factor-determined component and an error component. In the model, the factors do not affect the error.
3. The factor component of variance is a composition of the linear relationship coefficients and the covariance of the factors. The covariance/correlation of factors implies the factors may need to be considered in combination, since changes in one factor are linked to changes in other factors.
4. The combined effect can be studied with a spectral decomposition. There exists a transformation of factors $\Gamma = AF$, so that $R = (\tilde{B}A')\Gamma + \varepsilon$ and $\tilde{B}\Omega\tilde{B}' = \tilde{B}A'\Delta A\tilde{B}'$, where Δ is diagonal. The transformed factors Γ are independent, and risk can be interpreted from the coefficients $\tilde{B}A'$.

The systems model is presented with the decisions (weights in the system components) assumed as known. It is considered that the factors are independent of the decisions. Varying the decisions will result in different system outputs, but the factors do not change with the decisions. That is reasonable since the factors are features of the operating environment. It also enables us to compare decisions based on the output distribution since the factor effect applies equitably to each decision choice.

The linear factor model is an abstraction that is suitable for analyzing risk. However, it approximates the relationships in a real-world operating system. The test is the closeness of the abstract model to the real system. We will consider the fitting of the abstract model to data from real operations in the next section. First, let's look at examples of factors in operating systems:

- **Investing:** A portfolio is a system for investing capital in assets. In the financial market, investors buy and sell shares in assets at quoted prices. There are many macroeconomic factors affecting the financial market and the trading prices. Indeed, there have been so many proposed factors that it is called the "factor zoo." Some established factors are (1) the market index (S&P500); (2) market volatility (CBOE VIX); (3) credit spread (LIBOR and T-bill difference); and (4) bond yields (difference between the U.S. ten-year yield and the U.S. two-year yield).
- **Machine safety:** A complex machine, such as an aircraft, is a system composed of many interconnected components. The operational status (airworthiness) depends on important factors: (1) age or hours of operation; (2) time since last service overhaul; (3) machine model; and (4) machine operator.
- **Health status:** A health system (clinic, hospital, national service) transforms the health status of individuals. The outcomes of the system are dependent on many risk factors in the service population: (1) age; (2) socioeconomic status; (3) wealth; and (4) lifestyle.

Clearly, accounting for risk factors will improve our understanding of the systemic variations in system output. The improved knowledge of the operating environment will lead to better decisions in the objective of improved outcomes with controlled risk.

3.3 Estimating the Linear Factor Model

We are studying the output from a stochastic dynamic system and in particular the distribution of the rate of change R. It is hypothesized that the distribution for R depends on system factors

$F_j, j = 1, \ldots, m$. We will consider the linear factor model empirically. That is, observations on the system output are collected, and the best estimates for parameters in the linear factor model are calculated. There are three major tasks in model fitting:

1. Model Specification
2. Model Estimation
3. Model Validation

3.3.1 *Model specification*

The structure of the linear factor model is crucial for the estimation methodology and the interpretation of the fitted model, so we will review the model specification.

Consider that we have observations on the dependent variable R at times $t = 1, \ldots, T$. It is important that we look at the system output for a specified decision X, which gives weights to components in the system. The weights enabled us to write the output factor relationship by embedding the decisions in the output parameters. So, we initially consider observations on $R(X)$, written simply as R, the output from a system with the decision X.

We also have observations on factors $F_j, j = 1, \ldots, m$ at the same time, $t = 1, \ldots, T$. The factors do not depend on X. The data array for these observations is shown in Table 3.2.

The linear factor model postulates that our data were generated from the model: $r_i(X) = [\tilde{\beta}_0(X) + \tilde{\beta}_1(X) f_{i1} + \cdots + \tilde{\beta}_m(X) f_{im}] + \varepsilon_i(X)$, which we write without X as

$$r_i = [\tilde{\beta}_0 + \tilde{\beta}_1 f_{i1} + \cdots + \tilde{\beta}_m f_{im}] + \varepsilon_i, i = 1, \ldots, T.$$

Table 3.2. Data on system output and factors.

Time	R	F_1	$\cdots$	F_m
1	r_1	f_{11}		f_{1m}
$\vdots$	$\vdots$	$\vdots$		$\vdots$
T	r_T	f_{T1}		f_{Tm}

We have that $\mu_i = [\tilde{\beta}_0 + \tilde{\beta}_1 f_{i1} + \cdots + \tilde{\beta}_m f_{im}]$ is the conditional mean, given the factor values, and ε_i is the error or deviation from the mean. It is assumed that ε_i is white noise, i.e., $\varepsilon_i \sim N(0, \sigma^2)$. Then, $(\tilde{\beta}_0, \ldots, \tilde{\beta}_m, \sigma^2)$ are the parameters of the model to be estimated.

The model specification is based on assumptions which will need to be validated if it is a sound candidate for data generation. The data represent real output from the system, and the model is hypothetical, so invalid assumptions are problematic for the model. The assumptions are organized in Table 3.3.

With the assumptions in the table, it is possible to run the system, i.e., to generate data. The usual practice is to take the factor observations $(f_{ij}, i = 1, \ldots, T; j = 1, \ldots, m)$ as given and generate output for R_i conditional on the factor values. If the factor data are representative of the population distribution for factors, then that approach should be fine.

We have reviewed our model specification. The specification provides a rigorous foundation for drawing conclusions from our data. Later on, we will see the consequences of violations to our assumptions. For now, it is important to appreciate that the assumptions taken together provide the risk analyst with a powerful technique for drawing quantitative conclusions about risk. This will be illustrated in our case studies.

Table 3.3. Model assumptions.

Assumption	Notation	Interpretation
1. Linearity	$\mu_i = [\tilde{\beta}_0 + \tilde{\beta}_1 f_{i1} + \cdots + \tilde{\beta}_m f_{im}]$	The mean rate of change is linearly related to factors.
2. Unbiased	$E(\varepsilon_i) = 0$	The average error is zero.
3. Constant variance	$\mathrm{Var}(\varepsilon_i) = \sigma^2$	For each observation, the error variance is the same.
4. Factor Independence	$\mathrm{Cov}(F_j, \varepsilon_i) = 0$	The error does not depend on the factors.
5. Serial Independence	$\mathrm{Cov}(\varepsilon_i, \varepsilon_k) = 0$	The errors at different times are independent.
6. Normality	$\varepsilon_i \sim N(0, \sigma^2)$	The errors are normally distributed.

3.3.2 *Parameter estimation*

We have data on the system and the problem is to find the best parameter estimates based on the data. The statistical methodology is maximum likelihood, where the parameter values which maximize the probability of observing the data are determined. Consider the likelihood function

$$L\left((r_1,\ldots,r_T)|(\tilde{\beta}_0,\ldots,\tilde{\beta}_m,\sigma^2)\right)$$
$$= \frac{1}{(2\pi)^{\frac{T}{2}}\sigma^T} e^{-\frac{1}{2\sigma^2}\sum_{i=1}^{T}\left(r_i-[[\tilde{\beta}_0+\tilde{\beta}_1 f_{i1}+\cdots+\tilde{\beta}_m f_{im}]]\right)^2}.$$

We know that $\max_{\tilde{\beta}_0,\ldots,\tilde{\beta}_m,\sigma^2}\{L\}$ yields the same solution as $\max_{\tilde{\beta}_0,\ldots,\tilde{\beta}_m,\sigma^2}\{\ln(L)\}$, which reduces the likelihood maximization to least squares estimation:

$$\max_{\tilde{\beta}_0,\ldots,\tilde{\beta}_m,\sigma^2} \log L = \min_{\tilde{\beta}_0,\ldots,\tilde{\beta}_m} \sum_{i=1}^{T}\left(r_i - \left[\left[\tilde{\beta}_0 + \tilde{\beta}_1 f_{i1} + \cdots + \tilde{\beta}_m f_{im}\right]\right]\right)^2.$$

The least squares solution is simple to compute since it reduces to solving a system of linear equations. The least squares estimates have a closed form

$$b = (f'f)^{-1}f'r,$$

where $b = \begin{bmatrix} b_0 \\ \vdots \\ b_m \end{bmatrix}, f = \begin{bmatrix} 1 & \cdots & f_{1m} \\ \vdots & \ddots & \vdots \\ 1 & \cdots & f_{Tm} \end{bmatrix}, r = \begin{bmatrix} r_1 \\ \vdots \\ r_T \end{bmatrix}$.

(Appendix B shows the derivation of the least squares estimate b.)

If the fitting error is $e_i = r_i - [b_0 + b_1 f_{i1} + \cdots + b_m f_{im}]$, the fitted model is

$$r_i = [b_0 + b_1 f_{i1} + \cdots + b_m f_{im}] + e_i, \quad i = 1,\ldots,T.$$

The match between the theoretical model

$$r_i = [\tilde{\beta}_0 + \tilde{\beta}_1 f_{i1} + \cdots + \tilde{\beta}_m f_{im}] + \varepsilon_i, \quad i = 1,\ldots,T$$

and the fitted model is the basis for conclusions about the linear factor model and the impact of the factors on risk. Without the factors, the key ingredient of risk measures was the theoretical variance

$\sigma_R^2 = E(R - \mu_R)^2$ and the estimate $S^2 = \frac{1}{T-1}[(r - \bar{r}1)'(r - \bar{r}1)]$. Given the factors, the variance is decomposed so that part is explained by the factors, thereby quantifying the factor effect on the variation of R.

With $\bar{r} = \frac{1}{T}\sum_{i=1}^{T} r_i, \bar{f}_j = \frac{1}{T}\sum_{i=1}^{T} f_{ij}$, we have

$$\bar{r} = \bar{f}b.$$

If the sum of squared deviations for r (numerator in the variance estimate S^2) is

$$SST = (r - \bar{r}1)'(r - \bar{r}1) = \begin{bmatrix} r_1 - \bar{r} \\ \vdots \\ r_T - \bar{r} \end{bmatrix}' \begin{bmatrix} r_1 - \bar{r} \\ \vdots \\ r_T - \bar{r} \end{bmatrix},$$

which is the total error without the factors, then the total squared error with the factors is

$$SSE = (r - fb)'(r - fb).$$

Furthermore, with the factor deviations as

$$U = \begin{bmatrix} f_{11} - \bar{f}_1 & \cdots & f_{1m} - \bar{f}_m \\ \vdots & \ddots & \vdots \\ f_{T1} - \bar{f}_1 & \cdots & f_{Tm} - \bar{f}_m \end{bmatrix},$$

the deviations in the fitted values $\hat{r} = fb$ are

$$SSR = (\hat{r} - \bar{r}1)'((\hat{r} - \bar{r}1)) = \check{b}'U'U\check{b},$$

where $\check{b}' = (b_1, \ldots, b_m)$. The relevance of this sum of squares is the identity: $SST = SSR + SSE$. This mirrors the theoretical decomposition as shown in Table 3.4.

Table 3.4. Decomposition of variation.

Theory	$\sigma_{\tilde{R}}^2 = \tilde{B}'\Omega\tilde{B} + \tilde{\sigma}^2$
Estimated	$[(r - \bar{r}1)'(r - \bar{r}1)] = [\check{b}'U' \cdot U\check{b}] + [(r - fb)'(r - fb)]$

The squared error in the data SSE $= [(r - fb)'(r - fb)]$ is minimized, and the issue is how much variation has been allocated to the factors with $SSR = [b'U' \cdot Ub]$. The fraction allocated is

$$R^2 = \frac{SSR}{SST}.$$

This is an estimate of the factor effect in the sample. Obviously, we need to account for sampling variation in interpreting R^2, as well as the estimated coefficients b. Before considering inference, we will state important properties of least squares estimators in Table 3.5.

Properties 1, 2, and 3 characterize BLUE (best, linear, unbiased) estimators. Properties 4 and 5 relate to the variability of estimators, a key ingredient of risk. Clearly, the least squares methods are theoretically sound, and the estimation results are a good basis for analyzing risk factors.

The linear factor model parameter estimates are $\{(b_0, b_1, \ldots, b_m), S_e^2\}$, which yield estimates for the risk measures in Table 3.6. The estimates are provided for given values of the factors $f^0 = (1, f_1, \ldots, f_m)$. This determines the risk for the output rate R of a subsystem identified by $(f_1, \ldots, f_m)$. It is common practice in risk analysis to break risk down into subpopulations.

The parameter estimates and the risk measure estimates are determined from a sample of size T. The estimates are subject to sampling variation. It is reasonable to describe the results in the

Table 3.5. Properties of least squares estimators.

Property	Interpretation
1. Best	The OLS estimator b_i has minimum variance among the class of linear unbiased estimators.
2. Linear	The formulae for estimators are linear combinations of random variables.
3. Unbiased	The expected value of the estimates will be equal to their true values.
4. Consistent	The estimates will converge to their true values as the sample size increases to infinity.
5. Efficient	An estimator of a parameter is said to be efficient if no other estimator has a smaller variance.

Table 3.6. Estimated risk measures for given factors.

Measure	Estimate
Mean	$\hat{r}(f) = fb$
Variance	$S^2_{R(f)} = \frac{1}{T-m-1}[(r-fb)'(r-fb)]$
VaR	$\mathrm{VaR}_\alpha(R(f)) = fb + z_\alpha S_{R(f)}$
CVaR	$\mathrm{CVaR}_\alpha = fb + S_{R(f)} \cdot E_\alpha(Z)$

Table 3.7. Analysis of variance table.

Source	SS	df	MSS	F
Factors:	$SSR = (fb - \bar{r}1)'(fb - \bar{r}1)$	m	$MSR = \frac{SSR}{m}$	$F_0 = \frac{MSR}{S_e^2}$
Error	$SSE = (r - fb)'(r - fb)$	$T - m - 1$	$S_e^2 = \frac{SSE}{T-m-1}$	
Total	$SST = (r - \bar{r}1)'(r - \bar{r}1)$	$T - 1$	$S_R^2 = \frac{SST}{T-1}$	

data using the empirical distribution $R(f) \sim N(\hat{r}(f), S^2_{R(f)})$, but it is important to go further and consider the implications for the theoretical linear factor model. In particular, we wish to infer if the factors have a significant effect on output in the theoretical model.

3.3.3 *Statistical inference*

The effect of the factors on the output rate is modeled by the conditional mean $\mu_i = [\tilde{\beta}_0 + \tilde{\beta}_1 f_{i1} + \cdots + \tilde{\beta}_m f_{im}]$. With the least squares estimates for parameters, the fitted conditional means are $\hat{r}_i = [b_0 + b_1 f_{i1} + \cdots + b_m f_{im}]$, or $\hat{r} = fb$. As the observed factor values vary, the variation in the fits is $SSR = (fb - \bar{r}1)'(fb - \bar{r}1)$, where the mean of the fits is the overall mean $\bar{r}$. In Table 3.7, the variation in the observed output rates, fitted values, and errors is displayed, with $SST = SSR + SSE$.

The question becomes "Is the decomposition of the sum of squares evidence of a factor effect on output in the theoretical model?"

(1) Test on effect of all factors: $\{F_1, \ldots, F_m\}$

Consider the theoretical model and competing "no effect" and "effect" hypotheses for the set of factors $\{F_1, \ldots, F_m\}$:

$$\text{The null: } H_0 : \tilde{\beta}_1 = \tilde{\beta}_2 = \cdots = \tilde{\beta}_m = 0$$

$$\text{The alternative } H_a : \tilde{\beta}_j \neq 0 \quad \text{for some } j.$$

Recall that the theoretical effect of factors is $\tilde{B}'\Omega\tilde{B}$. If $\tilde{B} = 0$, then there is no theoretical effect. If the sample estimate is far enough from zero, there is sufficient statistical evidence to conclude that one or more of the parameters is not equal to zero. If the data are sampled from the null hypothesis, the variation in fitted values SSR is due to error variation. Then, the values $MSR = \frac{SSR}{m}$ and $\frac{MSE}{T-m-1}$ are both estimates of the variance of R. The denominators in the mean squared errors correspond to the number of free variables in the calculation of the sum of squares. For example, $SSR = (fb - \bar{r}1)'(fb - \bar{r}1) = [\check{b}'U' \cdot U\check{b}]$, which is determined by the m values $\check{b}' = (b_1, \ldots, b_m)$. The ratio of independent estimates of variance σ^2 is known to have an F distribution. In this case, the distribution has numerator df m and denominator df $(T - m - 1)$.

A summary of the test for the significance of factors $(F_1, \ldots, F_m)$ in the linear factor model proceeds as follows:

1. Hypotheses: $H_0 : \tilde{\beta}_1 = \tilde{\beta}_2 = \cdots = \tilde{\beta}_m = 0$

$$H_a : \tilde{\beta}_j \neq 0 \quad \text{for some } j.$$

2. Test statistic: $F_o = \frac{MSR}{MSE}$.
3. P-value if sampling from H_0:

$$P_o = Prob[F_{m,T-m-1} > F_o] = \text{ tail area.}$$

4. Decision: If $P_o < \alpha$, then there is a small chance the data is sampled from H_0. So reject H_0 and conclude there is sufficient evidence to support $H_a : \tilde{\beta}_j \neq 0$ for some j.

If the null hypothesis is rejected, so that the evidence in the data (r, f) supports the alternative, the conclusion is that the set of factors $(F_1, \ldots, F_m)$ affect the distribution for R. The interpretation of that effect is complicated. One major issue is that the factors are interrelated. That is a feature of observational studies, where the dependent and independent variables are observed simultaneously. For the matrix $U = \begin{bmatrix} f_{11}-\bar{f}_1 & \cdots & f_{1m}-\bar{f}_m \\ \vdots & \ddots & \vdots \\ f_{T1}-\bar{f}_1 & \cdots & f_{Tm}-\bar{f}_m \end{bmatrix}$, the covariation $U'U$ has off-diagonal elements. It is not possible to unpack the $SSR = [\check{b}'U' \cdot U\check{b}]$, attributing effects to individual factors. The coefficient b_j does not define the sensitivity of R to changes in F_j. The interrelationship implies that changes in F_j are accompanied by changes in other factors. If $U'U$ was diagonal, then the contribution of individual variables to SSR is separated, $SSR = SSR(F_1)+\cdots+SSR(F_m)$, and $R_j^2 = \frac{SSR(F_j)}{SST}$ is a measure of the effect of factor F_j on the distribution for outcome rate R. In particular, factor F_j impacts the mean of the normal distribution. That would provide a clear picture of F_j as a risk factor.

In the absence of a definitive statement on individual factors, we have an existence test for factor effects. We can consider sets $\{F_1, \ldots, F_{m-1}\}$ and $\{F_1, \ldots, F_{m-1}, F_m\}$ to estimate the incremental effect of F_m, when it is added to a model already having other variables. The incremental effect is $SSR(F_1, \ldots, F_{m-1}, F_m) - SSR(F_1, \ldots, F_{m-1})$. Note that if F_m is closely related to other variables, much of its effect will already be included in $SSR(F_1, \ldots, F_{m-1})$. In spite of this caveat, we will test the incremental effect of each factor (including it as the last variable).

(2) Testing for incremental effect of each factor

We will compare a reduced model $SSR(F_1, \ldots, F_{i-1}, F_{i+1}, \ldots, F_m)$ with a full model $SSR(F_1, \ldots, F_{i-1}, F_i, F_{i+1}, \ldots, F_m)$. The test requires running both the full and reduced models for each factor:

1. Hypotheses: $H_0 : \tilde{\beta}_i = 0$ (reduced) vs $H_a : \tilde{\beta}_i \neq 0$ (full).
2. Test Statistic: $F_o = \frac{SSR(\text{full})-SSR(\text{reduced})}{MSE(\text{full})}$.
3. P-value for F_o if data are sampled from $H_0 : P_o = Prob[F_{1,T-m-1} > F_o]$.
4. Decision rule: Reject H_0 if $P_o < \alpha$ (unlikely data sampled from H_0).

Note: The statistic $F_o = \frac{SSR(\text{full})-SSR(\text{reduced})}{MSE(\text{full})}$ has one degree of freedom in the numerator, the incremental effect of one factor F_i.

The best estimate of error variance is $MSE(\text{full}) = S_e^2$, so it is used in the denominator. An F statistic with 1 df in the numerator is equivalent to a t distribution: $F_{1,T-m-1} = [t_{T-m-1}]^2$. We prefer the F statistic since it exactly indicates the incremental effect of a factor. The formula for F_0 in the incremental test can be rearranged so that $F_o = [t_o]^2$, where $t_o = \frac{b_i}{S(b_i)}$, and t_o has $T - m - 1$ df. Except for b_i, the numerator terms in F_0 get moved to the denominator to become $S(b_i)$. If $U'U$ is diagonal, then the incremental effect only involves f_i, and $S(b_i)$ is specific to F_i. Otherwise, $S(b_i)$ is determined from all the factors.

The practice in most statistical software is to report $t_o = \frac{b_i}{S(b_i)}$. The F_o and t_o statistics are equivalent. The t distribution is bell shaped (and approximately normal), so it may fit with the usual reasoning in statistics. In the case here, it is very important to be clear that the test is on "incremental" effects of a factor. It is not possible to interpret b_i as the sensitivity of the outcome R to a change in the factor F_i. We will consider the interrelationship of the estimates b_i in a later section on multicollinearity.

3.3.4 *Validating error assumptions*

The objective in considering risk factors in risk analysis is to obtain a clear picture of the variation in outcomes from a stochastic system. If the variance is strictly idiosyncratic, then measuring risk from the empirical distribution of output is appropriate. However, if there are factors which define subsystems so that risk is conditional on the subsystem, then knowledge of factors is important. For example, if mortality rates in a health system are being studied, it is understood that factors such as age, gender, and socioeconomic status are relevant. Risk measures which condition on the relevant factors are required.

We have presented the linear factor model as a vehicle for exploring the relevance of factors to system outcomes. The intention is to draw conclusions about the factors. The model, data, and estimation methods must be valid if we are to reach correct conclusions. The validity checks we are presenting relate to assumptions about error. Violating the error assumptions can lead to incorrect decisions about factors.

Table 3.8. Model error validation.

Assumption	Notation	Impact of violation	Diagnostic test	Remediation
Constant error variance – homoscedasticity	$\mathrm{Var}(\varepsilon_i) = \sigma^2$	OLS is not efficient, that is, it does not have the minimum variance property.	White's test	Variable transformations Weighted least squares estimation
Uncorrelated Errors	$\mathrm{Cov}(\varepsilon_i, \varepsilon_j) = 0$	OLS estimates will be biased, inconsistent, and not efficient.	Durbin–Watson test Breusch-Godfrey test	Cochrane–Orcutt transformation Autoregressive model
Independence of factors and error	$\mathrm{Cov}(\varepsilon_i, F_j) = 0$	Model under-specification.	Correlation test	Add factor (s)
Normal errors	$\varepsilon_i \sim N(0, \sigma^2)$	Test statistics are invalid (for small samples).	Jarque–Bera Test	Variable transformation

The significance tests using the F or t statistics are based on assumptions about the error term ε_i in the linear factor model $r_i = [\beta_0 + \beta_1 f_{i1} + \cdots + \beta_m f_{im}] + \varepsilon_i$. Test decisions are based on P_o values obtained from tables for F and t which were created with the error assumptions satisfied. In Table 3.8, we repeat the assumptions and provide some remediation for violations.

1. Heteroscedasticity

The common variance estimate is an average of $e_i^2, i = 1, \ldots, T$. A plot of e_i^2 versus the fits $\hat{r}_i = [b_0 + b_1 f_{i1} + \cdots + b_m f_{im}]$ will give an eyeball check on error variance. A typical pattern is the trade-off from higher variance with greater mean (fit), so an increasing trend in variance may be visible.

A general statistical test for heteroscedasticity (non-homoscedasticity) was proposed by White (1980). White's test is a test of the null hypothesis of no heteroscedasticity against heteroscedasticity of unknown, general form. The test statistic is computed by an auxiliary regression using the residuals from the original equation. We regress the squared residuals on all possible (non-redundant) cross products of the regressors (factors). For example, suppose we estimated the following regression:

$$\hat{r}_i = [b_0 + b_1 f_{i1} + b_2 f_{i2}] + e_i,$$

where the b are the estimated parameters and e the residual. The test statistic is then based on the auxiliary regression:

$$e_i^2 = a_0 + a_1 f_{i1} + a_2 f_{i2} + a_3 f_{i1}^2 + a_4 f_{i2}^2 + a_5 f_{i1} \times f_{i2} + v_i,$$
$$i = 1, \ldots, T.$$

The value from the auxiliary regression $W_0 = T \times R_a^2$ is White's test statistic, computed as the number of observations times the centered R_a^2 from the test regression. White's test statistic is asymptotically distributed as a χ^2 with degrees of freedom equal to the number of slope coefficients in the test regression.

To carry out any of the heteroscedasticity tests in EViews, select View/Residual Tests/Heteroscedasticity tests. This will bring you to the following dialog:

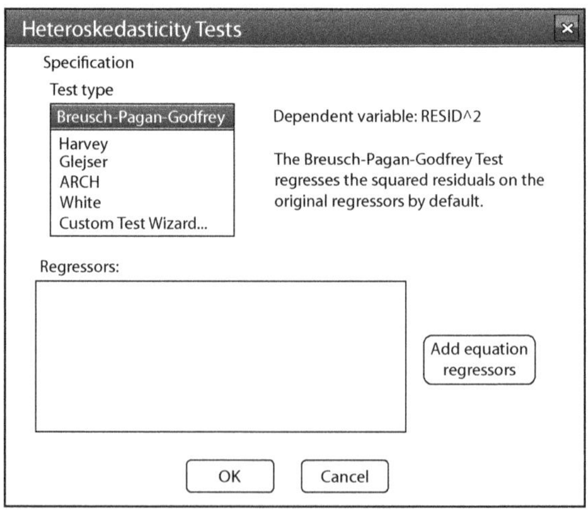

You may choose which type of test to perform by clicking on the name in the Test Type box. The remainder of the dialog will change, allowing you to specify various options for selected tests.

The White test lets you choose whether to include cross terms or not using the Include cross terms checkbox. The cross terms version of the test is the original version of White's test that includes all of the cross-product terms. However, the number of cross-product terms increases with the square of the number of right-hand side variables in the regression; with large numbers of regressors, it may not be practical to include all of these terms. The no cross terms specification runs the test regression using only the squares of the regressors.

If the null is rejected (there is evidence of heteroscedasticity), then a weighted least squares is performed. This involves weighting the data for each case i by a weight $w_i = \frac{1}{|e_i|}$ and performing least squares regression on the weighted data. By construction, the errors in the WLS have equal variance. Furthermore, the refitted equation usually has almost identical coefficient estimates to the unweighted estimates. We will have material on WLS in the next chapter.

2. Autocorrelation

The stochastic dynamic systems we are considering imply that there may be a serial relationship between observations. In the linear factor model, this is manifested in correlation in the errors/residuals. It is assumed that $\text{Var}(\varepsilon_i) = \sigma^2 I$, and a violation of the assumption can have significant consequences for OLS estimation. If the model has a different structure in the error term, then the OLS estimates will be biased, inconsistent, and not efficient.

Autocorrelation plots are a commonly used tool for checking randomness in a dataset. This randomness is ascertained by computing autocorrelations for data values at varying time lags. If the residuals for the estimated linear factor model are $\{e_1, \ldots, e_n\}$, then the k lagged autocorrelation is $q_k = \frac{\sum_{i=k+1}^{T} e_i e_{i-k}}{\sum_{i=1}^{T} e_i^2}$. If the residuals are random, then autocorrelations should be near zero for all time-lag separations.

A flexible test for autocorrelation is the Breusch–Godfrey test. If the population-lagged autocorrelations for $\{\varepsilon_i, i = 1, \ldots, T\}$ are

$\{\rho_i, i = 1, \ldots, k\}$, then the null (no autocorrelation) hypothesis is $H_0 : \rho_i = 0, i = 1, \ldots, k$. The test statistic for H_0 involves an auxiliary regression, where the residuals obtained from estimating the linear factor model are regressed on the original factors $F_i, i = 1, \ldots, m$, and k lags of the residuals, where k is the order of the test:

$$e_i = \left[\sum_{j=1}^{m} a_j f_{ij}\right] + \left[\sum_{j=1}^{k} g_j e_{i-j}\right] + v_i, \quad i = 1, \ldots, T.$$

If the coefficient of determination for this regression is R_g^2, the test statistic from this auxiliary regression is $LM_o = T \times R_g^2$. Under the null hypothesis of no autocorrelation, this statistic LM_o is asymptotically distributed as a χ_k^2, with k degrees of freedom. If $P_o = \Pr[\chi_k^2 > LM_o]$, then H_0 is rejected if $P_o < \alpha$.

To carry out the test in EViews, push **View/Residual Tests/Serial Correlation LM Test...** on the equation toolbar and specify the highest order of the AR or MA process that might describe the serial correlation. If the test indicates serial correlation in the residuals, LS standard errors are invalid and should not be used for inference. An autoregressive model is required.

3. Normality

Another important assumption for the error term is $\varepsilon_i \sim N(0, \sigma^2)$. This assumption is the basis for the exact distribution of F and t and the inference testing on the coefficients. We of course do not have actual independent observations of the error term. Rather, we have the residuals from the regression. There may be several influences in addition to observation error in the residuals.

A popular test for normality is the Jarque–Bera test. The test statistic JB is defined as

$$JB = \frac{T - m}{6}\left(S^2 + \frac{1}{4}(K - 3)^2\right),$$

where T is the number of observations, m is the number of factors, S is the skewness, and K is the kurtosis for the sample of residuals $\{e_1, \ldots, e_T\}$. The Jarque–Bera statistic has the χ^2 distribution with 2 degrees of freedom under the null hypothesis of normally distributed errors.

To display the histogram and Jarque–Bera statistics in E-Views, select **View/Residual Tests/Histogram-Normality**. Given an estimated equation, we select the residuals, then select View/ Residual Diagnostics/Histogram-Normality Test. This view displays a histogram and descriptive statistics of the residuals, including the Jarque–Bera statistic for testing normality. If the residuals are normally distributed, the histogram should be bell-shaped, and the Jarque–Bera statistic should not be significant. A small p value leads to rejection of the null hypothesis that the residuals come from a normal distribution.

We have analyzed the system outcome with the classical model: *outcome* = [*mean*] + [*error*]. The assumptions on the *error* are validated with the noted tests. If assumptions fail, then remedial modeling is appropriate, and we will consider options in the next chapter. The other component in the model is the *mean*, which is the primary interest in the analysis. We will turn our attention to some potential problems with the *linear factor* structure of the mean component.

3.4 Model Specification Issues

The goal in considering risk factors is to better understand the sources of variation in the system outcome. This section examines various limitations of the linear factor model specification and the implications of the limitations. The context of risk analysis is an important consideration in formulating a model. The first point is that there is usually no true model. That is, the dynamics of a system do not behave according to equations. Any postulated model is an abstract approximation. The second point is that knowledge of the system is obtained through observation. The data obtained from observation can present problems, particularly when studying relationships between factors and outcomes. Spurious associations, limits on the range of observed values, and exogenous disturbances may affect observed results. Statistical analysis is iterative, with equations being revised and data being expanded as knowledge and insight grow.

We will take the linear factor model as the initial formulation and consider its limitations. In the next chapter, we look at extensions. The various issues we examine under our general heading of model specification are as follows:

1. functional form,
2. omitting a relevant variable,
3. inclusion of an irrelevant variable,
4. multicollinearity.

1. Functional form

The linear form may be very limited if we contemplate an abstract model $R = f(X, F) + \varepsilon$. However, there are some ideas to consider when evaluating linearity:

1. A first-order Taylor series approximation around the mean is useful, particularly for rates.
2. The linear model is linear in the parameters, but not in the factors. A polynomial model can have powers and cross-products of the factors. The polynomial model is linear in the parameters. So, additional factor terms can be included to accommodate curvilinear relationships. Indeed, any curve can be approximated by a polynomial.
3. The linear model is a natural setting for categorical variables. The use of indicator variables to define classes places analysis of variance and analysis of covariance in the linear model framework.

The remarkable thing is that the linear model is sufficiently flexible to enable the analyst to study a full range of hypothetical relationships. The least squares estimation of parameters from observations is straightforward. The combination of a linear model and OLS is a powerful methodology for analyzing data. The real issues in the analysis arise from the data – the set of factors included and the number and character of observational units. Some issues with observational units were discussed under error assumptions. We will now look at issues around the set of factors.

2. Factor selection problems

The linear factor model has a preselected list of factors $F' = (F_1, \ldots, F_m)$ being proposed for their effect on the conditional mean $E(R|F = f) = f'\beta$. There is usually a rationale for the selection of factors, but in any specification, the set $\{F_1, \ldots, F_m\}$ is a subset of all possible factors impacting the distribution of R. For example, in financial research, there is a concept of the "factor zoo," a phrase describing the vast array of factors detailed by academics and investment practitioners alike.

It is a theoretical question of which factors are included in the linear factor model. In this section, we are considering a dynamic system where the factors are specified. The questions we analyze are under-specification and over-specification. That is, "Are there relevant factors which are not included?" and "Are there included factors which are not relevant?"

3. Model under-specification: Missing a relevant factor

In the linear factor model $R = F\beta + \varepsilon$, the factors affect the mean, but not the error. So, the factor effect is defined by $F\beta$. It may be the case that the dynamic system is fully defined by $F = (F_1, \ldots, F_m)$ and any variation in output beyond that attributed to F is random. However, it is possible the model omits a relevant variable either because we are unaware of its importance or because we lack data to measure its importance. That is likely in observational studies where data are recorded on the system as it operates. If an additional factor F_{m+1} has an impact on the output R, then its effect is included in ε. That contamination of error has consequences.

If F_{m+1} is related to $F = (F_1, \ldots, F_m)$, then the mean and error are not independent. The basis for estimation and testing is violated.

If F_{m+1} is not related to $F = (F_1, \ldots, F_m)$, then the mean and error are independent. However, $\varepsilon(F_{m+1}) \sim N(\mu(F_{m+1}), \sigma^2(F_{m+1}))$.

In either case, the estimation of parameters in the model using only factors $F = (F_1, \ldots, F_m)$ will be biased and inconsistent.

Model under-specification is almost inevitable. We mentioned the "factor zoo," which has more than 200 proposed factors affecting returns in financial models. Many of the noted factors are interrelated, and including factors which measure the same effect is redundant and furthermore introduces estimation problems (near-singularity). In a situation where there is a large set of potential risk factors, the goal is to find a subset that satisfies some specified criteria. Generally, the most important tool in selecting a subset of variables for a multiple linear regression model is careful logical analysis based on the analyst's knowledge of theory and research in the area of study. There are methods to select variables based on the data. The "Best Subsets" and "LASSO" techniques are available in statistical software (EViews) for subset selection. It is always important to keep in mind that the data are a sample and an "optimal" subset for the sample may not apply to another sample or the population.

With some caution, let's look at the "Best Subsets" technique. The idea is simple:

(1) For each model size k, estimate the parameters for each subset of k variables. From the subset of fitted models, select the one with the $\min_{\text{models}} MSE(model)$, where $MSE = mean\ squared\ error$.
(2) For the best size k subset model, calculate $AIC(k) = 2MSE + 2k$. Thus, AIC rewards goodness of fit (as assessed by the likelihood function), but it also includes a penalty that is an increasing function of the number of estimated parameters.
(3) Select the model size with $\{\min_k AIC(k)\}$.

The variable selection techniques can be part of a decision about missing a relevant variable. If a parsimonious model was determined through best subsets, then a new (missing) variable would need to improve on the AIC to expand the model. The attention is focused on the MSE, which is the estimate of error variance.

4. Model over-specification: Including an irrelevant variable

Following the concept of model parsimony noted earlier, the best subset technique will eliminate irrelevant variables, since irrelevant variables do not contribute to a reduction in MSE. In fact, the "t-test" for the incremental effect of an irrelevant variable F_j will fail to reject $H_0 : \beta_j = 0$.

We need to be cautious with the partial t-test, since a high correlation between variables may produce small t-values, even if the variables are part of the best subset. In the absence of an established theory about factors in a system, it is best to view the estimated coefficients $(b_1, b_2, \ldots, b_m)$ as a set of weights for combining the factors $(F_1, F_2, \ldots, F_m)$ into an estimated conditional mean for the rate R. The coefficients are typically not independent, but rather each coefficient depends upon the data for all factors.

5. Specification errors: Ramsey's reset test

We have discussed modeling errors within the context of the linear factor model. There are many variations on the model relating factors to outputs. The classical linear regression model is specified as

$$R = F\beta + \varepsilon,$$

where the disturbance vector ε is presumed to follow the multivariate normal distribution $N(0, \sigma^2 I)$.

RESET stands for Regression Specification Error Test and was proposed by Ramsey (1969). Specification error is an omnibus term which covers any departure from the assumptions of the standard model. Serial correlation, heteroskedasticity, and non-normality all violate the assumption that the disturbances are distributed as $N(0, \sigma^2 I)$. Tests for these specification errors have been described earlier. In contrast, RESET is a general test for the following types of specification errors:

- Omitted variables: F does not include all relevant variables.
- Incorrect functional form: some or all of the variables in R and F should be transformed to logs, powers, reciprocals, or in some other way.
- Correlation between F and ε: These may be caused, among other things, by measurement error in F, simultaneity, or the presence of lagged R values and serially correlated disturbances.

Under such specification errors, LS estimators will be biased and inconsistent, and conventional inference procedures will be invalidated. Ramsey showed that any or all of these specification errors produce a non-zero mean error vector for ε. Therefore, to test model specification, the null and alternative hypotheses of the RESET test are

$$H_0 : \varepsilon \sim N(0, \sigma^2 I),$$
$$H_a : \varepsilon \sim N(\mu, \sigma^2 I), \quad \mu \neq 0.$$

The test is based on an augmented regression:

$$R = F\beta + Z\gamma + \varepsilon.$$

The test of specification error evaluates the restriction $\gamma = 0$. That is, $H_0 : \gamma = 0$ versus $H_0 : \gamma \neq 0$. The critical question in constructing the test is to determine what variables should enter the Z matrix. Note that the Z matrix may, for example, be composed of variables that are not in the original specification of variables F, so that the test of $\gamma = 0$ is simply the omitted variables' test described earlier.

In testing for incorrect functional form, the nonlinear part of the regression model may be some function of the regressors included in F. For example, if a linear relation,

$$R = \beta_0 + \beta_1 F_1 + \varepsilon,$$

is specified instead of the true relation,

$$R = \beta_0 + \beta_1 F_1 + \beta_2 F_1^2 + \varepsilon,$$

the augmented model has $Z = F_1^2$. A more general example might be the specification of an additive relation,

$$R = \beta_0 + \beta_1 F_1 + \beta_2 F_2 + \varepsilon,$$

instead of the (true) multiplicative relation,

$$R = \beta_0 F_1^{\beta_1} F_2^{\beta_2} \varepsilon.$$

A logarithm transformation converts the multiplicative model to the additive model.

A Taylor series approximation of any nonlinear relation would yield an expression involving powers and cross-products of the explanatory variables. Ramsey's suggestion is to include powers of the predicted values of the dependent variable (which are, of course, a linear combination of powers and cross-product terms of the explanatory variables) in Z:

$$Z = (\hat{r}^2, \hat{r}^3, \hat{r}^4, \ldots),$$

where $\hat{r}$ is the vector of fitted values from the regression of R on F. The superscripts indicate the powers to which these predictions are raised. The first power is not involved since it is perfectly collinear with the F matrix.

The output from the test reports the regression equation, and the F-statistic and log likelihood ratio for testing the hypothesis that the coefficients on the powers of fitted values are all zero. A study by Ramsey and Alexander (1984) showed that the RESET test could detect specification error in an equation which was known a priori to be misspecified but which nonetheless gave satisfactory values for all the more traditional test criteria – goodness of fit, test of first-order serial correlation, and high t-ratios.

To apply the test in EViews, select **View/Stability Tests/ Ramsey RESET Test**... and specify the number of fitted terms to include in the test regression. The fitted terms are the powers of the fitted values from the original regression, starting with the square or second power. For example, if you specify 1, then the test will add $\hat{r}^2$ in the regression, and if you specify 2, then the test will add $\hat{r}^2$ and $\hat{r}^3$ in the regression, and so on. If you specify a large number of fitted terms, EViews may report a near-singular matrix error message since the powers of the fitted values are likely to be highly collinear. The Ramsey RESET test is applicable only to an equation estimated by least squares.

6. Multicollinearity

An ideal assumption that is made when using the OLS estimation method is that the explanatory variables are not correlated with one another. If there is no relationship between the explanatory variables, they are said to be orthogonal to one another. If the explanatory variables are orthogonal to one another, adding or removing a variable from a regression equation would not cause the values of the coefficients on the other variables to change. A problem occurs when the explanatory variables are very highly correlated with each other, and this problem is known as multicollinearity.

Perfect multicollinearity occurs when there is an exact relationship between two or more variables. In this case, it is not possible to estimate all of the coefficients in the model. For perfect multicollinearity, EViews would output an error message – singular matrix.

Near multicollinearity is much more likely to occur in practice, and would arise when there was a non-negligible, but not perfect, relationship between two or more of the explanatory variables.

A simple method for checking multicollinearity involves looking at the matrix of correlations between the individual variables. As a rule of thumb, we accept that multicollinearity is a problem if the correlation coefficient is greater than 0.7 in absolute value. That will usually remove the estimation problem of the singularity of $U'U$, where $U = \begin{bmatrix} f_{11}-\bar{f}_1 & \cdots & f_{1m}-\bar{f}_m \\ \vdots & \ddots & \vdots \\ f_{n1}-\bar{f}_1 & \cdots & f_{nm}-\bar{f}_m \end{bmatrix}$.

It is understandable that factors are interrelated. In economic and financial systems, the factors are macroeconomic variables that move in tandem. So, the estimated coefficients inform us how to bring the factors together. It is the resulting estimated conditional mean which is needed for risk computations.

It is worth stating that the presence of near multicollinearity does not affect the BLUE properties of the OLS estimator, i.e., it will still be consistent, unbiased, and efficient since the presence of near multicollinearity does not violate any of the regression assumptions 1–4.

There is still an issue of looking ahead – extrapolation/forecasting to the next period. The regression analysis summarizes the observed data. The next period has unknown factor values and unknown returns. A natural addition to the systems model is to include a forecasting equation for the factors. For example, a first-order autoregressive model for $F' = (F_1, \ldots, F_m)$ would provide next-period factor values to be used in the linear factor model. We will have more to say on this in Chapter 4.

3.5 Case Studies

The risk factors, as incorporated into a linear factor model, will be illustrated with a number of cases. The various aspects of modeling, estimation, testing, and validation will be demonstrated with a real-world application. EViews software is used for data analysis.

Case 3.1: Nova Scotia exports

Nova Scotia is a province of Canada situated on the Atlantic coast. It has a small population and is rich in resources, particularly fish. In this case, we will consider the annual export revenue of NS and look at the risk factors that affect the annual variation. Consider the export revenue of Nova Scotia as the outcome of a stochastic dynamic process. Let

$$Y_t = \text{export revenue in year } t\text{, chained in 2017 dollars.}$$

There are many exogenous economic factors impacting NS exports. We postulate that Nova Scotia's export demand depends on the economic health of its major trading partners. We expect that export demand is determined by the gross domestic product of Canada and the U.S., plus a time variable to capture other trends and dummy variables to account for the COVID-19 crisis in 2020 and 2021. We are selecting a small subset of exogenous factors, with the qualification that some of the modeling issues noted earlier could be relevant. The series will span the COVID years 2020–2021, which affected economic activity worldwide.

The factors are as follows:

$$\begin{aligned}
F_1 &= \text{Canada gross domestic product (constant dollars, billions),}\\
F_2 &= \text{U.S. gross domestic product (constant dollars, billions),}\\
F_3 &= \text{indicator for 2020: 1 for 2020, 0 otherwise,}\\
F_4 &= \text{indicator for 2021: 1 for 2021, 0 otherwise,}\\
t &= \text{Time indicator } 1981 = 1,\ 1982 = 2, \text{ etc.}
\end{aligned}$$

The proposed factor model is

$$Y_t = \beta_0 + \beta_1 F_{t1} + \beta_2 F_{t2} + \beta_3 F_{t3} + \beta_4 F_{t4} + \beta_5 t + \varepsilon.$$

Observations on the variables were collected for the years 1981 to 2022. The data are contained in the EViews workfile RiskBK31.

We explore the relationship between Nova Scotia exports and the factors through a series of graphs. In EViews, we first form a group (set of series) consisting of Nova Scotia exports, Canadian GDP, and US GDP.

Given the small size of the Nova Scotia exports, the graphs are separated. It appears that Nova Scotia exports grew in a linear fashion with Canadian GDP up to 2004, but thereafter, Nova Scotia exports "flatlined." Similar results are evident for the U.S. GDP.

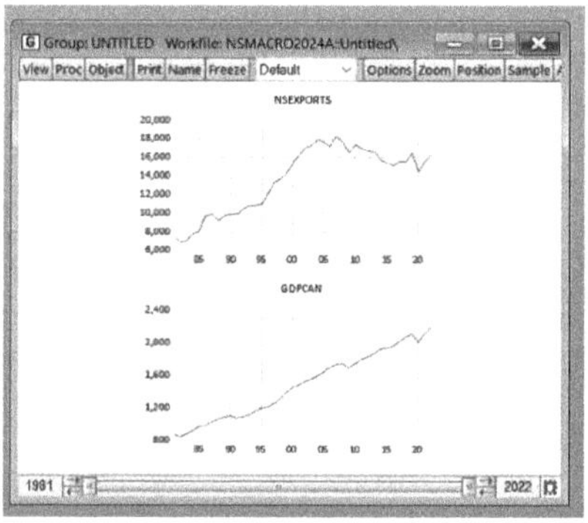

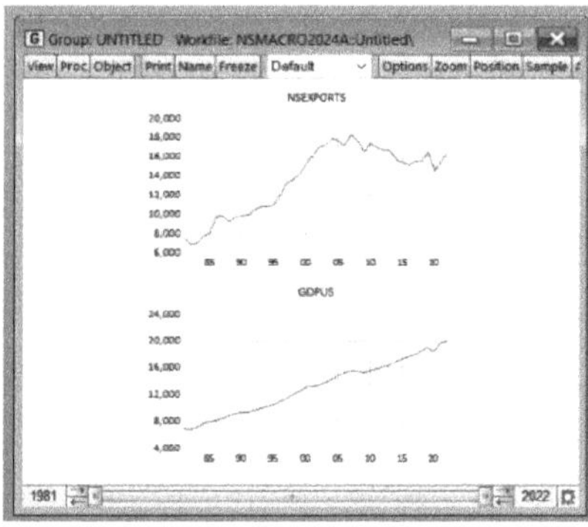

To estimate our multiple regression equation in EViews, we click on quick in the main task bar, then when the dialog box appears, click on estimate equation. First, type the Y variable (nsexports) followed by C, the constant (note that C is a reserved word in EViews that is only used to designate the constant), and then each of the postulated factors (F_1 = gdpcan, F_2 = gdpus, F_3 = xxdum2020, F_4 = xxdum2021, t = xxtime). Next, click on LS, Least Squares (NLS and ARMA), and fill in the sample 1981 to 2022. Click on OK, and we have our multiple regression output.

Dependent Variable: NSEXPORTS
Method: Least Squares
Date: 02/27/24 Time: 08:26
Sample: 1981 2022
Included observations: 42

Variable	Coefficient	Std. Error	t-Statistic	Prob.
GDPCAN	-25.50417	7.633139	-3.341243	0.0020
GDPUS	5.322283	0.938702	5.669835	0.0000
C	-6213.912	2796.991	-2.221642	0.0327
XXTIME	-567.6724	132.1931	-4.294265	0.0001
XXDUM2020	-3982.305	1417.180	-2.810022	0.0080
XXDUM2021	-5755.240	1462.207	-3.935994	0.0004

R-squared	0.879976	Mean dependent var	13624.14
Adjusted R-squared	0.863306	S.D. dependent var	3599.450
S.E. of regression	1330.796	Akaike info criterion	17.35651
Sum squared resid	63756671	Schwarz criterion	17.60474
Log likelihood	-358.4866	Hannan-Quinn criter.	17.44750
F-statistic	52.78783	Durbin-Watson stat	0.399011
Prob(F-statistic)	0.000000		

The fitted equation is

$$
\begin{aligned}
Y_t = &-6213.912 - 25.504F_{t1} + 5.3222F_{t2} - 3982.305F_{t3} \\
&- 5755.240F_{t4} - 567.672t.
\end{aligned}
$$

We have a high R-square, and the F statistic has a probability of 0.0, hence we reject the null hypothesis that the coefficients are all equal to zero. The t-tests are all statistically significant with low p values, so we again reject the null hypothesis that the coefficient equals 0 (conclude that the incremental effect of a variable, after the other variables, is significant).

Note the negative coefficient for Canadian GDPCAN in spite of the graph showing a positive effect. It is important to understand the values of factors, and especially $F_2 = GDPUS$. The United States' economy is very dominant since most of Nova Scotia's exports go to the US market – the test value is $t = 5.67$! The effect of the other variables is to adjust the growth provided by the US, so the coefficient estimates are negative.

The COVID years have had an additional negative effect on NSEXPORTS, and that effect has been documented in many economic analyses.

The results from the linear factor model estimation are convincing. There are checks on model assumptions that are an appropriate part of the model fitting.

We examine the issue of multicollinearity by calculating the correlation matrix for the explanatory variables. Notice that many correlations are all greater than .90, i.e., highly correlated. Certainly, greater than our heuristic rule of .7 implies multicollinearity could be an issue.

Correlation

	GDPCAN	GDPUS	EXPORTPRI	XXDUM2020	XXDUM2021	XXTIME
GDPCAN	1.000000	0.997578	0.972418	0.201049	0.239447	0.988873
GDPUS	0.997578	1.000000	0.977615	0.212724	0.256545	0.992006
EXPOR	0.972418	0.977615	1.000000	0.240132	0.295635	0.986955
XXDUM	0.201049	0.212724	0.240132	1.000000	-0.024390	0.227490
XXDUM	0.239447	0.256545	0.295635	-0.024390	1.000000	0.239931
XXTIME	0.988873	0.992006	0.986955	0.227490	0.239931	1.000000

The relationship between country GDPs and Nova Scotia EXPORTNS is totally expected. The estimation objective is to adjust the effect of the US economic growth on Canadian economic growth. As stated, most of the NS exports go to the US, so the appetite there is dominant. However, there are many Canadian political and economic forces impacting the NS economy, and the coefficient on GDPCAN captures that effect. The negative effect of the COVID years is also in line with expectations.

The time variable is highly correlated with the GDP variables, but it had an additional effect ($t = -4.29$). This is a trend adjustment for NS, since that economy is slower than both Canada and the US. There may be clearly defined factors for Nova Scotia that would also do the trend adjustment, but without additional information, we need the time variable.

For illustration, we include the redundant variable test for the COVID indicators.

Redundant Variables Test
Equation: EQ01
Redundant variables: XXDUM2020 XXDUM2021
Specification: NSEXPORTS GDPUS C XXDUM2020 XXDUM2021
Null hypothesis: XXDUM2020 XXDUM2021 are jointly insignificant

	Value	df	Probability
F-statistic	4.189704	(2, 38)	0.0227
Likelihood ratio	8.369316	2	0.0152

F-test summary:

	Sum of Sq.	df	Mean Squares
Test SSR	24647095	2	12323548
Restricted SSR	1.36E+08	40	3410496.
Unrestricted SSR	1.12E+08	38	2941388.

LR test summary:

	Value
Restricted LogL	-374.4606
Unrestricted LogL	-370.2759

Restricted Test Equation:
Dependent Variable: NSEXPORTS
Method: Least Squares
Date: 02/27/24 Time: 08:29
Sample: 1981 2022
Included observations: 42

Variable	Coefficient	Std. Error	t-Statistic	Prob.
GDPUS	0.781572	0.072644	10.75889	0.0000
C	3333.923	997.9863	3.340650	0.0018

R-squared	0.743184	Mean dependent var	13624.14
Adjusted R-squared	0.736764	S.D. dependent var	3599.450
S.E. of regression	1846.753	Akaike info criterion	17.92669
Sum squared resid	1.36E+08	Schwarz criterion	18.00944
Log likelihood	-374.4606	Hannan-Quinn criter.	17.95702
F-statistic	115.7538	Durbin-Watson stat	0.117837
Prob(F-statistic)	0.000000		

The test concludes that the COVID variables are not redundant.

Next, we test for heteroscedasticity. Click View/Residual Diagnostics/Heteroscedasticity Test. When the dialog box appears, select White.

Heteroskedasticity Test: White
Null hypothesis: Homoskedasticity

F-statistic	5.402361	Prob. F(4.37)	0.0016
Obs*R-squared	15.48550	Prob. Chi-Square(4)	0.0038
Scaled explained SS	8.250255	Prob. Chi-Square(4)	0.0828

Test Equation:
Dependent Variable: RESID^2
Method: Least Squares
Date: 02/27/24 Time: 09:37
Sample: 1981 2022
Included observations: 42
Collinear test regressors dropped from specification

Variable	Coefficient	Std. Error	t-Statistic	Prob.
C	3632377.	5120711.	0.709350	0.4826
GDPUS^2	0.043397	0.032176	1.348741	0.1856
GDPUS*XXDUM2020	–327.5229	147.2945	-2.223593	0.0324
GDPUS*XXDUM2021	–364.2726	146.4748	-2.486930	0.0175
GDPUS	–671.9608	838.6066	-0.801282	0.4281

R-squared	0.368702	Mean dependent var	2661256.
Adjusted R-squared	0.300454	S.D. dependent var	3073061.
S.E. of regression	2570273.	Akalke info criterion	32.46827
Sum squared resid	2.44E+14	Schwarz criterion	32.67513
Log likelihood	-676.8336	Hannan-Quinn criter.	32.54409
F-statistic	5.402361	Durbin-Watson stat	0.502520
Prob(F-statistic)	0.001576		

Under the F test, we reject the null hypothesis of homoscedasticity as shown in the screenshot. Therefore, we can go back to our equation specification and reestimate. Click on estimate, and when the dialog box opens, click on options and select Huber White as the covariance method. The screenshot shows the revised p values with the heteroscedasticity correction.

Dependent Variable: NSEXPORTS
Method: Least Squares
Date: 02/27/24 Time: 09:41
Sample: 1981 2022
Included observations: 42
Huber-White-Hinkley (HC1) heteroskedasticity consistent standard errors and covariance

Variable	Coefficient	Std. Error	t-Statistic	Prob.
C	2598.966	905.8084	2.869222	0.0067
GDPUS	0.851206	0.080110	10.62550	0.0000
XXDUM2020	−3829.071	649.0963	−5.899080	0.0000
XXDUM2021	−3808.951	732.1910	−5.202128	0.0000

R-squared	0.789584	Mean dependent var	13624.14
Adjusted R-squared	0.772972	S.D. dependent var	3599.450
S.E. of regression	1715.048	Akaike info criterion	17.82266
Sum squared resid	1.12E+08	Schwarz criterion	17.98615
Log likelihood	−370.2759	Hannan-Quinn criter.	17.88332
F-statistic	47.53142	Durbin-Watson stat	0.260643
Prob(F-statistic)	0.000000		

The t values are better in the enhanced model, but the R^2 is decreased. The AIC for both models is the same. An argument can be made that the enhanced model is preferred, even though the original model had features which are important to understand the outcome: $Y_t = GDPNS$. The sample size is moderate $T = 42$, so the heteroscedasticity may have an effect on the test statistics (t, F). The revised model is

$$Y_t = 2598.986 + 0.852F_{t2} \text{ if not COVID time,}$$

$$Y_t = -1230.084 + 0.852F_{t2} \text{ if 2020,}$$

$$Y_t = -1209.964 + 0.852F_{t2} \text{ if 2021.}$$

The attraction of this model is simplicity, with the GDPNS effectively driven by GDPUS. We will use the revised model for risk analysis. However, we need to check for the normality of residuals. Click on View/Residual Diagnostics/Histogram – Normality Test. Based on the Jarque–Bera test, we do not reject the null hypothesis of a normal distribution of errors.

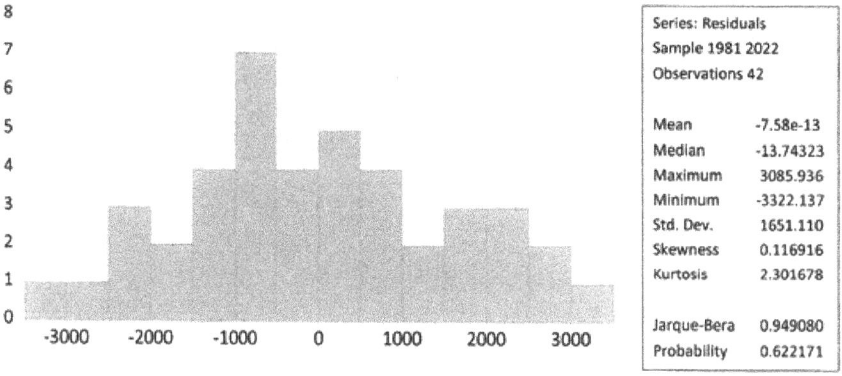

Risk measures

Given our final equation, we proceed to calculate risk measures for the outcome $Y(t)$. The data on Y provide an empirical distribution from which descriptive risk measures can be computed. In this application, we are looking forward to the next year – 2022. The analysis has produced an estimated distribution for returns – $(Y|F) \sim N(\hat{\mu}(Y|F), \hat{\sigma}(Y|F))$. If we specify value(s) for F, the normal formulas for risk measures can be applied.

So, the linear model for the Y variable has a conditional normal distribution, conditional on the values for the factors. Also, recall that the estimate of the variance of Y, conditional on the values for the factors, is the estimated variance from the residuals: $\sigma^2(Y|F) = \sigma^2(\varepsilon)$. Thus, once we specify values for the factor values, we have the two parameters required for specification of the normal distribution: $\mu = E(Y|F), \sigma^2(Y|F) = \sigma^2(\varepsilon)$.

We can proceed to calculate $(\text{VaR}_\alpha, \text{CVaR}_\alpha)$ under the assumption of a normal distribution:

(1) Forecast the next value $F_{43,2} = GDPUS(43)$. There are a variety of approaches to forecasting the next period: exponential smoothing, moving average, and autoregression. We will simply take the most recent value, $GDPUS(42)$, and set $GDPUS(43) = GDPUS(42)$. Forecasting factors will be discussed in Chapter 4.

(2) Given the forecast $F_{43,2} = 20,000$ in 2022 (see plot), we estimate

$$\hat{\mu}(Y_{43}|F_2 = 20,000) = 2598.986 + 0.852 \times 20,000 = 19,635.2.$$

(3) The estimated standard deviation, provided in the figure on page 99, is

$$\hat{\sigma}(\varepsilon) = 1651.11.$$

(4) Let $\alpha = .05$, and calculate $\text{VaR}_{.05}(Y_{43}) = \hat{\mu} + z_{.05}\hat{\sigma}$:

$$\text{VaR}_{.05} = 19,635.2 - 1.65 \times 1651.11 = 16{,}910.87.$$

(5) Calculate $\text{CVaR}_{.05}(Y_{43}) = \hat{\mu} + \hat{\sigma} \times E_{.05}(Z)$:

$$\text{VaR}_{.05} = 19,635.2 + 1651.11 \times (-2.06) = 16,233.9.$$

Comment

The VaR and CVaR are just numbers, devoid of interpretation. There is no benchmark for an unacceptable decline in NSEXPORTS. For example, if a 10% below average in exports is a problem, the benchmark is $y^* = 0.90 \times 19635.20 = 17671.68$. Then $\text{VaR}_{0.05} = 16{,}910.87 < 17{,}671.68$ and there is a problem, assuming a static forecast for the risk factor.

Forecasting the distribution for output NSEXPORTS and calculating risk measures is included here as an example. In practice, this exercise considers the economic viability of a political entity. Scenarios for risk factors would be considered, and alternative benchmarks would be proposed. Then, decisions/policies to mitigate risk would be determined, and the best decision implemented.

Case 3.2: Risk beta

The beta risk measure is a popular measure used by financial agencies to measure the risk of a firm's stock relative to the risk of the market. As an example of the beta estimation in EViews, we examine the monthly returns on the Toronto Stock Exchange of Shopify Inc. (shop pct). The simplest model specification is the so-called index model, which relates a stock's return to the market index. We postulate that a stock's return is a function of the intercept and the movement in the market as follows:

$$R_{t,i} = \beta_0 + \beta_1 R_{t,M} + \varepsilon,$$

where

$R_{t,i}$ = stock i return rate in month t,
$R_{t,M}$ = market index return rate (Toronto Stock Exchange Index - TSX) in month t,
β_0 = intercept specific to the firm,
β_1 = Beta risk measure to specify how much the firm's stock moves with the market,
ε = normally distributed error.

As shown in the description box in the following figure, Shoppct over the period 2000 month 1 to 2024 month 1 had an average rate of return of 0.043 and a standard deviation of 0.15. The Jarque–Bera probability is 0.236. Hence, we do not reject the null hypothesis that the data follow a normal distribution at the 5% level of significance.

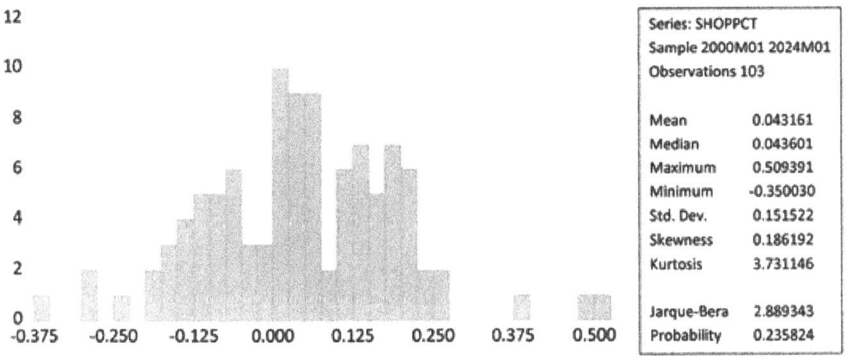

The regression results shown have statistically significant intercept and beta coefficient. Although R^2 is modest, stock returns for the firm are positively linked to the overall market. The beta reveals that an increase of 1% in the market rate is associated with a 1.89% increase in the stock rate (or alternatively, a 1% decrease results in a 1.89% decrease).

Dependent Variable: SHOPPCT
Method: Least Squares
Date: 01/18/24 Time: 11:16
Sample (adjusted): 2015M07 2024M01
Included observations: 103 after adjustments

Variable	Coefficient	Std. Error	t-Statistic	Prob.
C	0.035043	0.013252	2.644330	0.0095
SPTSXPCT	1.893751	0.345196	5.486010	0.0000

R-squared	0.229574	Mean dependent var	0.043161
Adjusted R-squared	0.221946	S.D. dependent var	0.151522
S.E. of regression	0.133653	Akaike info criterion	−1.167908
Sum squared resid	1.804185	Schwarz criterion	−1.116748
Log likelihood	62.14727	Hannan-Quinn criter.	−1.147187
F-statistic	30.09630	Durbin-Watson stat	1.786000
Prob(F-statistic)	0.000000		

This is a simple version of the linear factor model. The beta indicates if a stock is more ($\beta_1 > 1$) or less ($\beta_1 < 1$) volatile than the market. That is, the stock return has greater movement than the market. The market index R_M is a random variable, and the linear model implies that the variability of a stock is partly attributable to the co-movement with the market. Consider $E(R_M) = \mu_M$ and $E(R_M - \mu_M)^2 = \sigma_M^2$. Then, we have

$$\mu_i = \beta_0 + \beta_{1i}\mu_M$$
$$\sigma_i^2 = \beta_{1i}^2\sigma_M^2 + \sigma^2.$$

So, the beta coefficient β_{1i} indicates the enhanced volatility relative to the market if $\beta_{1i} > 1$.

If risk is the chance of R_i falling below a critical value, then the relationship to the market defined by β_{1i} is a risk measure since it affects the mean and variance of R_i.

Portfolio beta

The beta as the sensitivity of a stock return to the market index return is extendable to a portfolio. Recall that a portfolio is a combination of stocks. Consider a set of n stocks with random returns $(R_1, \ldots, R_n)$. With weights $X = (x_1, \ldots, x_n)$ being the investments in the stocks, the portfolio return is

$$R_P = \sum_{i=1}^{n} x_i R_i.$$

For the individual stocks, we have $R_i = \beta_{0i} + \beta_{1i} R_M + \varepsilon_i, i = 1, \ldots, n,$ and

$$R_P = \sum_{i=1}^{n} x_i \beta_{0i} + \sum_{i=1}^{n} x_i \beta_{1i} R_M + \sum_{i=1}^{n} x_i \varepsilon_i.$$

So, the portfolio return has the same linear dependence on the market return, with the parameters being functions of the investment weights. The portfolio mean and variance are

$$\mu_P = \sum_{i=1}^{n} x_i \beta_{0i} + \sum_{i=1}^{n} x_i \beta_{1i} \mu_M$$

$$\sigma_P^2 = \sum_{i=1}^{n} x_i^2 \beta_{1i}^2 \sigma_M^2 + \sum_{i=1}^{n} \sum_{j=1}^{n} x_i x_j \beta_{1i} \beta_{1j} \sigma_M^2 + \sum_{i=1}^{n} x_i^2 \sigma^2(\varepsilon_i).$$

The portfolio beta is a linear combination of the stock betas: $\beta_{1P} = \sum_{i=1}^{n} x_i \beta_{1i}$. The Market index component of portfolio return variance is

$$\beta_{1P}^2 \sigma_M^2 - \left[\sum_{i=1}^{n} x_i^2 \beta_{1i}^2 + \sum_{i=1}^{n} \sum_{j=1}^{n} x_i x_j \beta_{1i} \beta_{1j} \right] \sigma_M^2.$$

There is an important message in the formulas for the portfolio mean and variance. There is control over the distribution $R_P \sim N(\mu_P, \sigma_P^2)$ with the investment decisions. In particular, the portfolio beta, β_{1P}, is a measure of risk for the investment strategy $X = (x_1, \ldots, x_n)$.

Case 3.3: Applying regression to minimize risk with hedging

It is often the approach in applications of risk management that variance is the risk measure used in optimization problems where risk is minimized. An example of this is developing a hedging strategy. Hedging involves the use of "long" and "short" positions in assets. Having a long position means you own the asset. Investors maintain "long" security positions in the expectation that the asset will rise in value in the future. A short position is generally the sale of an asset you do not own. Investors who sell short believe the price of the asset will decrease in value.

Two questions have to be answered before a hedge can be established:

1. What assets in the portfolio should the short position be in?
2. What proportion of the value of the long position in the portfolio should the short position represent so as to minimize the variance of the overall portfolio?

The first question is simply answered by looking at the correlation coefficient of the changes in the price of the long position and the potential candidates for the short position. The candidate with the highest correlation with the long position should be chosen.

With regard to the second question, the proportion to go short is known as the hedge ratio. OLS regression can be used to derive the hedge ratio, which minimizes the portfolio variance.

Commodity hedging is a risk management strategy used by companies to protect against price fluctuations in essential commodities they need for their operations.

Minimum variance hedge ratio formula from regression:

> Consider that we have an asset A with price S and a similar asset B with price F. Suppose we expect to sell x_A units of asset A at time t_2 and choose to hedge at time t_1 by shorting futures contracts with x_F units of asset B. The hedge ratio is
>
> $$h = \frac{x_F}{x_A}.$$
>
> We want to determine the optimal hedge ratio. We will denote the total amount realized for the asset when the profit or loss on the hedge is taken into account by Y, so that
>
> $$Y = S_2 x_A - [F_2 - F_1]x_F,$$
>
> where S_1 and S_2 are the prices of asset A, and F_1 and F_2 are the futures prices of B, at times t_1 and t_2, respectively.

If $\Delta S = S_2 - S_1, \Delta F = F_2 - F_1$, then

$$Y = S_1 x_A - [\Delta S - h\Delta F]x_A.$$

Because S_1 and x_A are known at time t_1, the variance of Y is minimized when the variance of $[\Delta S - h\Delta F]$ is minimized. The variance of $[\Delta S - h\Delta F]$ is

$$V = \sigma_s^2 + h^2\sigma_F^2 - 2h\rho\sigma_S\sigma_F,$$

where ρ is the correlation coefficient between S and F. Minimizing V as a function of h gives

$$h_{\max} = \frac{\rho\sigma_F}{\sigma_S}.$$

This is a familiar formula. Consider the OLS regression model for the change in prices for asset B related to the change in prices for asset A:

$$\Delta F = b_0 + b_1\Delta S + e.$$

The slope estimate is $b_1 = \frac{\sum(\Delta F - \overline{\Delta F})(\Delta S - \overline{\Delta S})}{\sum(\Delta S - \overline{\Delta S})^2} = \frac{[\sum(\Delta F - \overline{\Delta F})(\Delta S - \overline{\Delta S})]}{[\sqrt{\sum(\Delta S - \overline{\Delta S})^2}]\times[\sqrt{\sum(\Delta F - \overline{\Delta F})^2}]} \times \frac{\sqrt{\sum(\Delta F - \overline{\Delta F})^2}}{\sqrt{\sum(\Delta S - \overline{\Delta S})^2}} = \hat{\rho} \times \frac{S_F}{S_S}$. So, the regression of the change in futures price on the change in asset price provides an estimate of the optimal hedge ratio.

Often, it is the case that a futures market does not exist for a particular commodity. In this case, the analyst picks an alternative with a high correlation to the commodity. This is known as cross hedging. The measure of risk associated with cross hedging is the variance. The analyst seeks to minimize the variance.

Step-by-step example of commodity hedging for an airline

1. **Identifying the risk**
   An airline company recognizes that fluctuations in jet fuel prices could significantly impact its costs. Since fuel is one of the largest expenses for an airline, even small changes in fuel prices can have a substantial effect on the company's financial performance.
2. **Choosing the hedging instrument**
   To hedge against the risk of rising jet fuel prices, the airline decides to use futures contracts. Futures are standardized

agreements to buy or sell a commodity at a predetermined price at a specified time in the future.

3. **Implementation of the hedge**
   a. Timing: The airline forecasts its fuel requirements for the next year and decides to hedge a portion of them. The decision on how much of the fuel consumption to hedge depends on the airline's risk management policy and market conditions.
   b. Transaction: Suppose the current price of jet fuel is $2 per gallon. The airline could enter into futures contracts where it agrees to buy jet fuel at $2 per gallon for delivery in six months. This is done through commodities exchanges that specialize in these types of financial instruments.
4. **Outcome scenarios**
   a. **Scenario A (Prices Rise):** If in six months the market price of jet fuel rises to $3 per gallon, the airline still pays $2 per gallon as per the futures contracts. The airline saves $1 per gallon, offsetting the higher costs it would have faced without the hedge.
   b. **Scenario B (Prices Fall):** If the market price falls to $1.5 per gallon, the airline must still purchase at $2 per gallon as agreed in the futures contracts, leading to a loss compared to market prices. However, the certainty provided by the hedge might outweigh this potential for overpayment, especially in budget planning.

Example

An airline expects to purchase two million gallons of jet fuel in one month and decides to use heating oil futures for hedging. Table 3.9 provides hypothetical data for 30 successive months, data on the change, ΔS, in the jet fuel price per gallon, and the corresponding change, ΔF, in the futures price for the contract on heating oil that would be used for hedging price changes during the month.

The change in oil futures was regressed on the change in jet oil with the model

$$\Delta F = \beta \times \Delta S + \varepsilon.$$

Table 3.9. Data on heating oil futures and jet oil.

Month	Change in futures price per gallon	Change in jet oil price per gallon
1	0.024	0.032
2	0.032	0.017
3	−0.043	−0.041
4	−0.002	0.005
5	0.041	0.023
6	−0.026	−0.016
7	−0.029	−0.013
8	−0.032	−0.01
9	0.045	0.04
10	−0.009	0.008
11	−0.033	−0.033
12	−0.008	−0.015
13	0.016	0.006
14	−0.024	−0.029
15	0.032	0.026
16	0.029	0.021
17	0.036	0.028
18	0.040	0.031
19	0.021	0.017
20	0.027	0.025
21	0.031	0.019
22	0.029	0.021
23	0.036	0.031
24	0.045	0.035
25	0.041	0.033
26	0.021	0.017
27	0.005	0.007
28	0.019	0.009
29	0.025	0.021

Table 3.10. Hedge Ratio Estimation.

Dependent variable: OILPCHANGE **Method: Least squares** **Date: 04/30/24 Time: 09: 15** **Sample: 115** **Included observations: 15**				
Independent Variable	**Coefficient**	**Std. Error**	**t-Statistic**	**Prob.**
FUELPCHANGE	**0.756998**	**0.084375**	**8.971840**	**0.0000**
R-Squared	0.851842	Mean-dependent var.		4.63E-19
Adjusted R-squared	0.851842	S.D.-dependent var.		0.024791
S.E. of regression	0.0099542	Akaike info. criterion		6.401846
Sum squared resied.	0.001275	Schwartz criterion		6.354643
Log likelihood	49.01385	Hannan-Quinn criter.		6.402349
Durban-Watson stat.	1.515844			

Regression through the origin was used based on the expectation that the constant was zero. The regression results are in Table 3.10.

The estimate of the optimal hedge ratio is $\hat{h} = 0.756998$. The recommended decision is to sell units of futures contracts in heating oil to hedge units of jet fuel oil at a ratio of 0.757.

3.6 Conclusion

Risk assessment with the normal model is based on the mean and variance of returns. If the variation in returns is dependent on observable risk factors, then the classical linear regression model is an attractive approach to understanding the mean and variance of returns. Least squares estimation minimizes the unexplained variation and correspondingly maximizes the explained variation. A systematic component of variation in returns is identified and the idiosyncratic variation is reduced. Furthermore, the estimated parameters in the linear factor model are elements of the formulas for risk measures for system output. The improved risk measures depend on the risk factors, so they are tailored to the system scenarios determined by risk factor levels.

In our presentation, the parameters in the linear factor model were linear functions of the decisions on system control. So, the risk measures are decision dependent, and are well suited for the "decisions have consequences" theme. The calculation of comparative or relative risk is facilitated by the model. In Chapter 5, we consider decision preferences based on risk comparisons.

The linear factor model is an ideal setting for analyzing the risk of system outcomes. However, it is hypothetical and may be a limited representation of an actual operating system. There are variations on the classical model, which address model shortcomings while maintaining the analytic facility that is important to quantitative risk analysis, where decisions are based on numeric evidence from observations on a system. We will consider some model variations in Chapter 4.

Bibliography

Buhlmann, H. (1970). *Mathematical Methods in Risk Theory.* Springer, Berlin.

Chen, N.F., Roll, R., and Ross, S.A. (1986). Economic forces and the stock market. *Journal of Business*, 59(3), 383–403.

Connor, G. and Korajczyk, R.A. (1995). The arbitrage pricing theory and multifactor models of asset returns. In R. Jarrow, V. Maksimovic, and W. Ziemba (eds), *Finance*, 87–144. Amsterdam: Elsevier Science B.V.

Draper, N.R. and Smith, H. (1998). *Applied Regression Analysis* (3rd ed.). John Wiley, New Jersey, USA.

Fama, E.F. (1968). Risk, return and equilibrium: Some clarifying comments. *Journal of Finance*, 23(1), 29–40.

Fama, E.F. and French, K.R. (1992). The cross-section of expected stock returns. *Journal of Finance*, 47(2), 427–465.

Fama, E.F. and French, K.R. (1993). Common risk factors in the returns on stocks and bonds. *Journal of Financial Economics*, 33(1), 3–56.

Fama, E.F. and French, K.R. (1996). Multifactor explanations of asset pricing anomalies. *Journal of Finance*, 51(1), 55–84.

Fama, E.F. and French, K.R. (1998). Value versus growth: The international evidence. *Journal of Finance*, 53(6), 1975–1999.

Fama, E.F. and French, K.R. (2015). A five-factor asset pricing model. *Journal of Financial Economics*, 116(1), 1–22.

Fox, J. (1997). *Applied Regression Analysis, Linear Models and Related Methods.* Sage Publications, Los Angeles, USA.

Guidolin, M. and Timmermann, A.G. (2006). An econometric model of nonlinear dynamics in the joint distribution of stock and bond returns. *Journal of Applied Econometrics*, 21(1), 1–22.

Hou, K., Karolyi, G.A., and Kho, B.C. (2006). What factors drive global stock return? Working paper, Ohio State University, Charles A. Dice Center for Research in Financial Economics, No. 2006–9.

Jones, C.M. and Kaul, G. (1996). Oil and the stock market. *Journal of Finance*, 51(2), 463–491.

MacLean, L., Richman, A., Richman, V., and Larsson, S. (2005). The dynamics of aircraft degradation and mechanical failure. *Journal of Transportation and Statistics*, 8(1), 1–11.

Middleton, L.P. and Satchell, S.E. (2001). Deriving the arbitrage pricing theory when the number of factors is unknown. *Quantitative Finance*, 1(5), 502–508.

Ramsey, J.B. (1969). Tests for specification errors in classical linear least-squares regression analysis. *Journal of the Royal Statistical Society. Series B (Methodological)*, 31(2), 350–371.

Ramsey, J.B. and Alexander, A. (1984) The econometric approach to business-cycle analysis reconsidered. *Journal of Macroeconomics*, 6(3), 347–355.

Rosenberg, B. and Rudd, A. (1982). Factor-related and specific returns of common stocks: Serial correlation and market inefficiency. *The Journal of Finance*, 37(2), 543–554.

Sen, A. and Srivastava, M. (2011). *Regression Analysis: Theory, Methods, and Applications* (4th printing). Springer-Verlag, Berlin.

White (1980). A heteroskedasticity-consistent covariance matrix estimator and a direct test for heteroskedasticity. *Econometrica* 48(4), 817–838.

Chapter 4

Risk Factors: Part II

4.1 Introduction

We have defined risk from the perspective of the outcome distribution of a stochastic system. If failure is defined as a system outcome falling below a sustainable threshold, then the probability and consequence of failure are the features that are necessary for risk control. The outcome of the system depends on characteristics of the system, which we associate with risk factors. Knowledge of system factors can greatly improve our understanding of the distribution of outcomes and the assessment of risk. The linear factor model was presented as a vehicle for incorporating risk factors into the distribution of the system outcome. In our discussion of the linear model, we identified some shortcomings. In this chapter, we explore alternative risk models that address some of the issues with the standard linear model. We will initially consider models for the percentiles of the empirical distribution, with the percentiles depending on risk factors. This facilitates an analysis of the dependence of risk measures on risk factors. We then look at generalized least squares for models which do not satisfy the assumptions of the classical linear model. The last section introduces hidden Markov models for switching phases or regimes in dynamic systems.

4.2 Probability Models

As we have stated, risk is the chance and consequence of undesirable outcomes from a stochastic system. In Chapter 3, the distribution for system outcomes was defined by a linear factor model, with the mean depending on specified risk factors. Formulas for standard risk measures also depend on the risk factors. The risk requirement of the system is that the risk measure exceeds a threshold. For the Value at Risk, the requirement is that $\{G(v) = \Pr[R \leq v] < \alpha\} \Leftrightarrow \{\text{VaR}_\alpha(R) = G^{-1}(\alpha) > v\}$, where v is a sustainability threshold. The risk requirement $\text{VaR}_\alpha(R) > v$ is equivalent to $\Pr[R \leq v] < \alpha$. The linear model focused on VaR_α, using a normal distribution for R. We will now consider models for the probability of the event $[R \leq v]$.

4.2.1 *The logistic model and risk*

With the risk concern being defined by outcomes below the downside threshold v, it is reasonable to classify outcomes depending on whether $[R < v]$ or $[R \geq v]$. With $G(v) = \Pr[R < v]$, a comparison of the chances of those events is given by the *odds ratio*: $\frac{G(v)}{1-G(v)}$. The ratio is commonly used in risk analysis. The "odds" are standard reporting statistics in games of chance such as horse racing and football, and evaluating negative outcomes from health systems.

The normal distribution for the outcome variable R was the framework for the linear factor model. Similar to the normal distribution is the logistic distribution for a threshold variable V, where $H(v) = \Pr[V \leq v]$. The logistic distribution function for V with parameters (μ, s) is

$$H(v) = \frac{1}{1 + e^{-\left(\frac{v-\mu}{s}\right)}},$$

where μ is the mean, and the variance is $\frac{\pi^2}{3}s^2$. The variance can be chosen so that the logistic distribution is very close to a normal distribution, i.e., $H(v) \approx G(v)$. With the logistic distribution, we have the odds ratio $\frac{H(v)}{1-H(v)} = e^{\left(\frac{v-\mu}{s}\right)}$. Then, $ln\left[\frac{H(v)}{1-H(v)}\right] = \left(\frac{v-\mu}{s}\right)$. The term $ln\left[\frac{H(v)}{1-H(v)}\right]$ is called the *logit*. The logit is linear in the mean. If $H(v) = p_v$, we can see that the inverse cumulative (quantile) is $v = H^{-1}(p_v) = \mu + s \times ln\left[\frac{p_v}{1-p_v}\right]$.

Not only does the logit conform (approximately) to the normal distribution but it is also very suited for analyzing quantiles. If we are considering risk factors $\{F_1, \ldots, F_m\}$ which affect the distribution of outcome R, and therefore the quantile $H^{-1}(\alpha)$, then a logistic model is

$$L_v(F) = ln\left[\frac{p_v}{1-p_v}\right] = [\theta_0 + \theta_1 F_1 + \cdots + \theta_m F_m] + \varepsilon.$$

Since p_v is linked to the threshold v, *the coefficients in the logistic model are specific to that threshold.* The logistic model is a bit different from the linear factor model. The focus is on the events $\{R \leq v\}$ versus $\{R > v\}$. The system output is classified as either one of those events, i.e., the outcome is binary. With the logit relationship $L_v(F) = F\theta + \varepsilon$, the uncertain event probability is predicted as $\hat{p}_v = \frac{1}{1+e^{-F\theta}}$. The event probability is partly determined by the combination of risk factors $[\theta_0 + \theta_1 F_1 + \cdots + \theta_m F_m]$. The assessment of the system operation is based on the estimated probability $\hat{p}_v$, so that $\hat{p}_v < \alpha$ implies that the system meets the risk control requirement.

The logistic model looks like the linear factor model from Chapter 3. However, the dependent variable $L_v = ln\left[\frac{p_v}{1-p_v}\right]$ is not observed. The observation is for $D_v = 1$ if $\{R \leq v\}$, $D_v = 0$ if $\{R > v\}$. The data comprise T observations: $\{(d_i, f_{i1}, \ldots, f_{im}), i = 1, \ldots, T\}$, as in Table 4.1.

In the formulation here, the classification variable D is defined by the rate of return R. Failure is the event "rate of return below the threshold." This classification has broad applications:

Table 4.1. System observations.

Trial	$\boldsymbol{D_v}$	**1**	$\boldsymbol{F_1}$	$\cdots$	$\boldsymbol{F_m}$
1	d_1	1	f_{11}	$\cdots$	f_{1m}
$\vdots$	$\vdots$	$\vdots$	$\vdots$	$\vdots$	$\vdots$
T	d_T	1	f_{T1}	$\cdots$	f_{Tm}

Investment system:	$D = 1$ if rate of return falls below threshold. The outcome for a period is the change in wealth.
Health system:	$D = 1$ if the morbidity rate exceeds a threshold. The outcome for a period is the change in health status.
Mechanical system:	$D = 1$ if failure rate exceeds a threshold. The outcome is the change in operating condition.
Sports system:	$D = 1$ if team loses a game. The outcome is the team strength.

In the systems model, the system has components that are affected by risk factors. It is considered that the system is controlled by decisions, where decisions are investments in components. So, we have $R(X) \Rightarrow D_v(X) \Rightarrow p_v(X)$. The investment in components is a "portfolio." Even in the sports system, the components are players, and the investment in players (e.g., playing time) is the portfolio. The logistic model provides the chance of failure for a given portfolio. We will consider preferred portfolios in the next chapter.

4.2.2 *Parameter estimation: Logistic regression*

The parameters in the logistic model, $\theta' = (\theta_0, \ldots, \theta_m)$, are estimated from the data $\{(d_i, f_{i1}, \ldots, f_{im}),\ i = 1, \ldots, T\}$. The methodology is maximum likelihood, assuming that the outcome D follows a binomial distribution. The likelihood function for θ is

$$\mathcal{L}(\theta \,|\, D, F) = \prod_{i=1}^{T} p_i^{d_i}(1 - p_i)^{1-d_i}.$$

The log likelihood is

$$\ell(\theta) = \sum_{i=1}^{T} [d_i f_{i \cdot} \theta - log((1 + e^{f_{i \cdot} \theta}))].$$

The maximum likelihood estimates are found by solving the problem $\max_\theta \ell(\theta)$. The log likelihood $\ell(\theta)$ is quite different from the linear factor model $\ell(\beta)$. The normality assumption gave a quadratic $\ell(\beta)$, and the derivatives (first-order conditions) produced linear equations, which had a closed-form solution – the multiple linear regression solution. For the logistic model, the first-order condition $\nabla_\theta \ell(\theta) = 0$

(the roots of log likelihood $\ell(\theta)$) does not have a closed-form solution. A standard numerical method to solve for the roots of a nonlinear equation is Newton Rapson, which iterates as

$$\theta^{t+1} = \theta^t - \frac{\nabla_\theta l(\theta^t)}{\nabla_{\theta\theta} l(\theta^t)'},$$

where $\nabla_\theta l(\theta^t)$ is the first derivative, $\nabla_{\theta\theta} l(\theta^t)$ is the second derivative, and t is the iteration number.

The numerical methods for the solution are available in E Views.

4.2.3 *Inference for the logistic model*

The analysis of the solution $\hat{\theta}$ follows the style of multiple regression. The comparison of likelihood values for various models replaces the comparison of sum of squares, since the loglikelihood is not quadratic:

(1) $R^2 = \frac{\ell(\hat{\theta}_0)-\ell(\hat{\theta})}{\ell(\hat{\theta}_0)}$, where $\hat{\theta}_0$ is the reduced model without factors ($H_0 : \theta_1 = \cdots = \theta_m = 0$), and $\hat{\theta}$ is the model with all m factors. If the factors have no effect, then $R^2 = 0$. If the factors are a perfect fit, then $\ell(\hat{\theta}) = 0$ and $R^2 = 1$.

(2) Likelihood ratio test for $H_0 : \theta_1 = \cdots = \theta_m = 0$.
The fitted reduced model $\hat{\theta}^0$ has all factors removed (only intercept) and the fitted full model $\hat{\theta}$ has all m factors. The statistic

$$\widehat{\Lambda} = -2(\ell(\hat{\theta}^0) - \ell(\hat{\theta}))$$

has an approximate χ^2 distribution with m degrees of freedom. If the observed statistic is $\widehat{\Lambda}_o$ and $P_o = \Pr[\widehat{\Lambda} > \widehat{\Lambda}_o] < \alpha$, then H_0 is rejected and the factors $\{F_1, \ldots, F_m\}$ affect the probability of failure.

(3) Likelihood ratio test for $H_0 : \theta_j = 0$.
The fitted reduced model $\hat{\theta}^j$ has the factor F_j removed, so has $(m-1)\,df$, and the fitted full model $\hat{\theta}$ has all m factors. The statistic

$$\widehat{\Lambda}^j = -2(\ell(\hat{\theta}^j) - \ell(\hat{\theta}))$$

has an approximate χ^2 distribution with 1 degree of freedom. If the observed statistic is $\widehat{\Lambda}^j_o$, and $P_o = \Pr[\widehat{\Lambda}^j > \widehat{\Lambda}^j_o] < \alpha$, then H_0 is rejected and the factor F_j has an incremental effect on

Table 4.2. Classification.

		Actual: D 0	1
Predicted: $\hat{D}$	0	k_{11}	k_{12}
	1	k_{21}	k_{22}

the probability of failure, in addition to the effects of the factors $\{F_1, \ldots, F_{j-1}, F_{j+1}, \ldots, F_m\}$.

This test can be used to determine if there is overfitting (too many factors), and some factors may be dropped.

(4) The inverted logit predicts the probability of failure for each case: $\hat{p}_i = \frac{1}{1+e^{-f_i\hat{\theta}}}$, where $f_i = (1, f_{i1}, \ldots, f_{im})$. A simple prediction rule is $\hat{d}_i = 1$ if $\hat{p}_i > 0.5$. The actual versus predicted classes are shown in Table 4.2.

With the total number of cases T and the correct classifications $(k_{11} + k_{22})$ the correct prediction fraction is $\left[\frac{k_{11}+k_{22}}{T}\right]$. The fraction is another measure of the performance of the logistic model.

4.2.4 *Logistic model: VaR and CVaR*

As noted, the logistic model was estimated from data $\{(d_i, f_{i1}, \ldots, f_{im}), i = 1, \ldots, T\}$, where $d_i = 1$ if $\{r_i < v\}$, $D = 0$ if $\{r_i \geq v\}$. The coefficients $\theta' = (\theta_0, \ldots, \theta_m)$ are linked to the threshold v, i.e., $v \Rightarrow p_v = \Pr[R < v] = \frac{1}{1+e^{-F\theta}}$. In this analysis, risk is acceptable if $p_v < \alpha$ or $v < \mathrm{VaR}_\alpha$.

With logistic regression, it is possible to vary v and obtain associated values p_v. Assume that we have identified $v_{\alpha T} = \mathrm{VaR}_\alpha$, and have selected values $\{v_1 < v_2 \cdots < v_{\alpha T} = \mathrm{VaR}_\alpha\}$. Then, repeated logistic regressions can determine the values $\{p_{v_1} < p_{v_2} < \cdots < p_{v_{\alpha T}} = \alpha\}$. The logistic regression for each v_i provides distinct/different coefficients for the factors. Recall that the observations on R, when ordered, give the empirical distribution: $\widehat{G} = \left\{\left(r_{(1)}, \frac{1}{T}\right), \left(r_{(2)}, \frac{2}{T}\right), \ldots, \left(r_{(T)}, \frac{T}{T}\right)\right\}$, which has the lower $\alpha - tail$: $\hat{G}_\alpha = \left\{\left(r_{(1)}, \frac{1}{T}\right), \left(r_{(2)}, \frac{2}{T}\right), \ldots, \left(r_{(j)}, \frac{\alpha T}{T}\right)\right\}$. The lower tail mean is an estimate $\widehat{\mathrm{CVaR}} = \frac{1}{j}\sum_{i=1}^{j} r_{(i)}$. This distribution and $\widehat{\mathrm{CVaR}}_\alpha$ did not account for the risk factors. The logistic regression provided another empirical $\alpha - tail$: $\overline{\overline{G}}_\alpha = \{(v_1, p_{v_1}), (v_2, p_{v_2}), \ldots, (v_{\alpha T}, \alpha)\}$, which accounts for the risk factors. The mean of that $\alpha - tail$ is an alternative estimate of $\overline{\overline{\text{CVaR}}}_\alpha = \frac{1}{\alpha}\sum_{i=2}^{\alpha T}\left(\frac{v_{i-1}+v_i}{2}\right)(p_{v_i} - p_{v_{i-1}})$.

We have presented the logistic model for an observed system output, which is classified as success/failure. The linear combination of risk factors with coefficients θ, which best predicts the probabilities of success/failure, is determined with logistic regression. If the outcome R is observed with data $\{r_1, \ldots, r_T\}$, we also have the classic OLS estimates b, with those coefficients determining the fitted normal distribution $R \sim N(\hat{\mu}, s_e)$ and the estimates for VaR and CVaR. We are presenting the logistic and normal models as alternatives without contrasting their performance.

There are applications where the observation is not on the system status R, but rather the system's success/failure, with the underlying status implied. Often, the status is not regularly monitored, and the total system on a trial is classified as a success/failure. To illustrate a system where the outcome measure is binary, we will consider an application of logistic regression involving basketball in Case 4.3.

4.3 Quantile Regression

The emphasis in risk analysis is on the lower tail of the outcome distribution for a stochastic system. The methods discussed so far used assumed probability distributions, the normal distribution with the linear factor model, and the logistic distribution with logistic regression. The assumptions are advantageous for analysis, and there is some evidence to support the bell shape for the outcome distribution. However, it is possible to proceed without assumptions and work with the empirical distribution. Estimated quantiles from the empirical distribution were discussed in Chapter 2. We will build on that approach by introducing risk factors in quantile regression.

4.3.1 *Quantile model*

Quantiles, denoted by $\tau, 0 \leq \tau \leq 1$, refer to the position where an observation falls within an ordered series: For example, the 0.10 quantile is the value of r that places 10th in ranked values, with

10% of the values below it and 90% of the values above it. More specifically, we define the τth quantile $Q(\tau)$ of a random variable R having a cumulative distribution $G(r)$ as follows:

$$Q(\tau) = inf_r\{G(r) \geq \tau\},$$

where inf_r is the smallest value of r satisfying the inequality.

In the case without factors, we had T observations on R: $\{r_1, \ldots, r_T\}$. Then, the τth quantile $Q(\tau) = q_\tau$ is found from the minimization

$$\min_q \left[\sum_{i=1}^{T} \rho_\tau(r_i - q) \right],$$

where the check function is $\rho_\tau(r) = \tau \times \max(r, 0) + (1 - \tau) \times \max(-r, 0)$. Equivalently,

$$Q(\tau) = \operatorname{argmin}_q \left[\tau \sum_{r_i > q} |r_i - q| + (1 - \tau) \sum_{r_i < q} |r_i - q| \right].$$

Having defined the unconditional quantiles as an optimization problem, it is straightforward to define quantiles conditional on factors in an analogous fashion. Consider that we have observations on the outcome and factors: $\{(r_i, f_{i1}, \ldots, f_{im}), i = 1, \ldots, T\}$. We want to obtain estimates of the conditional quantile function given observations on the factors, so we write

$$Q(\tau \mid f_i) = \beta_0(\tau) + \beta_1(\tau) f_{i1} + \cdots + \beta_m(\tau) f_{im} = f_i \beta(\tau),\ i = 1, \ldots, T.$$

With $f_i = (1, f_{i1}, \ldots, f_{im})$, we solve

$$\min_{\beta(\tau)} \left[\sum_{i=1}^{T} \rho_\tau(r_i - f_i \beta(\tau)) \right].$$

Equivalently,

$$Q(\tau|f) = \operatorname{argmin}_{\beta(\tau)} \left[\tau \sum_{r_i > f_i \beta(\tau)} |r_i - f_i \beta(\tau)| + (1 - \tau) \sum_{r_i < f_i \beta(t)} |r_i - f_i \beta(\tau)| \right].$$

This minimization problem is solved as a linear programming problem. With input data $\{(r_i, f_{i1}, \ldots, f_{im}), i = 1, \ldots, T\}$, an E Views module solves for the conditional quantile $\hat{Q}(\tau \mid f)$ and the coefficient estimates $\hat{\beta}(\tau) = (\hat{\beta}_0(\tau), \ldots, \hat{\beta}_m(\tau))$.

Although the minimization step is different, the quantile estimate is analogous to the conditional mean estimate from OLS. If $\tau = 0.5$, then $Q(0.5|f)$ is the conditional median, which is an alternative estimate for location.

4.3.2 *Quantile model inference*

The estimation of quartiles with quantile regression is based on a sample of data on system factors and the system outcome. Proceeding from fitted values to inference about the effect of the factors on system outcome is the next step:

[1] Goodness of fit with factors

Koenker and Machado (1999) define a goodness-of-fit statistic for quantile regression that is analogous to the coefficient of determination from conventional regression analysis. For the linear quantile specification, $Q(\tau \mid F) = F\beta(\tau)$, we write the factors and coefficient vector as $F = (1, P^*)$ and $\beta(\tau) = (\beta_0(\tau), \beta^*(\tau))'$, so that

$$Q(\tau \mid F) = \beta_0(\tau) + F^* \beta^*(\tau).$$

There are two comparison models, with and without the factors. The estimated model with factors has absolute error

$$\widehat{V}(\tau) = \sum_{i=1}^{n} \rho_\tau(r_i - \hat{\beta}_0(\tau) - f_i \hat{\beta}^*(\tau)).$$

The absolute error for the model without factors is

$$\tilde{V}(\tau) = \sum_{i=1}^{n} \rho_\tau(r_i - \tilde{\beta}_0(\tau)).$$

The measure of fit with factors is

$$R^1(\tau) = 1 - \frac{\widehat{V}(\tau)}{\tilde{V}(\tau)}.$$

$R^1(\tau)$ lies between 0 and 1, and measures the improvement in estimating the τth quantile using the factors $F = (F_1, \ldots, F_m)$.

[2] Hypothesis tests on factors

The sum of absolute deviations can be used in the same way as the sum of squared errors in the standard regression model to test the significance of the factors in their effect on the quantile. The deviation of an observation from the quantile is $u_i = r_i - Q(\tau \mid f_i)$, and the absolute deviation is $\rho_\tau(u_i)$, where ρ_τ is the check function.

The hypotheses on the set of factors $\{F_1, \ldots, F_m\}$ are $H_0 : \beta_j = 0, j = 1, \ldots, m\,(restricted)$ versus $H_a : not\,all\,zero\,(full)$. The sum of deviations under H_0 is $\tilde{V}(\tau) = \sum_{i=1}^{T} \rho_\tau(r_i - \tilde{\beta}_0(\tau))$. The sum of deviations under H_a is $\widehat{V}(\tau) = \sum_{i=1}^{T} \rho_\tau(r_i - \hat{\beta}_0(\tau) - f_i\hat{\beta}^*(\tau))$. The reduction in deviations with the factors is $L(\tau \mid F) = 2[\tilde{V}(\tau) - \widehat{V}(\tau)]$. If the deviations have an exponential distribution $g(u_i) = \tau(1-\tau)exp(\rho_\tau(u_i))$, then $L(\tau \mid F)$ has an approximate χ^2_m distribution with m degrees of freedom. So, a P-value, $P_o = \Pr[\chi^2_m > L_o(\tau \mid F)]$, provides evidence for a decision on factor effect: $P_o < \alpha \Rightarrow reject\,H_0 \Rightarrow$ factors have an effect.

The exponential distribution for absolute deviations is plausible. Without that assumption, the statistic is adjusted to $L^a(\tau|F) = \frac{2[\tilde{V}(\tau) - \widehat{V}(\tau)]}{\tau(1-\tau)\hat{s}(\tau)}$, where $\hat{s}(\tau) = \frac{\hat{F}^{-1}(\tau+\delta) - \hat{F}^{-1}(\tau-\delta)}{2\delta}$ is a slope estimate of the inverse empirical distribution at τ.

The difference of the sum of deviations statistic can also be used to test $H_0 : \beta_j = 0\,(all\,factors\,except\,F_j)$ versus $H_0 : \beta_j \neq 0\,(all\,factors)$ to determine the incremental effect of each factor when added to a model with the other factors already included.

[3] Multivariate distribution

Koenker and Bassett (1978) derive asymptotic normality results for the vector of quantile regression estimates $\hat{\beta}^*(\tau) = (\hat{\beta}_1, \ldots, \hat{\beta}_m)'$. Under mild regularity conditions, we have

$$\sqrt{n}(\hat{\beta}(\tau) - \beta(\tau)) \sim N(0,\ \tau(1-\tau)s(\tau)^2 J^{-1})$$

where $J = \lim_{T\to\infty}\left(\frac{R'R}{T}\right)$, and $s(\tau) = \frac{1}{g(G^{-1}(\tau))}$.

In the formula, $s(\tau)$ is the derivative of the quantile function or the inverse of the density function evaluated at the τth quantile. We provided an estimate of $s(\tau)$ earlier.

The multivariate distribution can be used to test various hypotheses about $\beta^*(\tau)$.

4.3.3 *Risk measures with quantile regression*

Quantile regression is an alternative to the standard regression model where the errors are assumed to have a normal distribution. It can be applied to any problem which considers the relationship between an outcome and independent factors. Our interest is in risk, which focuses on the lower tail of the outcome distribution from a stochastic system. Quantile regression is suited to the analysis of lower quantiles and provides alternative estimates of the risk measures VaR_α and CVaR_α.

We have the empirical distribution, $\hat{G} = \{(r_{(1)}, \frac{1}{T}), (r_{(2)}, \frac{2}{T}), \ldots, (r_{(T)}, \frac{T}{T})\}$, which has the lower $\alpha - tail$, $G_\alpha = \{(r_{(1)}, \frac{1}{T}), (r_{(2)}, \frac{2}{T}), \ldots, (r_{(k)}, \frac{\alpha T}{T})\}$. The lower tail mean is an estimate $\widehat{\text{CVaR}}_\alpha = \frac{1}{\alpha T}\sum_{i=1}^{k} r_{(i)}$. This distribution and $\widehat{\text{CVaR}}_\alpha$, did not account for the risk factors.

Quantile regression estimates the τth quantile $Q(\tau|F)$. For $\tau = \alpha$, we obtain an estimate $\widetilde{\text{VaR}}_\alpha = Q(\alpha|f)$, which accounts for the risk factors $\{F_1, \ldots, F_m\}$. This estimate is based on the empirical distribution and does not make theoretical distribution assumptions.

Applying the method to a set of values $\{\tau_1 \leq \cdots \leq \tau_h = \alpha\}$, we have another empirical $\alpha - tail$, $\check{G}_\alpha = \{(Q(\tau_1|f), \tau_i), (Q(\tau_2|f), \tau_2), \ldots, (Q(\tau_h), \alpha)\}$, which accounts for the risk factors. The quantiles $Q(\tau_i|f)$ are not observations, just as the fitted values $\hat{r}_i(f)$ from OLS regression are not observations. However, they are as close as possible to the ordered observed values, and they account for the factors. The mean of that $\alpha - tail$ is an alternative estimate of conditional value at risk

$$\widetilde{\text{CVaR}}_\alpha = \frac{1}{\alpha T}\sum_{i=2}^{h}\left(\frac{q_{i-1}+q_i}{2}\right)(\tau_i - \tau_{i-1}).$$

We have presented alternative models for evaluating risk measures. The application advantage for the models is noted in Table 4.3.

4.4 Regime-Switching Model

We have been considering models for a stochastic dynamic system, where the internal system is composed of an interrelated set of

Table 4.3. Models for evaluating Risk Measures.

Model	Error assumption	Application
Linear factor	Normality	This model works directly with the observed output $\{r_1, \ldots, r_n\}$. Least squares regression is quite robust and can be adapted to many variations/transformations. The software and output are familiar and understandable. It is possible that the estimates of VaR_α and $C\text{VaR}_\alpha$ are understated. However, the large sample properties are good.
Logit	Binomial	In some applications, the system status is not known or recorded. For example, with machines, the status only becomes noted when there is maintenance or repair. The available record is from breakdowns/failures. At time points, the status record is binary: (success, failure). So, the binary outcome (with unobserved status) is an obvious model for analysis.
Quantile	None	The system output $\{r_1, \ldots, r_n\}$ is observed, but there are indications that normality is not a property of the system. A non-parametric approach avoids distribution assumptions and provides robust estimates by working with the empirical distribution.

components which are controlled by decisions. We have interpreted the decisions as component weights representing the investments in the operating status of the components. In addition to the intrinsic components, the operation of the system is impacted by exogenous factors. It is proposed that the exogenous factors affect the component operation, and through the components, the system output is affected. The equations defining the output factor relationship were linear.

4.4.1 Regimes

So, the outcome for a system of m components with decisions $\{x_1, \ldots, x_m\}$, given exogenous factors $F' = (F_1, \ldots, F_K)$, is

$$\tilde{R}(X, F) = F\tilde{\beta} + \tilde{\varepsilon},$$

where the factor effect across the components of the system is aggregated as $\beta_j = \sum_{i=1}^{m} x_i\beta_{ij}, j = 1, \ldots, m$.

For the system design with m components and weights $x_i, i = 1, \ldots, m$, it is considered that the system operates in the same environment during trials/times. That is, the relationship $F\tilde{\beta}$ applies at each time. The systematic variation in output comes from varying F, not varying β.

It is possible (and even likely) that the time series of returns is cyclical. One way to interpret the cycles is that the effect of exogenous factors F on returns R, as measured by β, changes between cycles. It is usual to identify known periodic cycles/seasons with indicator variables that generate season-dependent β. In the case of unknown (hidden) aperiodic cycles, an indicator of the cycle/regime would be a random variable, and there would be a distribution over the possible cycles/regimes.

The concept of regimes to reflect the cyclical behavior of time series is common in financial analysis. It is well supported that financial markets have periods of expansion and contraction. The market phases are random in duration, with the switching triggered by unobserved phenomena. The phases can be described as regimes, with the switching between regimes being probabilistic. This regime switching is also plausible in mechanical systems where random shocks impact the operating environment, or in health systems where unexpected technological innovations or health policies change the operating environment.

We are focused on the risk of undesirable output from a system and the impact of selected risk factors. Assuming there are unobserved or latent regimes, it is proposed that the parameters in the linear factor model will change as the regime changes. Although the regimes are latent, incorporating regimes into the linear model will affect the measurement of systemic and idiosyncratic variation, and correspondingly, risk assessment.

Table 4.4. Regime indicators.

Regime	D_1	D_2	$\cdots$	D_K
1	1	0	$\cdots$	0
$\vdots$	$\vdots$	$\vdots$	$\ddots$	$\vdots$
K	0	0	$\cdots$	1

Consider that there are K hidden regimes in the system operation, with indicators D_k, $k = 1, \ldots, K$. So $D_k = 1$, for regime k, $D_k = 0$ otherwise. Table 4.4 displays the indicator values.

Within regimes (conditional), the linear factor model is

$$\tilde{R}(X, F|k) = F\tilde{\beta}_k + \tilde{\varepsilon}_k.$$

Across regimes (unconditional), the mixture model is

$$\tilde{R}(X, F) = \sum_{k=1}^{K} D_k(F\tilde{\beta}_k + \tilde{\varepsilon}_k).$$

The complication in this mixture is that D_k is latent (unobservable). However, information about the regime at any iteration of the system can be extracted from the data on observed variables $(R, F_1, \ldots, F_m)$. The procedure is to assume the regime-switching process follows a Markov chain: $\{D(t), t = 1, \ldots, T\}$. That process assigns probabilities to switches/transitions from one regime to another in an iteration. Using the indicators as regime labels, the transition probabilities are $p_{ij} = Prob[D(t) = D_j|D(t-1) = D_i]$. The matrix of transition probabilities is $P = [p_{ij}]$. The Markov assumption is somewhat reasonable, with the transition to the next regime only depending on the current regime, and not the complete history of prior regimes. It is restrictive in that the transition probabilities are fixed over time/iterations.

4.4.2 *Estimation of parameters*

The advantage of the Markov assumption is that it enables the estimation of all parameters $\{P; (\tilde{\beta}_k, k = 1, \cdots K)\}$. The estimation procedure is called the Baum–Welsh algorithm, a modification of the Expectation Maximization algorithm (Dempster *et al.*, 1977). The procedure is iterative:

1. Consider the data on $(R, F_1, \ldots, F_m)$ and assume the number of regimes is K.
2. Assume an initial distribution for regimes $\pi(0) = \{\pi_1(0), \ldots, \pi_K(0)\}$.
3. Given the regime probabilities as weights, use weighted least squares to estimate the parameters in the mixture model: $(\tilde{\beta}_k, k = 1, \ldots, K)$.
4. With the $(\tilde{\beta}_k, k = 1, \ldots, K)$ estimates, use Bayes's theorem to calculate the transition probabilities and the updated distribution for regimes.
5. Return to step 3.
6. Stop when the estimates converge (to within a tolerance value).

The results of the estimation are parameter estimates of the linear factor model by regime and Markov transition probabilities between regimes. An illustration of the output is shown in Table 4.5 for two regimes ($K = 2$).

Table 4.5. Parameter estimates for linear factor model and transition matrix.

	K	Constant	F_1	$\cdots$	F_m	ε
Single regime	1	$\tilde{\beta}_0$	$\tilde{\beta}_1$	$\cdots$	$\tilde{\beta}_m$	$\tilde{\sigma}^2$
Two regimes	1	$\tilde{\beta}_{10}$	$\tilde{\beta}_{11}$	$\cdots$	$\tilde{\beta}_{1m}$	$\tilde{\sigma}_1^2$
	2	$\tilde{\beta}_{20}$	$\tilde{\beta}_{21}$	$\cdots$	$\tilde{\beta}_{2m}$	$\tilde{\sigma}_2^2$

		Time t regime	
		1	**2**
Time $t-1$ regime	**1**	p_{11}	p_{12}
	2	p_{21}	p_{22}

4.4.3 *Inference*

In the EM algorithm, the linear factor model parameter estimates are determined by a conditional log likelihood maximization. With the assumption of normality for the error term, the maximization is equivalent to a weighted least squares calculation. If the conditional log likelihood in regime k of the data at time t is $\mathcal{L}_k(t)$, and the posterior probability for regimes are $\widehat{\pi}_k(t), k = 1, \ldots, K$, then the posterior log likelihood evaluated at the optimal parameter estimates is $\mathcal{L}_K(\widetilde{\beta}, \widetilde{\sigma}) = \sum_{k=1}^{K} \left\{ \sum_{t=1}^{T} \widehat{\pi}_k(t) \mathcal{L}_k(t) \right\}$. This posterior likelihood is the basis of inference. If competing hypotheses (H_0, H_a) are nested, then the difference $D(H_0, H_a) = -2\mathcal{L}_{K_0}(\widetilde{\beta}, \widetilde{\sigma}|H_0) + 2\mathcal{L}_{K_a}(\widetilde{\beta}, \widetilde{\sigma}|H_a)$ is a test statistic. We use that statistic to test several hypotheses.

1. Number of regimes:

For the linear model with m factors, we have hypotheses
$H_0 : K = 1$,
$H_0 : K > 1$.

We compare $K = 1$ and $K = 2$ to determine if there are multiple regimes. The test statistic is $D(H_0, H_a) = -2\mathcal{L}(\widetilde{\beta}, \widetilde{\sigma}|H_0) + 2\mathcal{L}(\widetilde{\beta}, \widetilde{\sigma}|H_a)$, which under the null hypothesis H_0 is approximately χ^2_d, where the degree of freedom d is the difference in the number of free parameters in the models $\{H_0\colon \widetilde{\beta}_0 + \sum_{j=1}^{m} \widetilde{\beta}_j F_j\}$ and $\{H_a\colon D_1(\widetilde{\beta}_{10} + \sum_{j=1}^{m} \widetilde{\beta}_{1j} F_j) + D_2(\widetilde{\beta}_{20} + \sum_{j=1}^{m} \widetilde{\beta}_{2j} F_j)\}$. If $\Pr[\chi^2_d > D(H_0, H_a)] < \alpha$, then reject H_0, and conclude there are multiple regimes.

There may be evidence for more than 2 regimes, so the test can be repeated for contrasts $\{(K, K+1), K = 2, \ldots\}$, to choose the number K where H_0 cannot be rejected. Equivalently, we can calculate the Bayes Information Criterion (BIC)

$$BIC(K) = -2\mathcal{L}_K(\widetilde{\beta}, \widetilde{\sigma}) + \delta \ln(T),$$

where δ is the number of slope parameters in the K regime model. $K^* = \operatorname{argmin}_K\{BIC(K)\}$ selects the number of regimes.

2. Total factor effect

There are many possibilities for the effect of the factors $F_j, j = 1, \ldots, m$ on the outcome in the K regimes. We will consider the factors as a set and test the effect of all factors versus no factors in a k regime model. The hypotheses are

$$H_0\text{: } \widetilde{\beta}_{k1} = \widetilde{\beta}_{k2} = \cdots = \widetilde{\beta}_{km} = 0, \quad \textit{for each } k, k = 1, \ldots, K,$$
$$H_a\text{: } \quad \textit{for at least one } (k, j), \widetilde{\beta}_{kj} \neq 0.$$

The reduced model H_0 implies that the regime means for R do not depend on the factors, whereas the full model H_a allows the regime means to depend on the factors in some fashion. The contrast between full and reduced hypotheses is an extension of the "all variables" test in the linear factor model without regimes.

The test statistic under the null hypothesis H_0 is $D(H_0, H_a) = -2\mathcal{L}(\widetilde{\beta}, \widetilde{\sigma}|H_0) + 2\mathcal{L}(\widetilde{\beta}, \widetilde{\sigma}|H_a)$, which under the null hypothesis H_0 is approximately χ^2_d, where the degree of freedom is the difference in the number of free parameters in the models $\{H_0 : D_1(\widetilde{\beta}_{10}) + \cdots + D_K(\widetilde{\beta}_{K0})\}$ and $\{H_a : D_1(\widetilde{\beta}_{10} + \sum_{j=1}^{m} \widetilde{\beta}_{1j} F_j) + \cdots + D_K(\widetilde{\beta}_{K0} + \sum_{j=1}^{m} \widetilde{\beta}_{Kj} F_j)\}$. If $\Pr[\chi^2_d > D(H_0, H_a)] < \alpha$, then reject H_0, and conclude the factors $\{F_j, j = 1, \ldots, m\}$ have a significant effect on the conditional mean of R in at least one regime.

3. Partial factor effect

The effect of individual factors is complicated by the correlation between factors. However, we can check the incremental effect of a factor after accounting for the effect of all other factors. The competing hypotheses are

$$H_0 : \widetilde{\beta}_{kl} = 0, k = 1, \ldots, K,$$
$$H_a : \textit{for at least one } k, \widetilde{\beta}_{kl} \neq 0.$$

The null hypothesis gives the reduced model with factors $\{F_1, \ldots, F_{l-1}, F_{l+1}, \ldots, F_m\}$, and the alternative hypothesis has the full model with factors $\{F_1, \ldots, F_m\}$.

The test statistic under the null hypothesis H_0 is $D\,(H_0, H_a) = -2\mathcal{L}(\widetilde{\beta}, \widetilde{\sigma}|H_0) + 2\mathcal{L}(\widetilde{\beta}, \widetilde{\sigma}|H_a)$, which under the null hypothesis H_0 is approximately χ^2_d, where the degrees of freedom is the difference in the number of free parameters in the models $\{H_0 : D_1(\widetilde{\beta}_{10} + \sum_{j\neq l} \widetilde{\beta}_{1j}) + \cdots + D_K(\widetilde{\beta}_{K0} + \sum_{j\neq l} \widetilde{\beta}_{Kj})\}$ and $\{H_a : D_1(\widetilde{\beta}_{10} + \sum_{j=1}^{m} \widetilde{\beta}_{1j} F_j) + \cdots + D_K(\widetilde{\beta}_{K0} + \sum_{j=1}^{m} \widetilde{\beta}_{Kj} F_j)\}$. If

$\Pr[\chi_d^2 > D(H_0, H_a)] < \alpha$, then reject H_0, and conclude the factor F_l has a significant effect on the conditional mean of R in addition to the factors $\{F_1, \ldots, F_{l-1}, F_{l+1}, \ldots, F_m\}$.

4.4.4 *Risk measures*

The reason for introducing factors into the model for the distribution of system output is to reduce the idiosyncratic variation. As well, the effect of factors on risk is regime dependent, and the probabilities for regimes are known (or estimated). Let the regime probabilities in a trial be $\underset{\sim}{\pi_k}, k = 1, \ldots, K$, and consider the linear factor model by regime: $\widetilde{R}_k = \widetilde{R}(X, F|k) = F\widetilde{\beta}_k + \tilde{\varepsilon}_k, k =, \ldots, K$. Let $g_k(r)$ be the normal density for $\widetilde{R}_k$. The distribution of $\ln(R(X, F))$ is a mixture of normal with density $g(r) = \pi_1 g_1(r) + \cdots + \pi_K g_K(r)$. The mixture distribution accommodates deviations from normality, and is also amenable to an analysis of risk measures.

1. Value at risk

From the definition of value at risk, we have

$$\int_{-\infty}^{\mathrm{VaR}_\alpha} g(r)\,dr = \alpha \Leftrightarrow \sum_{k=1}^{K} \pi_k \left[\int_{-\infty}^{\mathrm{VaR}_\alpha} g_k(r)dr\right] = \alpha.$$

So, finding VaR_α requires solving the equation

$$\sum_{k=1}^{K} \pi_k \Phi\left(\frac{\mathrm{VaR}_\alpha - \mu_k}{\sigma_k}\right) = \alpha,$$

where Φ is the cumulative standard normal distribution. If $z_k = \frac{\mathrm{VaR}_\alpha - \mu_k}{\sigma_k}$, and $erf_k(\mathrm{VaR}_\alpha) = \Phi(z_k)$, then numerically solving for VaR_α is straightforward.

2. Conditional value at risk

For the CVaR_α, we have

$$\begin{aligned}\mathrm{CVaR}_\alpha &= \frac{1}{\alpha}\int_{-\infty}^{\mathrm{VaR}_\alpha} rg(r)dr \\ &= \frac{1}{\alpha}\sum_{k=1}^{K} \pi_k \left[\int_{-\infty}^{\frac{\mathrm{VaR}_\alpha - \mu_k}{\sigma_k}} (\mu_k + z\sigma_k)\,\phi(z)\,dz\right].\end{aligned}$$

Again with $z_k = \frac{\mathrm{VaR}_\alpha - \mu_k}{\sigma_k}$, calculate $\alpha_k = \int_{-\infty}^{\frac{\mathrm{VaR}_\alpha - \mu_k}{\sigma_k}} \phi(z)\,dz$ and $\mu_{k\alpha} = \int_{-\infty}^{\frac{\mathrm{VaR}_\alpha - \mu_k}{\sigma_k}} z\phi(z)\,dz$. Then,

$$\mathrm{CVaR}_\alpha = \frac{1}{\alpha}\sum_{k=1}^{K} \pi_k \left[\alpha_k \mu_k + \sigma_k \mu_{k\alpha}\right].$$

The calculation of CVaR_α is straightforward, although it does not have the simple closed form provided for the linear factor model without regimes.

4.4.5 *Model assumptions*

The regime-switching linear factor model is a generalization of the model in Chapter 3. It has some assumptions that are important for analysis, but may limit the practicality of the model.

Number of regimes: The number of regimes must be specified in the model formulation. That is an important part of the number of parameters in the model. Since the maximum likelihood will increase with the number of parameters, it is customary to use a penalized likelihood criterion such as AIC or BIC to limit the number of regimes. The best choice for the number of regimes is the one with the minimum BIC (or AIC) value.

Normality: We have continued with the standard linear factor model within regimes, where the error has a normal distribution. So, the conditional distribution of returns is normal, but the unconditional distribution (across regimes) is a mixture of normal distributions. In that way, non-normal characteristics such as skewness and kurtosis are captured.

Linearity: The linear factor model within regimes is proposed. The linearity together with normality within regimes makes the conditional maximization likelihood step in the EM algorithm a weighted least squares calculation. So, the regime generalization clearly follows the analytic methods we described in Chapter 3.

Stationary transition matrix $\boldsymbol{P}$: The Markov regime-switching model uses a stationary transition matrix for regime switching. An additional level of randomness is introduced with the model, and characteristics such as the mean time between regime switches are the same over time.

Time-varying volatility: The regime-switching model has a constant idiosyncratic variance within a regime, but the idiosyncratic variance changes with a regime change. This time-varying volatility is significant for financial time series. We will have more on volatility later.

4.5 Case Studies

We have presented some important alternatives to the classical linear factor model for the output of a stochastic system. The alternative models will be illustrated with case studies of actual operating systems.

Case 4.1: Logistic regression with bank loan default

Logistic regression is a powerful tool for risk measurement because it estimates the probability of a critical event directly and allows an assessment of the importance of the explanatory factors to the risk in the dependent variable. This case study uses logistic regression to identify risky bank loans.

We obtain data on a large number of past bank loans in addition to information about the loan applicants. Data with these characteristics are available in a dataset donated to the UIC Machine Learning Repository (http://archive.ics.uci.edu/ml) by Hans Hofmann of the University of Hamburg. The dataset contains information on loans obtained from a credit agency in Germany.

The credit dataset includes 1,000 examples of loans, plus a set of numeric nominal features indicating the characteristics of the loan and the loan applicant. The outcome variable indicates whether the loan went into default. The variables are listed in Table 4.6.

The dataset is in the EViews workfile riskbk41. The first step in the estimation process is to select Quick from the main toolbar. Next, as shown in the following screenshot, the variables are entered in the dialog box beginning with Y = default, and then the factors $\{F_1, \ldots, F_6\}$. Now, select the method Binary and select Logit. Select OK to obtain the maximum likelihood estimation results.

Table 4.6. Credit variables.

Variable	Description
Y	Default: indicates whether the loan applicant was able to meet the agreed payment terms or if they went into default. 0 = went into default; 1 = loan was paid, with $p = Prob[Y = 1]$.
F_1	Credit history: history of compliance with previous or concurrent credit contracts, 1 = critical; 0 = good.
F_2	Dependents: 1 = Yes; 0 = No.
F_3	Empduration: employment duration in years with current employer.
F_4	Housing: type of housing debtor lives in; 1=own, 0=rent or other.
F_5	Months loan: months of loan duration.
F_6	Years residence: years at residence.

Several factors that were significant were identified and the final model is provided in the dialog box.

Dependent Variable: DEFAULT
Method: ML - Binary Logit (Newton-Raphson / Marquardt steps)
Date: 02/28/24 Time: 10:19
Sample: 1 1000
Included observations: 1000
Convergence achieved after 4 iterations
Coefficient covariance computed using observed Hessian

Variable	Coefficient	Std. Error	z-Statistic	Prob.
CREDITHISTORY	0.783037	0.156623	4.999501	0.0000
EMPDURATION	0.158863	0.027665	5.742313	0.0000
HOUSING	0.801276	0.129585	6.183402	0.0000
MONTHSLOAN	−0.028494	0.004873	−5.847967	0.0000

Mean dependent var	0.700000	S.D. dependent var	0.458487
S.E. of regression	0.439116	Akaike info criterion	1.142612
Sum squared resid	192.0515	Schwarz criterion	1.162243
Log likelihood	−567.3059	Hannan-Quinn criter.	1.150073
Deviance	1134.612	Restr. deviance	1221.729
Avg. log likelihood	−0.567306		

Obs with Dep=0	300	Total obs	1000
Obs with Dep=1	700		

The equation for predicting the probability of default is

$$\hat{p} = \frac{1}{1 + exp\left(-\left(0.783F_1 + 0.159F_3 + 0.801F_4 - 0.028F_5\right)\right)}.$$

Table 4.7. Model classification.

		Observed	
		Non-default : $Y = 0$	Default: $Y = 1$
Predicted	Non-default $\hat{Y} = 0$	90	210
	Default: $\hat{Y} = 1$	210	490

With the equation, the predicted probability of default for each of the 1000 samples is calculated: $\{\hat{p}_1, \ldots, \hat{p}_{1000}\}$. To convert the probability to a classification of default/non-default, we use a criterion: $\{\hat{p}_i > 0.5 \Rightarrow \hat{Y} = 1\}$, $\{\hat{p}_i \leq 0.5 \Rightarrow \hat{Y} = 0\}$. To find the prediction performance for the equation in EViews, in the dial box select: View:;Expectation - Prediction ... greater then .5/OK. As shown in the following screenshot, the logistic regression scored 26.67 percent correct for the dependent variable with default = 0 and 90.43% correct for the dependent variable with default = 1.

The model correctly predicts the loan outcome in 58% of the samples (Table 4.7). The risk factors have modest predictive power. To illustrate the VaR calculation, consider a loan applicant with risk factor values $F_1 = 0$ (credit history good), $F_3 = 5$ (five years current employment), $F_4 = 0$ (renter), $F_5 = 12$ (one year loan):

$$\hat{p} = \frac{1}{1 + exp\,(-\,(0.783 \times 0 + 0.159 \times 5 + 0.801 \times 0 - 0.028 \times 12))}$$
$$= 0.613.$$

If our critical value was $\alpha = .5$, then this loan prospect was too risky.

Case 4.2: Chance of winning in basketball

A competitive game is composed of a sequence of events. In basketball, the event is a possession of the ball. The possession ends when the ball is turned over to the competing team. So, possessions alternate. The play on an offensive possession is intricate, with the 5 players on the floor having important roles. On defense, the effect of blocking out offensive players around the basket produces successful rebounds and a change of possession. Although the on-floor choreography is complicated, the end result is clear – a change of possession with a score or change of possession without a score.

The scorecard for the possession will record those activities which directly affect the outcome. A focus on the scorecard and box score assumes that the strategic movements and physical abilities of players lead to favorable offensive and defensive opportunities, and that in turn produces a winning box score. The box score is the routine data collected on players and teams in a competition. The box score data is available for a long history of sports competitions, and that game summary is a convenient basis for analyzing game outcomes.

We will consider box score items as we do factors. It is the record of player activities, and the performance of players on a team is determined by their contribution to the team box score.

Composite measures: Team strength

It is the multidimensional profile for players and teams that is of interest, and in particular the connection of that profile to game success will be explored. We will consider linear combinations of the box score components as composite measures of performance.

Suppose there are m items in the box score and let the box score for team j be

$$F_j^{'} = (F_{j1}, \ldots, F_{jm}).$$

The approach is to generate a linear combination of the box score components with weights $\theta = (\theta_{j1}, \ldots, \theta_{jm})$. The weights capture the relative importance of a component to team success. Teams differ in their composition, with varying player abilities and strategies for game success. So, the relative importance of the box score components should differ by team. Then, team j strength is defined by

$$Y_j = \theta_{j0} + \theta_{j1} F_1 + \cdots + \theta_{jK} F_m + \varepsilon.$$

Team strength is variable, and there is an element of chance in the observation of strength in a game competition. The objective in a competition is to "win" the game, so the objective is to find weights that define a value Y_j which is closely related to winning.

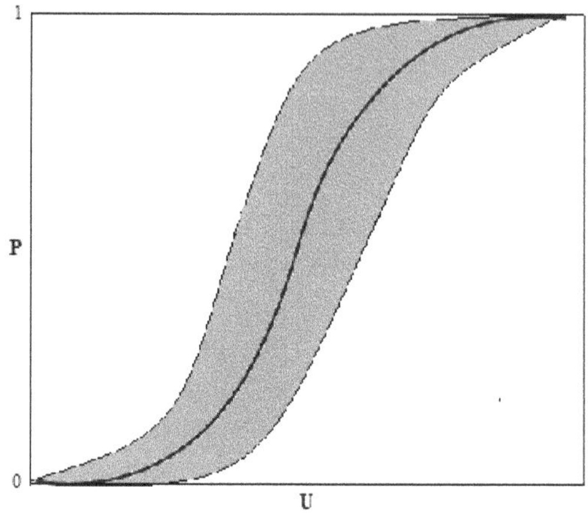

Figure 4.1. Win probability vs team strength.

With a specific box score, there is a chance of winning, with the assumption that the chance increases as the value increases. Let $P_j =$ the probability of winning, and consider the relationship between P_j and Y_j represented in Figure 4.1.

The sigmoid shape is a theoretical function for the improvement in performance with team strength, possibly from learning or training. The improvement through practice is a player phenomenon, and the team improves with individual player development.

Winning in a team competition is a team success, and the initial hypothesis is that as the team box score value increases, the success rate increases – implied by the sigmoid function. Suppose there are n games, the observed box score for team j in game i is $\{f_{ij1}, \ldots, f_{ijm}\}$, and the team strengths are $y_{ij} = \theta_{j0}+\theta_{j1}f_{ij1}+\cdots+\theta_{jm}f_{ijm} + \varepsilon_i$.

With the logistic function, the probability of winning game i is

$$p_{ij} = \frac{1}{1 + e^{-[\theta_{j0}+\theta_{j1}f_{ij1}+\cdots+\theta_{jm}f_{ijm}+\varepsilon_i]}}.$$

Therefore, $y_{ij} = ln\left(\frac{p_{ij}}{1-p_{ij}}\right) = \theta_{j0} + \theta_{j1}f_{ij1} + \cdots + \theta_{jm}f_{ijm} + \varepsilon_i$, and logistic regression can be performed to find the estimates

$$\left(\hat{\theta}_{j0}, \hat{\theta}_{j1}, \cdots \hat{\theta}_{jm}\right).$$

The fitted team strength values for games are $\{\hat{y}_{ij}, i = 1, \ldots, n\}$, where $\hat{y}_{ij} = \hat{\theta}_{j0} + \hat{\theta}_{j1} f_{ij1} + \cdots + \hat{\theta}_{jm} f_{ijm}$.

By inverting the logits, we have

$$\hat{p}_{ij} = \frac{1}{1 + e^{-\hat{y}_{ij}}}.$$

These are the estimated win probabilities for the n games based on the box scores. The estimated probability can be converted to predicted wins $\hat{W}_i$ and losses $\hat{L}_i$ and a comparison of predicted and actual W_i/L_i for the set of n games is a validation of the team strength values and the estimated linear weights.

The 1989–90 NBA Season

The NBA team analysis will be applied to the game box score data for the 1989–90 regular season. The data are found on the site NBA.com/boxscores. For each NBA team, the team linear weights were estimated from the 82 games played using logistic regression. Then, the team weights were applied to the team box scores for each game in the 1989–90 season, to give fitted logit values $Y_{ij}, i = 1, \ldots, 82$ for each team. The logits were classified by the winning team and the losing team in games. The plot of winning and losing logits is shown in Figure 4.2.

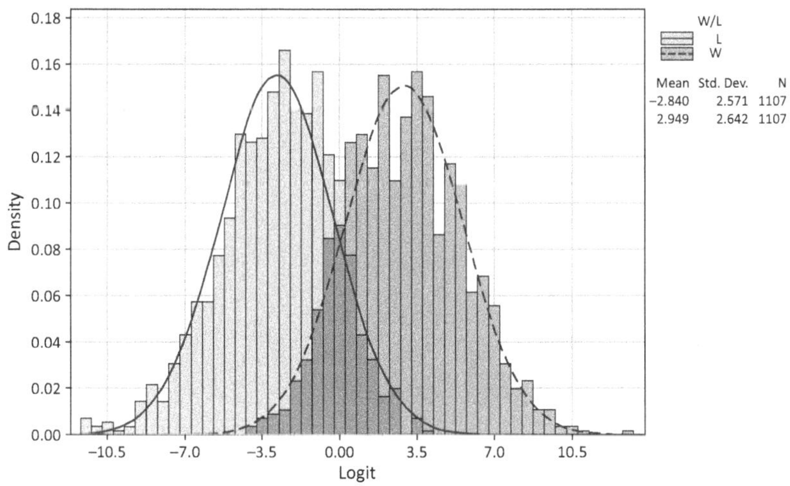

Figure 4.2. Game logits by win/loss result.

Table 4.8. Predicted wins.

	$\hat{L}$	$\hat{W}$
L	970	137
W	149	958

Clearly, there is a difference between winning and losing logits and by implication a difference between winning and losing box scores. The linear weights produce an aggregate score that discriminates between winning and losing. Note that the distribution of logits is close to normal, so the logistic model is valid.

The logit is converted to a probability of winning/losing, with Table 4.8 showing the classification of actual wins/losses and predicted wins/losses. The association is very high (88%). The evidence is strong that creating an aggregate score from team box scores using linear weights estimated with logistic regression is warranted.

The probability of winning in a game between teams can be calculated from the logit model. Consider a game between team A with team strength $y_A = \theta_{A0} + \theta_{A1}f_{A1} + \cdots + \theta_{Am}f_{Am}$ and team B with team strength $y_B = \theta_{B0} + \theta_{B1}f_{B1} + \cdots + \theta_{Bm}f_{Bm}$. The predicted probability of team A winning is $p_{AB} = \frac{1}{1+\exp(-(y_A - y_B))}$. For example, if $y_A = 3.5$ and $y_B = 1.5$, then $p_{AB} = 0.88$. That is, the chance of Team A winning is 88 percent. Gambling on games is based on this type of calculation. Of course, the team strengths of the respective teams would be based on box scores up to the time of the game and would be updated after each game.

Case 4.3: VaR estimation with quantile regression

Quantile regression is a natural alternative to estimating VaR. In this case study, we illustrate applying the EViews software to estimating the VaR at the 10% level of significance for the Shopify data. The equation expresses VaR as a function of the market index.

Estimation of the quantile regression starts by clicking on Quick and selecting the estimate equation. When the dialog box appears, insert shoppct c sptsxpct, where shoppct is the estimated monthly returns for Shopify stocks over the 2015 month 7 to 2024 month 1 (103 observations), c is the regression constant, and sptsxpct is the stock returns for the Toronto Stock Exchange Index. In the method section, select QREG from the drop-down menu. Enter .1 in the Quantile to estimate.

Quantile Equation Estimation Dialog Box: tau = 0.1

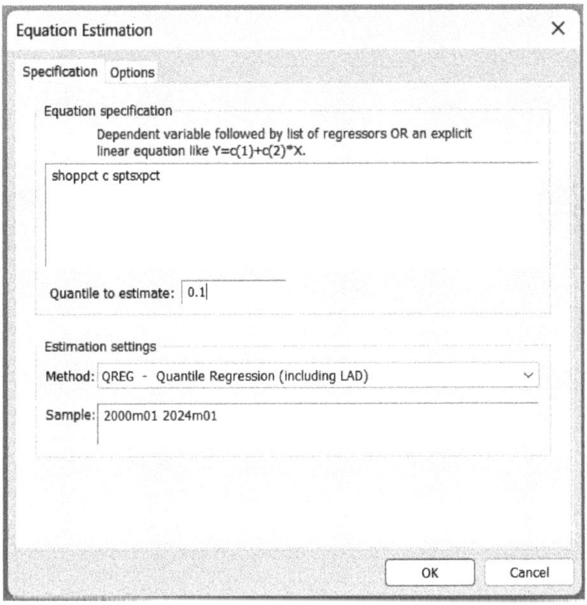

As shown in the screen shot, the estimated equation has an explanatory power of 9% – rather low but each of the coefficients is statistically significant with low p values implying to reject the null hypothesis that coefficients equal zero.

The Jarque–Bera test indicates the residuals come from a normal distribution, since $P = 0.61$ implies we do not reject the null hypothesis of a normal distribution.

The quantile regression with the coefficient value of 2.63 shows that the Shopify return is highly volatile relative to the market, not a surprising result.

Quantile Regression Estimation of Shopify Stack Return: Tau – 0.1

Equation: UNTITLED Workfile: RISKBK3.21::Untitle...

View | Proc | Object | Print | Name | Freeze | Estimate | Forecast | Stats | Resids

Dependent Variable: SHOPPCT
Method: Quantile Regression (tau = 0.1)
Date: 02/08/24 Time: 13:40
Sample (adjusted): 2015M07 2024M01
Included observations: 103 after adjustments
Huber Sandwich Standard Errors & Covariance
Sparsity method: Kernel (Epanechnikov) using residuals
Bandwidth method: Hall-Sheather, bw=0.073811
Estimation successfully identifies unique optimal solution

Variable	Coefficient	Std. Error	t-Statistic	Prob.
C	-0.134534	0.025572	-5.260934	0.0000
SPTSXPCT	2.638259	0.749184	3.521511	0.0006

Pseudo R-squared	0.090127	Mean dependent var	0.043161
Adjusted R-squared	0.081119	S.D. dependent var	0.151522
S.E. of regression	0.216606	Objective	2.419445
Quantile dependent var	-0.143335	Restr. objective	2.659103
Sparsity	0.758477	Quasi-LR statistic	7.021619
Prob(Quasi-LR stat)	0.008053		

Quantile Residuals Shopify Stock Return

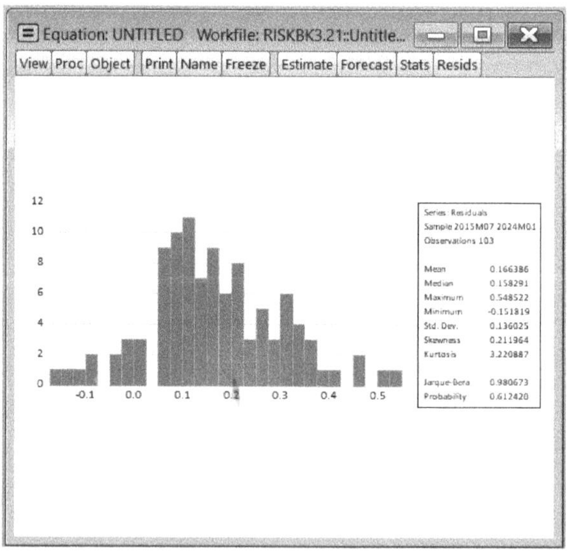

We have the conditional quantile given the market index f as

$$Q(0.1 \mid f) = -0.134534 + 2.638259f.$$

Consider the market rate of return $f = 0.065$. Then, $Q(0.1 \mid f = 0.065) = 0.037$. That is, for Shopify, the $\text{VaR}_{.1} = 0.037$ if $TSX = 0.065$.

Case 4.4: Returns on exchange-traded funds by regime

It is well established that financial time series exhibit cyclical patterns. In this case, we will consider the identification of cycles or switching regimes in the US stock market. The assets studied are the Sector Select Exchange-Traded Funds (ETFs). The returns on the ETFs are related to a set of macroeconomic factors with a regime-dependent linear factor model.

The results in this example are based on the paper by Maclean and Zhao (2021).

Recall within the regime (conditional), the linear factor model is for regime k,

$$R = F\beta_k + \varepsilon_k.$$

The parameters in the model are P = the transition matrix in the Markov process for regimes, and $\{(\mu_k, \Sigma_k), k = 1, \ldots, K\}$ = the regime dependent mean vector and covariance matrix for return rates. In the model, $\mu_k = F\beta_k$.

The factors and assets considered are shown in Tables 4.9 and 4.10.

Weekly data on the factors F_t and the asset returns R_t were recorded for the years between 1999 and 2019. The EM algorithm

Table 4.9. Macroeconomic factors.

F	Definition
F_1	(SPX): annualized logarithmic return on the S&P 500 Index
F_2	(VIX): annualized logarithmic change in the Volatility Index
F_3	(TB3): weekly risk-free return
F_4	(YSD): difference in 20 year bond yield and 2-year note yield
F_5	(LMT): difference in the three-month LIBOR and three-month T- Bill rates
F_6	(UER): logarithmic changes in the Unemployment Rates

Table 4.10. Assets: sector select funds.

R	**Definition**
R_1	XLY: CSM.DISCRTNY.SLT. SECT. SPDR FUND
R_2	XLY: CSM.DISCRTNY.SLT. SECT. SPDR FUND
R_3	XLP: CONSUMER STAPLES SELECT SECTOR SPDR FUND
R_4	XLE: ENERGY SELECT SECTOR SPDR FUND
R_5	XLF: FINANCIAL SELECT SECTOR SPDR FUND
R_6	XLV: HEALTH CARE SELECT SECTOR SPDR FUND
R_7	XLI: SECT.SPDR TST.SBI INTER INDS
R_8	XLB: MATERIALS SELECT SECTOR SPDR FUND
R_9	XLK: TECHNOLOGY SELECT SECTOR SPDR FUND
R_{10}	XLU: SECTOR SPDR TST.SBI INT- UTILS

Table 4.11. Average value of the economic indicators by regime.

Market	**SPX**	**VIX**	**TB3**	**LMT**	**YSD**	**UER**
Bear	−0.0956	−0.0492	0.0054	0.0166	0.0073	0.0027
Transition	0.0854	0.0961	0.0029	0.0083	0.0040	−0.0009
Bull	0.1339	−0.1045	0.0032	0.0257	0.0022	−0.0023

was used to estimate parameters. This requires a specification of the number of regimes K. The optimal number of market regimes using the BIC criterion was $K = 3$.

The average value of the economic indicators by regime is given in Table 4.11. From the table, it is observed that the factors have different indications in different market regimes.

An important question is how the probabilities of the regimes change as the financial market changes from one regime to another. The regime-switching dynamics are defined by the transition matrix $\hat{P}$. The labeling of the financial market regimes follows from the statistics on factors:

	Bear	Transition	Bull
Bear	0.9799	0.0059	0.0142
Transition	0.0095	0.9842	0.0063
Bull	0.0072	0.0096	0.9831

Table 4.12 presents asset return distribution parameters within each regime for the multi-regime model. For comparison, Table 4.13 has estimates for a single-regime model. In the model, the asset return distribution rates are normal, and the mean and covariance fully define the distributions.

The estimates for regimes are quite different. The mean rates for the bear market are negative, while they are strongly positive for the bull market. Also, the standard deviations are greater in the bear market. The single-regime estimates are sort of between the regime estimates.

For each of the ETFs, we can calculate the VaR_α with the formula

$$f(\text{VaR}_\alpha) = \sum_{k=1}^{K} \pi_k \phi \left(\frac{\text{VaR}_\alpha - \mu_k}{\sigma_k} \right) = \alpha.$$

For illustration, consider the market index SPY. Assume the regime probabilities are Bear – 0.2, transition – 0.4, and Bull −0.4. With the approximation to the normal cumulative $\phi(z) = 1 - 0.24015e^{-0.5616z^2}$, and $\alpha = .1$, we have for $x = \text{VaR}_1$ the equation

$$f(x) = 0.2\left(e^{-0.5616\left(\frac{x+0.08}{0.25}\right)^2}\right) + 0.4\left(e^{-0.5616\left(\frac{x-0.10}{0.12}\right)^2}\right)$$
$$+ 0.4\left(e^{-0.5616\left(\frac{x-0.15}{0.11}\right)^2}\right) - 3.75 = 0.$$

The value at risk for a specified α is determined by the root x from the equation $f(x) = 0$.

As indicated earlier, the CVaR_α is the average of the VaR_τ for $\tau \leq \alpha$. So, we can estimate CVaR_α by solving for VaR_{τ_i}, $\tau_1 < \tau_1 \ldots \leq \alpha$ and averaging the VaR_{τ_i}.

We have indicated an approach for finding the risk measures for an asset in a regime-switching market. A portfolio is defined by the investment strategy $X = (x_1, \ldots, x_n)$, and the portfolio risk measures would be a weighted average of the asset measures. We will consider portfolio strategies and their risk values in Chapter 5.

There is a very important risk issue in these estimates. Risk and the values of the various risk measures would be very different by regime. Ignoring the regime is missing a significant risk component associated with the regime indicators. Furthermore, the probabilities

Table 4.12. Annualized ETF statistics, by market regime.

Bear market										
ETF	**SPY**	**XLY**	**XLP**	**XLE**	**XLF**	**XLV**	**XLI**	**XLB**	**XLK**	**XLU**
Mean	−0.0793	−0.0616	−0.0275	−0.0437	−0.1405	−0.0287	−0.0698	−0.0506	−0.0980	−0.0467
Standard Deviation	0.2470	0.3006	0.1944	0.3146	0.3937	0.2332	0.2800	0.3153	0.3594	0.2407
Correlation	1.0000	0.8595	0.6230	0.6722	0.8317	0.8107	0.9116	0.7632	0.8466	0.6568
		1.0000	0.6076	0.5323	0.7952	0.7063	0.8489	0.7558	0.6479	0.5182
			1.0000	0.4674	0.5381	0.5488	0.5926	0.5345	0.3260	0.5296
				1.0000	0.5206	0.4873	0.6728	0.7419	0.4338	0.5889
					1.0000	0.6071	0.7894	0.6779	0.5771	0.5168
						1.0000	0.7420	0.5985	0.6578	0.5615
							1.0000	0.8340	0.7124	0.6216
								1.0000	0.5220	0.5633
									1.0000	0.4322
Transition market										
Mean	0.1043	0.0878	0.0823	0.0638	0.0908	0.0690	0.1024	0.0834	0.1567	0.1405
Standard Deviation	0.1215	0.1393	0.1014	0.2195	0.1641	0.1242	0.1443	0.1745	0.1530	0.1259
Correlation	1.0000	0.8971	0.7020	0.6934	0.8658	0.7976	0.8795	0.8305	0.8929	0.3677
		1.0000	0.6425	0.5487	0.7498	0.6763	0.7746	0.7155	0.8294	0.2702
			1.0000	0.3685	0.4904	0.5961	0.5679	0.5388	0.6037	0.5607
				1.0000	0.5907	0.4332	0.6226	0.6780	0.4996	0.2616

					1.0000	0.6779	0.8058	0.7350	0.6830	0.1666
						1.0000	0.6553	0.5956	0.6571	0.3558
							1.0000	0.8253	0.7314	0.2247
								1.0000	0.6972	0.2594
									1.0000	0.2530
Bull market										
Mean	0.1526	0.2096	0.1230	0.1544	0.1565	0.1788	0.1846	0.1702	0.1189	0.1163
Standard Deviation	0.1134	0.1304	0.0975	0.1813	0.1428	0.1227	0.1359	0.1579	0.1641	0.1265
Correlation	1.0000	0.8524	0.7124	0.6526	0.8571	0.7501	0.8932	0.7984	0.8450	0.5551
		1.0000	0.6637	0.4940	0.7128	0.6428	0.7953	0.7178	0.6525	0.4063
			1.0000	0.3722	0.5751	0.5883	0.5952	0.4743	0.4713	0.5110
				1.0000	0.5344	0.3727	0.6233	0.6666	0.4310	0.4034
					1.0000	0.6099	0.7782	0.6620	0.6177	0.4311
						1.0000	0.6485	0.5677	0.5518	0.4021
							1.0000	0.8045	0.6895	0.4827
								1.0000	0.6185	0.4160
									1.0000	0.4145

Table 4.13. Annualized ETF statistics, single regime.

ETF	SPY	XLY	XLP	XLE	XLF	XLV	XLI	XLB	XLK	XLU
Mean	0.0634	0.0859	0.0623	0.0636	0.0411	0.0793	0.0781	0.0732	0.0601	0.0708
Standard Deviation	0.1709	0.2042	0.1377	0.2428	0.2572	0.1675	0.1969	0.2255	0.2433	0.1722
Correlation	1.0000	0.8642	0.6536	0.6665	0.8378	0.7965	0.9034	0.7808	0.8520	0.5922
		1.0000	0.6236	0.5222	0.7766	0.6893	0.8280	0.7414	0.6728	0.4599
			1.0000	0.4263	0.5351	0.5664	0.5909	0.5249	0.3942	0.5324
				1.0000	0.5235	0.4508	0.6488	0.7104	0.4384	0.4812
					1.0000	0.6134	0.7862	0.6791	0.5961	0.4501
						1.0000	0.7100	0.5930	0.6352	0.4951
							1.0000	0.8271	0.7102	0.5306
								1.0000	0.5650	0.4823
									1.0000	0.4046

for the uncertain regimes are estimated by the Markov process for regimes. In fact, the prior probabilities for regimes in a subsequent period are calculated based on the observed factors in previous periods. There is a credible basis for inferring the most likely regime in the next period. The additional risk from regime uncertainty is reduced.

4.6 Conclusion

In the discussion of the risk associated with the outcome from a stochastic system, the focus is on the probability of failure (an undesirable outcome) and the consequences of the failure. The linear factor model with normal error is a very attractive model for analyzing risk. However, there are situations where the linear model is not appropriate, either because the model assumptions are violated or the data on outcomes are categorical. The goal in the current chapter was to present alternative models for risk analysis, while retaining the ability to incorporate important aspects of the system, such as risk factors and decisions.

The models that are based on the classification of outcomes as success/failure are important since, for many applications, it is the failure that is observed. The logistic model has many similarities to the linear factor model. It is suitable for comparing the risk of alternative systems, which may be distinguished by differing decisions on system maintenance. However, the decisions on investments in components are not explicit, and a detailed analysis of the system's decision is not clear. Comparisons of systems differentiated by decisions would be based on analysis of data that are differentiated by decisions.

Risk analysis using quantile regression is data based. The empirical distribution is the basis of quantile estimates. In the case where there are associated risk factors, conditional (on factors) empirical distribution is used to compute quantile estimates linked to risk factors.

The adaptation of the linear model to cyclical patterns or alternating regimes is a move toward time-varying parameters in the stochastic outcomes from the system. The concept of time-varying volatility is considered further in Chapter 6.

Bibliography

Agresti, A. (2002). *Categorical Data Analysis.* Wiley-Interscience, New York.

Amemiya, T. (1985). Qualitative response models. In *Advanced Econometrics*, 267–359. Basil Blackwell, Oxford.

Ang, A. and Bekaert, G. (2002). International asset allocation with regime shifts. *Review of Financial Studies*, 15(4), 1137–1187.

Angrist, J.D. and Pischke, J. (2009). Quantile regression. In *Mostly Harmless Econometrics: An Empiricist's Companion*, 269–291. Princeton University Press, New Jersey.

Bassett, G.W. and Chen, H. (2001). Portfolio style: Return-based attribution using quantile regression. *Empirical Economics*, 26, 293–305.

Basak, S. and Shapiro, A. (2001). Value at risk based risk management: Optimal policies and asset prices. *Review of Financial Studies*, 14, 371–405.

Berkson, J. (1944). Application of the logistic function to bio-assay. *Journal of the American Statistical Association*, 39(227), 357–365.

Birkes, D. and Dodge, Y. *Alternative Methods of Regression*, John Wiley, New York.

Cai, Z. (2002). Regression quantiles for time series. *Econometric Theory*, 18, 169–192.

Chekhlov, A., Uryasev, S., and Zabarankin, M. (2005). A drawdown measure in portfolio optimization. *International Journal of Theoretical and Applied Finance*, 8(1), 13–58.

Chordia, T. and Shivakumar, L. (2002). Momentum, business cycle, and time-varying expected returns. *Journal of Finance*, 57(2), 985–1019.

Costa, G. and Kwon, R.H. (2019). Risk parity portfolio optimization under a Markov regime-switching framework. *Quantitative Finance*, 19(3), 453–471.

Cox, D.R. (1958). The regression analysis of binary sequences (with discussion). *Journal of the Royal Statistical Society Series B*, 20(2), 215–242.

Cramer, J.S. (2002). The origins of logistic regression. Tinbergen Institute Technical Report, 119, 167–178.

Cuoco, D., He, H., and Issaenko, S. (2008). Optimal dynamic trading strategies with risk limits. *Operations Research*, 47, 1209–1227.

Dempster, A.P., Laird, N.M., and Rubin, D.B. (1977). Maximum likelihood from incomplete data via the EM algorithm. *Journal of the Royal Statistical Society Series B*, 39, 1–38.

De Santis, G. and Gerard, B. (1997). International asset pricing and portfolio diversification with time-varying risk. *Journal of Finance*, 52(5), 1881–1912.

Draper, N.R. and Smith, H. (1998). *Applied Regression Analysis* (3rd ed.). John Wiley, New York.

Fox, J. (1997). *Applied Regression Analysis, Linear Models and Related Methods*. Sage Publications, Los Angeles, CA.

Greene, W.H. (2003). *Econometric Analysis* (5th ed.). Prentice Hall, New Jersey.

Hamilton, J.D. (1989). A new approach to the economic analysis of non-stationary time series and the business cycle. *Econometrica*, 57(2), 357–384.

Hammerschmid, R. and Lohre, H. (2018). Regime shifts and stock return predictability. *International Review of Economics & Finance*, 56, 138–160.

Hosmer, D. (2013). *Applied Logistic Regression*. Wiley, Hoboken, New Jersey.

Koenker, R. (2005). *Quantile Regression*. Cambridge University Press, Cambridge, UK.

Liu, P., Xu, K., and Zhao, Y. (2011). Market regimes, sectorial investments, and time-varying risk premiums. *International Journal of Managerial Finance*, 7(2), 107–133.

Loffler, G. (2003). The effects of estimation error on measures of portfolio credit risk. *Journal of Banking and Finance*, 27(8), 1427–1453.

MacKinlay, A.C. and Pastor, L. (2000). Asset pricing models: Implications for expected returns and portfolio selection. *The Review of Financial Studies*, 13(4), 883–916.

Ma, Y., MacLean, L., Xu, K., and Zhao, Y. (2011). A portfolio optimization model with regime-switching risk factors for sector exchange traded funds. *Pacific Journal of Optimization, Pacific Journal of Optimization* 7(2), 281–296.

MacLean, L. and Zhao, Y. (2021). Kelly investing with risk control in a regime-switching market. *Quantitative Finance*, 22(1), 75–94. DOI: 10.1080/14697688.2021.1993617

MacLean, L., Zhao, Y., and Zhang, O. (2025). Mean-variance optimization with inferred regimes. *Annals of Operations Research*, 346(1), 341–368.

MacLean, L. and Ziemba, W. (2022). *Sports Analytics*. World Scientific Publishing Co., Singapore.

MacLean, L. and Ziemba, W. (2021). Who are the most important players in team sports. *Journal of Prediction Markets*, 15(3), 33–83.

Olabiyi, O. and Annamalai, A. (2012). Invertible exponential-type approximations for the Gaussian probability integral Q(x) with applications. *IEEE Wireless Communications Letters*, 1(5), 544–547.

Schaller, H. and van Norden, S. (1997). Regime switching in stock market returns. *Applied Financial Economics*, 7(2), 177–191.

Sen, A. and Srivastava, M. (2011). *Regression Analysis: Theory, Methods, and Applications* (4th printing). Springer-Verlag, Berlin.

Taylor, J. (1999). A quantile regression approach to estimating the distribution of multiperiod returns. *Journal of Derivatives*, 24, 64–78.

Theil, H. (1969). A multinomial extension of the linear logit model. *International Economic Review*, 10(3), 251–259.

Tversky, A. and Kahneman, D. (1993). Advances in prospect theory: Cumulative representation of uncertainty. *Journal of Risk and Uncertainty*, 5(4), 297–323.

Vliet, P. and Blitz, D. (2011). Dynamic strategic asset allocation: Risk return across economic regimes. *Journal of Asset Management*, 12, 360–375.

Zucchini, W. and MacDonald, I. (2009). *Hidden Markov Models for Time Series: An Introduction Using R*. CRC Press, Taylor & Francis Group, Oxfordshire, UK.

Chapter 5

Risk Control

5.1 Introduction

Risk has been explored in the setting of a dynamic stochastic system designed to produce outputs. The outputs are random variables with distributions affected by various sources. Quantitative methodology defines the system through equations that relate the output variables to system characteristics, including operational decisions. It is the effect of decisions on output variables that is the focus of the current chapter. The approach is prospective rather than retrospective. It is possible to analyze the historical data on output variables, factors, and decisions to estimate the effect of decisions. Our interest is in the decisions that are to be made currently and the impact on system output variables going forward.

We will assume that historical data have been used to estimate the parameters in equations, which define the dependence of output variables on factors and decisions. It is also assumed that the parameters in factor–output equations are not impacted by decisions. That will enable the determination of decisions, conditional on the parameters. There are many approaches to decision-making which control risk. We will develop two models, one with an emphasis on utility theory and another with an emphasis on risk theory.

5.2 System Structure: Factors and Decisions

We have analyzed the output from a system with a general system structure, composed of a set of interrelated components.

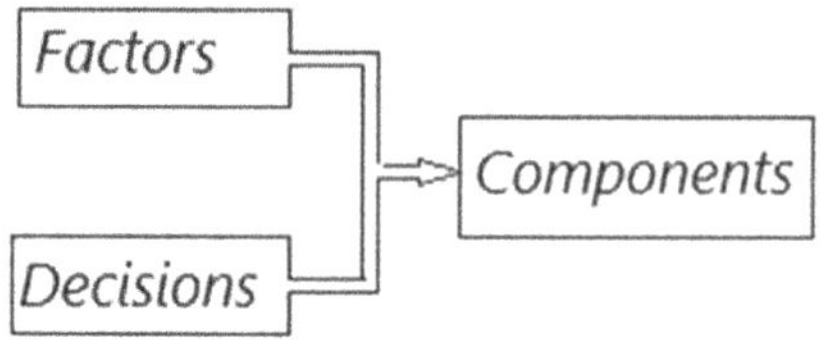

Figure 5.1. System structure.

The components are affected by risk factors and decisions which represent the importance of components to the total system outcome. A simple framework for the system structure is given in Figure 5.1.

The analysis of risk focused on the output of a system. The internal structure of the system was not explored. The components and decision weights assigned to components defined the system. The factors were exogenous and were filtered through the system to find the impact on the system output. The decisions that define the system are controls on the system output. In the evaluation of decisions, it is required that system output be ordered, so that systems and the decisions that define them can be compared. We will present the internal system's equations for components and decisions, which are defined by the linear factor model used in previous chapters.

Consider that there are n components and the state of a component at trial t is $S_i(t), i = 1, \ldots, n$. To link the dynamics of the components to the system outcome dynamics, we assume that the units of measure for a component state are such that the change in outcome for the system can be calculated from changes in component states: $\frac{S_i(t+1)}{S_i(t)} = 1 + \frac{\Delta S_i(t)}{S_i(t)} = 1 + R_i(t)$. So, $(1 + R_i(t))$ is the random variable for the change in status for component i and the rate $(R_i(t))$ is a per-unit change in system status: $\frac{\Delta S_i(t)}{S_i(t)}$. It is considered that the component status is affected by the risk factors. A first-order approximation of the factor effect is given by the system of linear equations $R_i(t) = [\beta_{i0} + \beta_{i1}F_1(t) + \cdots + \beta_{im}F_m(t)] + \varepsilon_i(t), i = 1, \ldots, n$. Since we will analyze the output from a trial of a system, we will drop the time argument and write in matrix form $R = [\beta F] + \varepsilon$. It is assumed that $\varepsilon \sim MVN(0, \Sigma)$.

The control over the system output comes from allocations to components. Consider that there is a system maintenance budget y. The decisions are allocations of the budget to components:

$\{(y_1, \ldots, y_n), \sum_{k=1}^{K} y_i = y\}$. Actually, the free decisions are $x_i = \frac{y_i(t)}{y(t)}$, $i = 1, \ldots, n$ the fraction of the budget allocated to components. We have a change in the system output $\sum y_i(1 + R_i) = y(\sum x_i(1 + R_i)) = y(1 + \sum x_i R_i)$. Then, the change from investment is

$$1 + R(X) = \left(1 + \sum x_i R_i\right). \tag{5.1}$$

In this equation, we consider that the system rate incorporates the sensitivity of the system state to changes in component states. That is, with the system state $S = h(S_1, \ldots S_n)$, the rate of change is $\Delta S = \frac{\partial h}{\partial S_1}\Delta S_1 + \cdots + \frac{\partial h}{\partial S_n}\Delta S_n$. We assume $R_i \approx \frac{\partial h}{\partial S_i}\Delta S_i$.

With the investment X, the system rate is composed of component rates as $R(X) = \sum_{i=1}^{n} x_i R_i$, where $R_i = [\beta_{i0} + \beta_{i1}F_1 + \cdots + \beta_{im}F_m] + \varepsilon_i$, $i = 1, \ldots, n$. The decision $X = (x_1, \ldots, x_n)$ determines the system output, and comparing decisions $X_1 = ((x_{11}, \ldots, x_{1n}))$ and $X_2 = ((x_{21}, \ldots, x_{2n}))$ is based on the ordering of random outcomes $R(X_1)$ and $R(X_2)$.

5.3 Stochastic Order: Comparing Decisions

The output from a stochastic dynamic system has been structured so that the defining feature is the maintenance decision for components of the system. If we want to determine preferred decisions, we need an order relation for random variables. That is a complex concept since the range of values for different random variables overlaps, and in many cases, covers the full real line. Random variables are defined by their probability distributions. The preference for random variables can be expressed in terms of the characteristics of their distributions with the order relations of stochastic dominance.

First-order stochastic dominance (FSD) is defined by the cumulative distribution.

Let $R(X_1)$ and $R(X_2)$ be random variables with distribution functions G_1 and G_2, respectively. Then, $R(X_1)$ FSD $R(X_2)$ iff $G_1(r) \le G_2(r)$, $\forall\, r$. Alternatively, $R(X_1)$ FSD $R(X_2)$ iff $G_1^{-1}(p) \ge G_2^{-1}(p)$, $0 \le p \le 1$.

In most cases, the cumulative distribution functions would not be ordered, but would rather intersect at various values of r. A reasonable approach to intersecting distributions is to consider the area between them. If the intersection(s) is such that when accumulating area, the positive is not offset by the negative, then second-order stochastic dominance holds.

Let $R(X_1)$ and $R(X_2)$ be random variables with distribution functions G_1 and G_2, respectively. Then, $R(X_1)$ SSD $R(X_2)$ iff $\int_{-\infty}^{y} G_1(r)dr \le \int_{-\infty}^{y} G_2(r)dr,\ \forall\, y$. Alternatively, $R(X_1)$ SSD $R(X_2)$ iff $\int_0^\alpha G_1^{-1}(p)dp \ge \int_0^\alpha G_2^{-1}(p),\ 0 \le \alpha \le 1$.

Obviously, first-order stochastic dominance implies second-order stochastic dominance. The mean of a random variable in terms of its inverse distribution is $\mu = \int_0^1 G^{-1}(p)dp$. The calculation $\int_0^\alpha G^{-1}(p)dp = L(\alpha)$ defines the incomplete mean, and the graph $\{(\alpha, L(\alpha), 0 \le \alpha \le 1\}$ is called the absolute Lorenz curve (Lorenz, 1905). SSD is based on an ordering of Lorenz curves. As with the distribution functions, it is possible that the Lorenz curves intersect and the random variables cannot be ordered by SSD. Dominated and undominated curves ($\mathrm{H}(p) = G^{-1}(p)$–distribution, $L(p)$–Lorenz) are shown in Figure 5.2.

The integration process can be continued with the calculation of the cumulative area between the curves to get higher orders of dominance. The dominance becomes weaker, but more random variables are ordered by higher orders.

The ordering defined by stochastic dominance is linked to the preference relation from expected utility. Hanoch and Levy (1969) show that stochastic dominance can be defined by classes of utilities as characterized by higher-order derivatives of the utility, with $u^{(k)}$ being the kth derivative. Consider the class of utilities $U_k = \{u|((-1)^{j-1}u^{(j)} \ge 0, j = 1, \ldots, k\}$. So, U_1 is the class of monotone non-decreasing functions, U_2 is the class of monotone non-decreasing, concave functions, and so on.

(i) Let $R(X_1)$ and $R(X_2)$ be random variables with distribution functions G_1 and G_2, respectively. Then, $R(X_1)$ FSD $R(X_2)$ iff

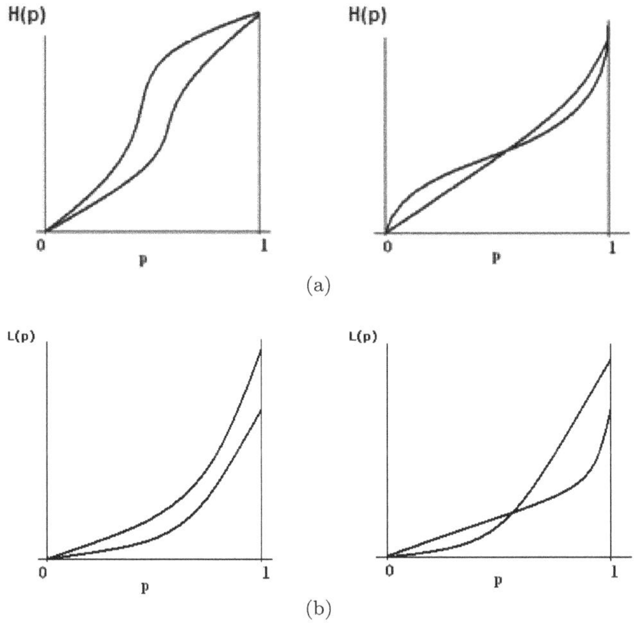

Figure 5.2. (a) First-order stochastic dominance. (b) Second-order stochastic dominance.

either

$$G_1^{-1}(p) \geq G_2^{-1}(p), \quad 0 \leq p \leq 1, \quad \text{or}$$
$$Eu(R(X_1)) \geq Eu(R(X_2)) \quad \text{for all } u \in U_1.$$

(ii) Let $R(X_{1)}$ and $R(X_2)$ be random variables with distribution functions G_1 and G_2, respectively. Then, $R(X_{1)}$ SSD $R(X_2)$ iff either

$$\int_0^\alpha G_1^{-1}(p)dp \geq \int_0^\alpha G_2^{-1}(p), \quad 0 \leq \alpha \leq 1, \quad \text{or}$$
$$Eu(R(X_1) \geq Eu(R(X_2)) \quad \text{for all } u \in U_2.$$

With second-order dominance, the distributions can cross many times as long as the order of area between the distributions is maintained. For distributions which cross just once, second-order dominance depends on the means: If $G_1(r) \leq G_2(r),\ r < r_0$ and $G_1(r) \geq$

$G_2(r)$, $r \geq r_0$, then $R(X_1)$ SSD $R(X_2) \Leftrightarrow E(R(X_1)) \geq E(R(X_2))$ (Hammond, 1974).

In certain cases, second-order dominance is characterized by the first two moments of the distributions.

Let $R(X_1)$ and $R(X_2)$ be random variables with distribution functions G_1 and G_2, and (means, variances) given by (μ_1, σ_1^2) and (μ_2, σ_2^2), respectively. Let $\mu_1 > \mu_2$ and assume

$$G_1(r_1) = G_2(r_2) \quad \text{for all } r_1, r_2 \text{ such that } \frac{r_1 - \mu_1}{\sigma_1} = \frac{r_2 - \mu_2}{\sigma_2},$$

$$G_1(r^*) > G_2(r^*) \quad \text{for some } r^*.$$

Then, $R(X_1)$ SSD $R(X_2)$ iff $\sigma_1^2 \leq \sigma_2^2$.

The higher orders of stochastic dominance can be continued with the classes of utilities based on derivatives of the utility function. So, $R(X_1)$ kth order dominates $R(X_2)$ iff $Eu(R(X_1)) \geq Eu(R(X_2))$ for all $u \in U_k$. Again, the higher-order dominance is weaker, but an interesting class of utilities arises when $k \to \infty$. The sign of successive derivatives alternates, which characterizes the class of power utilities: $\{u_\alpha(r) = \frac{1}{\alpha} r^\alpha, \alpha < 1\}$. The special member of this class is the log utility, when $\alpha \to 0$, which is the utility of Bernoulli (1738), and it dominates other power utilities in the sense that maximizing log of terminal wealth gives the maximal growth rate of capital.

The dominance described earlier is for a single period, usually the final period of accumulated capital. However, the capital is accumulated from investments over time and the trajectory to final wealth could be important in the assessment of utility. Levy and Paroush (1974) extend the notions of stochastic dominance to the multi-period case (see also Huang, Vertinsky and Ziemba (1978)). Two situations are discussed. In one case, inter-temporal utility is assumed to be additive, so that for the multi-period capital stream $(r_1, \ldots, r_T)$ the utility is $u(r_1, \ldots, r_T) = \sum_{t=1}^{T} u_t(r_t)$.

> Consider multi-period capital streams $R^T(X_1) = (R_1(X_1), \ldots, R_T(X_1))$ and $R^T(X_2) = (R_1(X_2), \ldots, R_T(X_2))$, with multivariate distributions $G_1(r)$ and $G_2(r)$. Let G_{t1} and G_{t2} be the marginal distributions for period $t, t = 1, \ldots, T$. Then, necessary and sufficient conditions for $R^T(X_1)$ FSD $R^T(X_2)$ are $G_{t1}(r) \leq G_{t2}(r)$, $\forall r, t = 1, \ldots, T$.

So, in the case of additive utility, the ordering of marginal distributions allows the stochastic dominance result to extend to multiple periods. This result does not require temporal independence. The second-order (and higher-order) dominance would follow by considering the area between (integration) for marginal distributions.

A second case considered by Levy and Paroush involves the geometric process where the final rate of return is the product of period returns: $R^T(X) = R_1(X) \times \cdots \times R_T(X)$. So, each period provided a rate of return. The utility is for the final return $u(1 + R^T(X))$.

Consider multi-period capital streams $R^T(X_1) = (R_1(X_1) \times \cdots \times (X_1))$ and $R^T(X_2) = (R_1(X_2) \times \cdots \times R_T(X_2))$, with multivariate distributions $G_1(r)$ and $G_2(r)$. Then, necessary conditions for $R^T(X_1)$ FSD $R^T(X_2)$ are

(i) $G_{1,t|t-1,\ldots,1}(r_t|r_{t-1}, \ldots, r_1) \leq G_{2,t|t-1,\ldots,1}(r_t|r_{t-1}, \ldots, r), t = 1, \ldots, T$, where $G_{i,t|t-1,\ldots,1}$ is the conditional distribution at time t, and
(ii) the conditional distribution $G_{i,t|t-1,\ldots,1}(\cdot|r_{t-1}, \ldots, r)$ is non-decreasing in $r_{t-1}, \ldots, r_1$.

This is a very common situation, where the terminal return is evaluated but the returns by period are serially correlated. The condition is necessary but not sufficient.

5.4 Efficient Decisions

The order relations provide a setting for comparing decisions in a stochastic dynamic system. Conditional on the design components and risk factors, the differences in outcome distributions can be attributed to decisions. If efficient distributions are un-dominated, then efficient investment strategies are ones whose outcomes at a specified time are un-dominated. Dyvbig and Ross (1982) put this in terms of utility functions in a class, such as U_k.

If $(1 + R_T(X))$ is the return at time T from an investment strategy X in the feasible set of strategies Λ, then $(1 + R_T(X^*))$ is kth order efficient if there exists a utility $u \in U_k$ such that

$$Eu(1 + R_T(X^*)) = \max_{X \in \Lambda} Eu(1 + R_T(X)). \tag{5.2}$$

5.4.1 *Mean–variance efficiency*

Efficiency applies to any order of stochastic dominance, although risk aversion and SSD are standard. The set of efficient strategies is characterized by stochastic dominance, but in general, efficient strategies are difficult to calculate. The special case of normally distributed random variables is tractable and has received a lot of attention.

Let $(1 + R(X_1))$ and $(1 + R(X_2))$ be normally distributed random variables with means μ_1, μ_2 and variances σ_1^2, σ_2^2, respectively. Then, the following are equivalent:

(i) $Eu(1 + R(X_1)) \geq Eu(1 + R(X_2))$ for any utility $u \in U_2$.
(ii) $\mu_1 \geq \mu_1$ and $\sigma_1^2 \leq \sigma_2^2$.

Second-order dominance and efficiency are determined by the parameters in the normal distribution. Markowitz (1952) originated the concept of mean–variance efficiency, and it has been a cornerstone of portfolio theory. The set of MV efficient points, called the efficient frontier, is determined from the problem for each mean μ_0,

$$\mathrm{P}(\mu_0): \min_X\{\sigma^2(X))|\mu(X) \geq \mu_0,\ X \text{ feasible}\}. \tag{5.3}$$

A depiction of the MV frontier is given in Figure 5.3. Also shown is the tangency (market) portfolio and the capital market line, where the market portfolio is blended with the risk-free asset for risk control.

The market portfolio is determined by the Sharpe ratio:

$$\varphi(X) = \frac{\mu(X) - r}{\sigma(X)}. \tag{5.4}$$

If the market portfolio is X_M, then $X_M = \operatorname{argmax}\{\varphi(X)\}$. The Sharpe ratio is often used as a measure of the risk–return trade-off. That is,

for decisions X_1 and X_2, we have X_1 dominated by X_2, denoted $X_1 \ll X_2$ if $\varphi(X_1) < \varphi(X_2)$.

There are decisions X which have the same $\varphi(X)$, so it involves classes of decisions which are ordered. The ρ equivalence class is $X(\rho) = \{X|\varphi(X) = \rho\}$. A sample Sharpe ratio would be a random variable. Taking into account variation, there are ranges of values

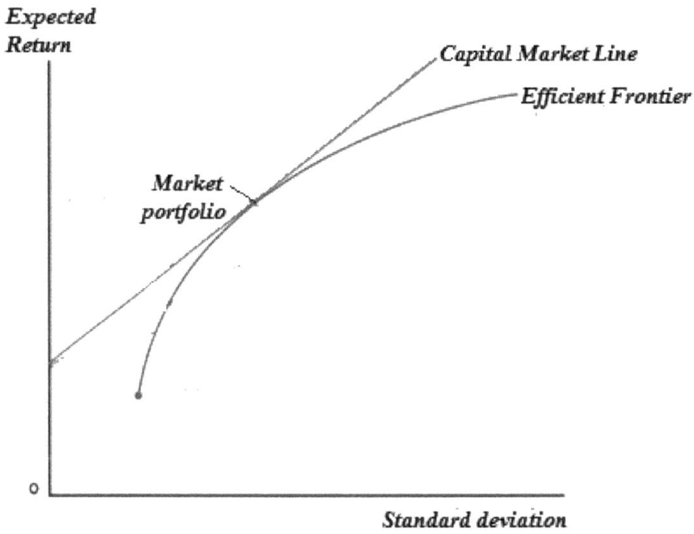

Figure 5.3. Mean–variance efficient frontier.

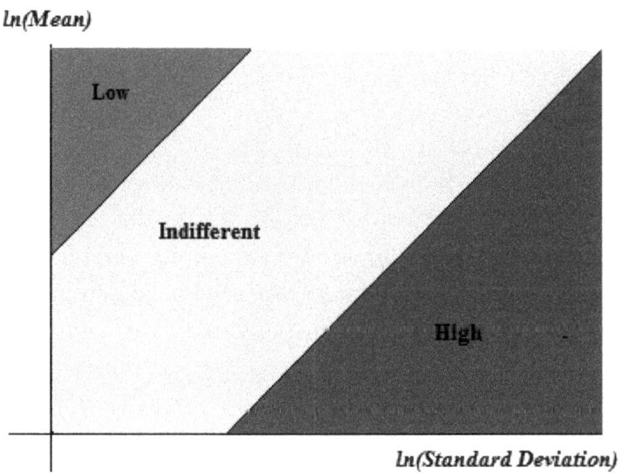

Figure 5.4. Risk zones.

around the market Sharpe ratio which would classify the risk as indicated in Figure 5.4. The indifference separation lines are from limits on the range of expected $\ln(\varphi)$ values.

Markowitz's (μ, σ^2) criterion is neither necessary nor sufficient for second-order dominance in general, as additional conditions on the distribution are required. The actual requirement is that the distributions need to be members of a two-parameter family, with parameters being independent non-decreasing functions of μ and σ^2.

5.4.2 *Growth–security efficiency*

In addition to mean–variance efficiency, the other tractable case of efficiency follows from the power utilities: $u_\alpha(1+R(X)) = \frac{1}{1-\alpha}(1+R(X))^{1-\alpha}$. The power efficient points are defined as

$$X_\alpha = \operatorname{argmax}\{E[u_\alpha(1+R(X))]\} \tag{5.5}$$

for some α. If the distribution of returns is lognormal (and the rate of return is approximately normal), the power efficient points have the form $X_\alpha = \frac{1}{1-\alpha}X^*$, where $X^* = \operatorname{argmax}\{E[\ln(1+R(X))]\}$. This class of strategies has generated a lot of interest. X^* is the optimal growth or Kelly strategy, and X_α is fractional Kelly. Many properties of this strategy are reported in MacLean, Thorp, and Ziemba (2011).

The fractional Kelly solution is also applicable to the risk-constrained problem:

$$X_\alpha = \operatorname{argmax}\{E\ln(1+R(X))|\Pr[1+R(X) < w] < \alpha\}. \tag{5.6}$$

The power utility approach does not assume a form for the distribution of returns. It has been noted that the solutions to the Mean–Variance and Growth–Security problems are very similar. We have been emphasizing the normal distribution in our analysis. Mean–Variance efficiency aligns with second-order stochastic dominance when returns are normal. If normality is assumed with the risk-constrained growth problem, we can see that the optimal solutions for the different problems are equivalent. If $\ln(1+R(X) \approx R(X)$ is $N(\mu(X),\sigma(X))$, then $\max_X\{E(R(X))|\Pr[R(X) \leq \text{VaR}] < \alpha\}$ becomes $\max_X\{\mu(X)|\mu(X) + z_\alpha\sigma(X) \leq \text{VaR}\}$ or $\max_X\{\mu(X)|\sigma(X) \leq \frac{\text{VaR}-\mu(X)}{Z_\alpha}\}$. The solution to this problem is fractional Kelly and is on the mean–variance efficient frontier. With an optimal solution X^*, let

$$\text{VaR}_\alpha(R(X^*)) = \mu(X^*) + z_\alpha\sigma(X^*).$$

In the normal case, the growth–security problem has an efficient frontier as shown in Figure 5.5.

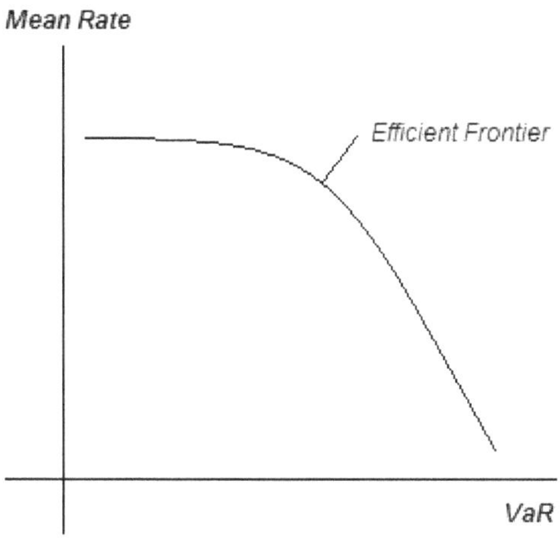

Figure 5.5. Growth–security Frontier.

5.4.3 *Downside risk efficiency*

For many stochastic systems, the focus is on the downside. If the status of components in a system degrades to the extent that the system output is critically low, then there is a system failure. So, the chance of failure and the consequence of failure need to be controlled by decisions. Assume failure is defined by the event $\{R(X) < r^*\}$, where r^* is an operating threshold and the size of a failure is $(r^* - R(X))$. The chance of failure is $\alpha(X) = F(r^*|X) = \Pr[R(X) \leq r^*]$. Corresponding risk measures are $r^* = \mathrm{VaR}_\alpha(X)$ and $\mathrm{CVaR}_\alpha(X) = E(r^* - R(X)|R(X) < r^*)$, the expected failure size (shortfall).

For strategies X_1 and X_2 and the threshold r^*, the risk measures are $(\mathrm{VaR}_{\alpha_1}(X_1), \mathrm{CVaR}_{\alpha_1}(X_1))$ and $(\mathrm{VaR}_{\alpha_2}(X_2), \mathrm{CVaR}_{\alpha_2}(X_2))$, respectively. To order the decisions, we will convert to the equivalent $(\alpha_1(X_1), \mathrm{CVaR}_{\alpha_1}(X_1))$ and $(\alpha_2(X_2), \mathrm{CVaR}_{\alpha_2}(X_2))$. The ranking of risk for stochastic processes is typically based on the *Risk Priority Number*

$$\psi(X) = \alpha(X) \times \mathrm{CVaR}_{\alpha(X)}(X). \tag{5.7}$$

We determine that

for decisions X_1 and X_2, we have X_1 dominating X_2, denoted $X_1 \ll X_2$ if $\psi(X_1) < \psi(X_2)$.

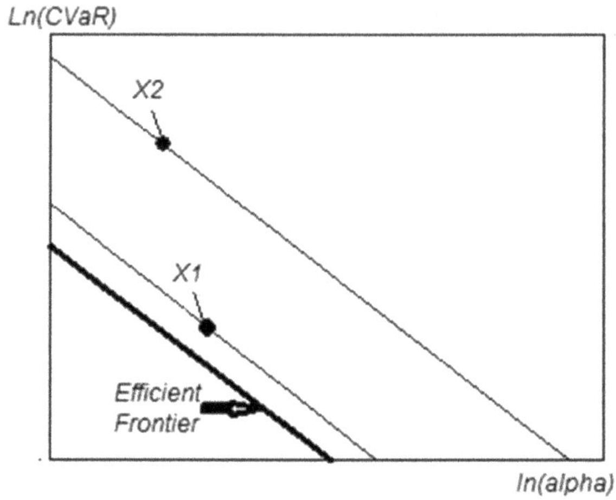

Figure 5.6. Probability–consequence.

It can be shown that the order using the risk priority number is consistent with second-order stochastic dominance (SSD) (MacLean, *et al.*, 2019). There are decisions X which have the same $\psi(X)$, so it involves classes of decisions which are ordered. The γ equivalence class is $X(\gamma) = \{X|\psi(X) = \gamma\}$. The equivalence classes are presented in a probability–consequence diagram shown in Figure 5.6.

The measures are presented on a log scale, so that $\ln[\psi(X)]$ is linearized. In the figure, $\ln[\psi(X_1)] < \ln[\psi(X_2)]$, and $X_1 \ll X_2$. Although the chance of failure is greater with decision X_1, the size of the failure for decision X_2 outweighs that disadvantage. The efficient frontier is defined by the minimum risk priority value: $\gamma^* = \min_X \psi(\mathrm{X})$, so that $X(\gamma^*) = \{X|\psi(X) = \gamma^*\}$.

The probability–consequence diagram in the figure is conceptual. It does provide a template for assessing decisions on the performance of stochastic systems. Taking into consideration the variation in the measures (VaR_α, CVaR_α), there are zones created from the ideal risk priority number as depicted in Figure 5.7.

5.5 Case Studies

We will illustrate the various efficiency concepts with applications to decisions in real-world stochastic systems.

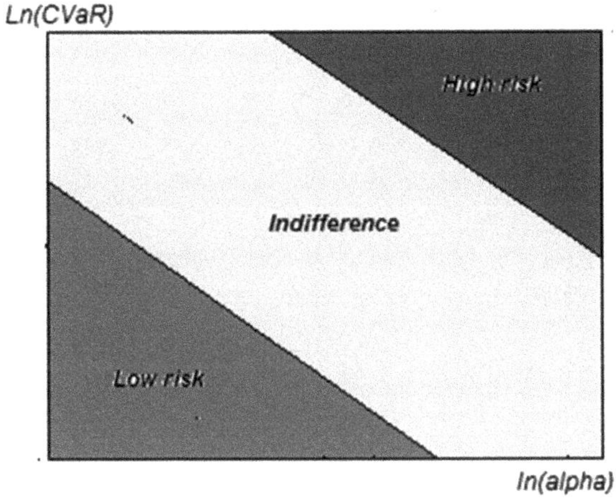

Figure 5.7. Risk zones.

Case 5.1: Investing in risky assets – mean–variance optimization with regimes

This case is based on results in the paper by MacLean, Zhao, and Zhang (2025). We will present a general mean–variance model for investing in financial assets and apply the model to investment in Exchange-Traded funds. The financial market will be characterized by risk factors and regimes. The returns on assets are affected by the risk factors and regimes. The presentation has the following steps:

1. a dynamic financial market that has a cyclical pattern, so that there are alternating regimes.
2. an autoregressive equation for risk factor dynamics and a linear factor model for returns on assets. The model distributions for asset returns within regimes are normal.
3. investment decisions based on the mean and variance of asset returns.
4. estimation of the parameters in model equations using data on a set of risk factors and financial assets (exchange-traded funds).
5. calculation of weekly investment decisions for investing in assets.
6. comparison of the performance of model-based investment decisions with alternative decisions.

Financial market model

Suppose there are m observable factors $F = [F_1, F_2, \ldots, F_m]$, which characterize the financial market. It is considered that there are unobserved or hidden regimes $\{M_1, \ldots, M_K\}$ impacting the dynamics of the financial market. The regimes change from period to period according to a Markov chain with transition probabilities $P = (p_{ij})$. The Markov chain is embedded in the following first-order hidden Markov vector autoregressive model:

$$F_t = A_{M_t} + F_{t-1}B_{M_t} + Z_tC_{M_t},$$

where A_{M_t}, B_{M_t}, and C_{M_t} are regime-dependent coefficients. This model is based on the assumption that the current values of market factors depend on the previous period values, as well as the current regime. There is strong empirical support for the autoregressive behavior of financial markets, and the movements depend on the type of market (e.g., bull or bear).

Suppose there are n risky assets and one risk-free asset. Let R_t be the rates of return on the risky assets and r_t the risk-free rate in period t. In addition to F_t, there are also asset/firm-specific predictors G_t, which may impact returns (e.g., Fama and French, 1993). Then, we propose the following transition–regression model for characterizing asset returns that are dependent on the factors and the transition of regimes from time $t-1$ to t:

$$R_t = \alpha_{M_t,M_{t-1}} + F_t\beta_{M_t,M_{t-1}} + G_t\delta_{M_t,M_{t-1}}U_t\gamma_{M_t,M_{t-1}},$$

where U_t is a standard normal random row vector. It is considered that the returns on assets depend on the regime sequence. In particular, the returns are different depending on whether the regime changes or the regime continues.

Conditional on the available information and the regime sequence $M_{t-1} = i, M_t = j$, the one-period mean return vector and the covariance matrix at time t are

$$\overline{R}_{tij} = \alpha_{ij} + \overline{F}_{tj}\beta_{ij} + G_t\delta_{ij},$$
$$V_{ij} = \beta'_{ij}C'_jC_j\beta_{ij} + \gamma^2_{ij}.$$

In the equation for the conditional mean, the factors are forecast as $\overline{F}_{tj} = A_j + f_{t-1}B_j$, based on the autoregressive model.

The following are important points to make about the proposed model for asset returns:

- The distribution for asset returns, conditional on the regime transition, is normal.
- The autoregressive model is formulated such that the factors for the next period can be forecast.
- There are standard statistical techniques for estimating the parameters in the model equations.
- The mean and covariance for rates of return provide sufficient information on asset returns to form investment decisions.

Investment decisions

We are concerned with the investment decision made at the end of period $t-1$ or the beginning of period t. The decision is designed to control the return distribution for the coming period t. Let X_t be the portfolio weight (row) vector in the risky assets and $(1 - X_t I)$ the weight in the risk-free asset, when the decision is made for period t. The portfolio rate of return is

$$R_p(X_t) = R_t X_t' + r_{0t}(1 - X_t I),$$

where I is a column vector of 1's. The conditional mean and variance of the portfolio rates of return in risky assets, given $M_{t-1} = i$ and $M_t = j$, are

$$\mu_{ij}(X_t) = \overline{R}_{tij} X_t',$$
$$\sigma_{ij}^2(X_t) = X_t V_{ij} X_t'.$$

The conditional portfolio return in risky assets follows a normal distribution: $N(\mu_{ij}(X_t),\ \sigma_{ij}(X_t))$. Of course, this is conditional on the transition, and forecasting the transition is an important part of the mean–variance analysis.

Based on the Capital Asset Pricing Model theory, all investors will invest only in the risk-free asset and an optimal portfolio of risky assets, which is determined by maximizing the Sharpe ratio. We will focus on the portfolio of risky assets. That is, if $\tilde{X}_t = (x_{0t}, X_t)$, with $x_{0t} = 1 - X_t I$, we will consider X_t. The constraint $\mu(X) \geq \mu_0$ in the Markowitz problem will reduce the fraction invested in the market portfolio (Sharpe). With the regime transition $i \to j$, the optimal Sharpe ratio problem is

$$\max_{X_t} \left[\frac{\mu_{ij}(X_t) - r_{0t}}{\sigma_{ij}(X_t)} \right]$$
$$s.t. \quad X_t I = 1.$$

It is well known that the optimal solution to this optimization model is

$$X_t^* = \frac{V_{ij}^{-1}(\overline{R}_{tij} - r_{0t})}{I' V_{ij}^{-1}(\overline{R}_{tij} - r_{0t})}.$$

The formulation we have presented has resulted in an explicit formula for the optimal portfolio decision at time t. Implementation of the decision formula required estimates of the parameters in the autoregressive equation, the linear factor model, and the regime transition matrix. Those procedures will be considered with data on factors and asset returns.

US Financial Market Data – 2016–2023.

The data for estimating the parameters in the financial market models and testing MVO portfolio performance contain weekly observations covering the time 01-January-2016 to 07-July-2023. For analysis, the in-sample estimation period spans 01-January-2016 to 26-June-2020 and the out-of-sample investment model testing period spans 03-July-2020 to 07-July-2023. The following five financial/economic factors are used for estimating the autoregressive model. The factors focus on dimensions of market risk: equity risk, credit risk, interest rate risk, and commodity risk:

SPX: logarithmic changes in the weekly S&P 500 price index.
VIX: logarithmic changes in the weekly CBOE volatility index.
CDS: changes in the credit spread between the three-month LIBOR and the three-month U.S. T-bill rate.
YDS: changes in the yield spread between the U.S. ten-year yield and the U.S. two-year yield.
MOR: logarithmic changes in the total mortgage applications.

Table 5.1 gives summary statistics for the weekly observations on the factors over the sample period.

Table 5.1. Sample statistics for factors.

Statistic	SPX	VIX	CDS	YDS	MOR
Mean	0.0020	−0.0016	−0.0007	−0.0053	−0.0004
SD	0.0250	0.1599	0.0676	0.0744	0.0486
Skewness	−0.9749	1.3008	1.7597	0.8235	0.2550
Kurtosis	10.6012	8.9532	23.2830	7.3455	4.8143
KS-test (p-value)	0.0013	0.0018	0.0000	0.0026	0.1931

Table 5.2. Sample statistics for ETFs.

Statistic	XLE	XLF	XLI	XLK	XLV	XLB	XLP	XLRE	XLY	XLU
Mean(%)	0.254	0.233	0.244	0.206	0.422	0.210	0.267	0.257	0.168	0.161
SD (%)	4.352	3.301	3.043	2.804	2.951	2.441	3.084	2.974	2.093	3.132
Skew	0.537	0.059	0.187	0.004	0.382	0.407	0.097	0.521	0.885	0.159
Kurt	8.053	8.938	10.12	15.45	6.013	6.594	6.567	10.39	7.819	16.76
KS- (p)	0.0028	0.0268	0.0073	0.0029	0.0810	0.0405	0.0114	0.0013	0.0140	0.0040

The linear factor model relates the returns on tradable assets to the market factors. In this application, the following ten Sector Select ETFs (SPDRs) are considered for analyzing returns:

XLE: ENERGY SELECT SECTOR SPDR FUND
XLF: FINANCIAL SELECT SECTOR SPDR FUND
XLI: SECT.SPDR TST.SBI INTER INDS
XLK: TECHNOLOGY SELECT SECTOR SPDR FUND
XLV: HEALTH CARE SELECT SECTOR SPDR FUND
XLB: MATERIALS SELECT SECTOR SPDR FUND
XLP: CONSUMER STAPLES SELECT SECTOR SPDR FUND
XLRE: REAL ESTATE SELECT SECTOR SPDR FUND
XLY: CSM.DISCRTNY.SLT. SECT. SPDR FUND
XLU: SECTOR SPDR TST.SBI INT-UTILS

Table 5.2 presents the sample statistics and normality tests on asset returns for the full sample with weekly data from 01-January-2016 to 07-July-2023.

The statistics from the sample on factors and asset returns indicate that considering the sample period as a single regime is questionable, and the models with multiple regimes could improve the inputs to mean–variance investment decisions.

Table 5.3. In-sample estimated parameters for the two-regime autoregressive model.

Market Regime	**Parameter**	**SPX**	**VIX**	**CDS**	**YDS**	**MOR**
BULL	A	0.0030***	−0.0179***	−0.0019*	−0.0101***	−0.0037**
	B	−0.0010	1.4989***	0.0197	−0.0665	0.5152***
		−0.0597***	−0.3520***	0.0052	0.0201*	0.0064
		−0.0361***	0.1573*	−0.0272	−0.1054**	0.0730*
		−0.0082	−0.3044**	−0.0164	−0.1933***	−0.0808**
		0.0095	0.1733*	−0.1060***	−0.0295	−0.1837***
	C	0.0108	−0.0131	0.0004	0.0071	0.0048
			0.1291	0.0006	−0.0006	−0.0021
				0.0397	0.0045	−0.0018
					0.0437	−0.0032
						0.0352
BEAR	A	−0.0035**	0.0712***	−0.0218***	0.0331***	0.0256***
	B	−0.2481***	−0.6087**	−0.9277***	−0.2378**	0.3863***
		−0.1470***	0.2058***	0.1721***	0.0958***	−0.0162*
		−0.0529***	−0.4963***	0.4150***	−0.2058***	−0.1990***
		−0.2251***	−0.2533*	1.1589***	0.0514*	0.2464***
		−0.1543***	−0.6637**	0.4104***	−0.0211	0.2236***
	C	0.0369	0.0100	−0.0393	−0.0017	0.0348
			0.2964	0.0167	0.0114	−0.0002
				0.0672	0.0038	−0.0069
					0.0808	−0.0168
						0.0477

In Table 5.3 are provided estimates for an autoregressive model with 2 regimes. The estimates for parameters in the linear factor model with regime transitions is given in Table 5.4.

Parameter estimates

Model Validation

Model	# Parameters	Log likelihood	BIC	AIC
Single Regime	45	2696.0	−5123.5	−5290.0
HMM	93	2876.1	−5197.0	−5507.2

Transition matrix

$$P = \begin{bmatrix} 0.9446 & 0.0554 \\ 0.3405 & 0.6595 \end{bmatrix}.$$

Although we have established a preference for a two-regime model, we will also estimate a single-regime model for comparison. In that

Table 5.4. In-sample estimated parameters for the transition asset pricing model.

Transition	Parameter	XLE	XLF	XLI	XLK	XLV	XLB	XLP	XLRE	XLY	XLU
BULL-BULL	α	−0.008	−0.000	−0.001	0.002	0.001	0.000	0.000	−0.000	0.004	0.002
	β	1.012	1.163	0.982	0.238	1.141	0.997	1.050	1.054	0.578	0.578
		−0.001	0.004	−0.006	0.016	−0.003	−0.000	−0.001	0.002	−0.005	−0.000
		−0.033	−0.014	−0.000	0.029	−0.001	0.022	−0.014	−0.007	0.034	0.055
		0.107	0.103	0.056	−0.119	−0.036	−0.059	−0.014	0.038	−0.027	−0.117
		0.038	−0.029	0.040	0.003	−0.014	0.033	−0.004	0.015	0.003	0.007
	δ	0.020	−0.001	−0.004	−0.006	0.002	0.001	−0.000	−0.000	−0.014	−0.001
		0.001	0.001	0.004	0.001	−0.001	−0.001	−0.000	0.001	0.001	−0.002
	γ	0.017	0.011	0.012	0.015	0.008	0.011	0.008	0.009	0.011	0.016
BULL-BEAR	α	−0.022	0.009	0.013	0.007	−0.003	0.004	−0.005	0.009	0.005	0.012
	β	1.350	1.267	1.291	0.438	1.028	1.020	0.946	1.196	0.745	0.509
		0.018	−0.004	−0.004	0.017	0.001	−0.008	−0.004	−0.005	0.007	−0.001
		0.319	−0.018	0.093	0.086	−0.043	−0.038	0.013	0.065	0.061	−0.019
		0.019	0.174	−0.039	−0.082	−0.041	−0.022	−0.013	0.099	−0.082	−0.046
		0.059	−0.064	−0.021	0.063	0.033	−0.015	−0.005	−0.072	0.060	0.062
	δ	0.137	−0.009	0.014	−0.026	−0.006	−0.007	0.011	0.010	−0.019	−0.067
		−0.031	0.005	−0.014	−0.005	−0.001	0.008	0.003	−0.006	−0.009	0.007
	γ	0.023	0.011	0.012	0.013	0.011	0.010	0.011	0.009	0.007	0.012

(*Continued*)

Table 5.4. *(Continued)*

Transition	Parameter	XLE	XLF	XLI	XLK	XLV	XLB	XLP	XLRE	XLY	XLU
BEAR-BULL	α	−0.006	0.016	0.003	0.002	−0.001	−0.009	0.002	0.001	−0.005	0.017
	β	1.177	1.911	1.522	0.970	0.819	0.802	0.593	1.626	0.754	1.314
		0.053	−0.040	−0.034	−0.023	−0.013	−0.003	0.031	−0.035	0.011	−0.037
		−0.097	−0.206	−0.190	−0.042	0.086	0.055	0.074	−0.151	0.024	−0.125
		0.118	0.004	0.086	−0.056	−0.022	−0.002	0.089	0.042	−0.080	−0.108
		−0.098	−0.232	−0.052	−0.244	0.086	0.003	0.133	−0.016	−0.125	−0.140
	δ	−0.018	−0.100	−0.068	−0.036	0.018	0.053	0.034	−0.049	0.022	−0.076
		0.006	0.008	0.022	0.013	0.001	−0.019	−0.005	0.015	−0.003	0.001
	γ	0.014	0.015	0.011	0.012	0.008	0.007	0.008	0.008	0.005	0.013
BEAR-BEAR	α	−0.017	0.004	0.001	−0.001	0.004	−0.002	0.011	0.017	−0.016	−0.004
	β	1.195	1.365	1.130	1.154	0.985	0.769	1.185	1.342	0.560	1.268
		0.003	−0.037	0.008	0.061	−0.007	0.023	−0.032	−0.020	0.055	0.048
		−0.100	−0.033	−0.006	0.065	0.013	0.033	0.022	−0.005	0.038	0.010
		−0.105	0.203	0.101	−0.128	0.053	−0.087	0.073	0.020	−0.149	0.061
		−0.078	−0.173	−0.043	−0.035	0.002	0.039	−0.035	−0.175	0.114	0.017
	δ	0.004	−0.031	0.013	0.013	0.001	0.025	−0.014	−0.042	0.038	0.029
		0.058	0.026	−0.005	0.001	−0.005	−0.020	−0.001	0.023	−0.006	−0.022
	γ	0.039	0.020	0.023	0.031	0.011	0.017	0.012	0.019	0.013	0.030

Table 5.5. Average optimal weights in the ETFs for alternative models.

Model	XLE	XLF	XLI	XLK	XLV	XLB	XLP	XLRE	XLY	XLU
Single-Regime	0.0449	0.1616	0.0193	0.0839	0.4431	0.0981	0.0256	0.0292	0.0453	0.0491
HMM with Inference	0.0438	0.0569	0.1395	0.2119	0.2277	0.0563	0.0428	0.0367	0.0448	0.1397
Transition Model with Inference	0.0646	0.0229	0.0721	0.2016	0.2144	0.0456	0.0489	0.0324	0.1781	0.1193

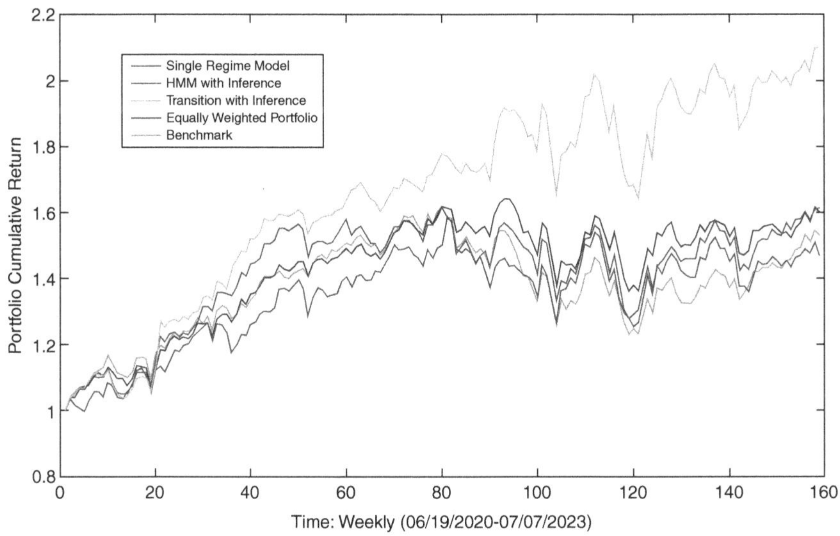

Figure 5.8. Cumulative wealth with various portfolio strategies.

case, the factors, F_t, jointly follow the simple multivariate autoregressive model, and asset return vector R_t follows a simple multivariate regression model:

Average optimal portfolio weights

The predicted mean and variance of asset returns are determined for the next week as formulated in model equations, for the single regime, HMM, and transition model, respectively. For the regime switching models, the mean and variance in the inferred regime are used in the MVO decisions. The inferred regime is the most likely one based on regime probabilities. Table 5.5 presents the average portfolio weight

Table 5.6. Out-of-sample portfolio performance comparison.

Performance	SR	HMMwI	TMwI	EWP	Benchmark
Mean Excess Return	0.3148	0.2527	**0.4845**	0.2989	0.2732
Standard Deviation	2.7240	2.6510	**2.8032**	2.3015	2.4392
Sharpe Ratio	0.1156	0.0953	**0.1728**	0.1299	0.1120

in each of the ETFs for the out-of-sample period. The weights in the optimal risky (Sharpe) portfolio are calculated as shown in the Sharpe formula for each week. This gives an indication of the relative weights in each asset in the risky portfolio. The investment decisions differ depending on the model.

The figures in Table 5.6 are based on the weekly portfolio performance data in percentage.

The mean–variance approach to determining portfolio weights was applied to investing in exchange-traded funds. Different models for the returns on investment in assets were considered: single regime, multiple regimes, and transition between regimes. Those models extract different information from the data on returns. Investment decisions depend on the estimated parameters for the alternative models. So, the decisions differ, as does the performance of the associated portfolios. From the wealth trajectories in Figure 5.8, the transition model proves to be a better model for returns based on the portfolio performance. The Sharpe ratio is the combined risk measure for ordering the portfolio risk in mean–variance analysis. The dominance of the TMwI portfolio is the result of improved estimation.

Case 5.2: Investing in risky assets – growth–security optimization

This case is based on the paper by MacLean and Zhao (2021). An investment portfolio of assets is constructed with a view to controlling downside risk. The risk measures employed are VaR and CVaR. The approach to decisions is to maximize the expected growth rate while keeping the rate of return above a minimum acceptable threshold. The presentation has the following outline:

1. A dynamic financial market is defined, with asset returns depending on unobservable regimes. The conditional distribution for

returns within regimes is normal, and the unconditional distribution across regimes is a mixture of normal distributions.
2. There is a minimum acceptable threshold (failure level), and investment decisions are designed to exceed the threshold with high probability, while achieving strong growth.
3. The parameters in model equations are estimated using data on financial assets (ETFs).
4. Programs for the calculation of optimal decisions for investing in assets are formulated.
5. There is a comparison of the performance of model-based investment decisions with alternatives.

Financial market

Consider a competitive financial market with n assets whose prices are stochastic dynamic processes and a single asset whose price is non-stochastic. Let the vector of prices at time $t, t = 1, \ldots, T$ be

$$P'(t) = (P_0(t), P_1(t), \ldots, P_n(t)),$$

where $P_0(t)$ is the price of the risk-free asset, with a rate of return r_t at time t. The variation in the price of risky assets follows from (1) the dynamics of economic factors defining the state of the financial market and (2) the unknown trading activity on assets. Economic factors such as interest rates, yield differentials, and market frictions characterize financial market states. It is assumed that the states over time $M(t), t = 1, \ldots, T$ follow a discrete state, discrete time Markov process. The states will be referred to as regimes: $\{k = 1, \ldots, K\}$. The transitions of the Markov process are driven by a matrix $Q = (q_{ij})$. Suppose the market is in regime k at time t, and the returns within regime are $\{(1 + R_{jk}), j = 1, \ldots, n\}$. Assume the returns are lognormally distributed within regime with mean of the random rates of return $\mu' = (\mu_{1k}, \ldots, \mu_{nk})$ and covariance Σ_k. So, the returns depend on the regime, but the distributions are the same within regime. If y_j units of capital are invested in asset j at time t, then the return is $(1 + R_{jk})y_j$.

The investment model assumes that the investment capital is the wealth at the beginning of a period, w_{t-1}, and a decision $x_j, j = 1, \ldots, n$, on the fractions of investment capital allocated to assets is made at each point in time. An investment strategy is the vector process

$$\{\tilde{X}(t) = (x_o(t), X(t))', t = 1, \ldots, T\}$$
$$= \{(x_0(t), x_1(t), \ldots, x_n(t))', t = 1, \ldots, T\},$$

with $x_0(t)$ the investment fraction in the risk-free asset.

If the regime is k and the investment strategy is $\tilde{X}(t)$, the conditional wealth at the end of period t is $W_k(t) = w_{t-1}(1+R_k(t))\tilde{X}(t) = w_{t-1}(1 + R_k(X(t)))$. The focus in the returns process is on the rate. The rate of return $R_k(X(t)) \approx \ln(1+R_k(X(t)))$ for period t in regime k is approximately normal with mean $\mu_k(\tilde{X}(t)) = (\mu_k - re))'\tilde{X}(t) + r - \frac{1}{2}\sigma_k^2(t)$ and variance $\sigma_k^2(t) = X(t)'\Sigma_k X(t)$. Although the investor is making decisions at discrete time points, the financial market is virtually continuous in activity. The linear change in a discrete-time random walk is calibrated to the continuous model at the discrete points.

There are K possible regimes, and assume the distribution for regimes at time t is $\pi'(t) = (\pi_1(t), \ldots, \pi_K(t))$, with $\pi(t) = Q \cdot \pi(t-1)$. The conditional rate of return is approximately normal, and the unconditional rate of return is approximated by a normal mixture. That is, $\Pr[R(X(t)) \leq r] = \sum_{k=1}^{K} \pi_k(t)\Pr[R_k(X(t)) \leq r]$.

Investment: Kelly portfolio

The problem under consideration is the selection of investment decisions at points in time, with knowledge of past decisions and returns, the distributions over uncertain regimes, and asset prices for the next time period. For decision $X(t)$ at time t, the wealth generated in that period is $W(t) = w(t-1) \cdot (1 + R(X(t))$, which may take unacceptable values depending on the manifest regime and prices on assets. So, the decision at time t is constrained by a minimum acceptable (MAG) threshold to keep the wealth path to the horizon under control. With MAG threshold $w^*(t)$, it is required that $\Pr[W(t) \geq w^*(t)] \geq 1 - \alpha$. Equivalently, in terms of rate of growth and deficits, with $b(t) = \frac{w^*(t)}{w(t-1)}$, the deficit constraint is

$$\sum_{K=1}^{m} \pi_k(t) \cdot \Pr[R_k(X(t)) \leq \ln(b(t))] \leq \alpha.$$

Let α_k be the failure rate below the threshold in regime k, so that $\mathrm{VaR}_{\alpha_k}(R_k(X(t))) = \ln(b(t))$. In addition to the rate of failures, we are concerned with the size of shortfalls, given by $[\ln(b(t)) - (R_k(X(t))]^+$, where $[\ln(b(t)) - (R_k(X(t))]^+ = 0$ if $(R_k X(t)) \geq \ln(b(t)$. In terms of the expected size of shortfalls,

$$E[\ln(b(t)) - (R(X(t))]^+ \\ = \sum_{k=1}^{m} \pi_k(t)[\mathrm{VaR}_{\alpha_k}(R_k(X(t))) - \mathrm{CVaR}_{\alpha}(R_k(X(t)))].$$

The expected shortfall is captured by the gap between the VaR and CVaR. The expected value of the rate of return with decision $X(t)$ is $\sum_{k-1}^{m} \pi_k \cdot E(R_k(X(t))$. This value is penalized for the expected shortfall from decision $X(t)$, giving the objective

$$\sum_{k-1}^{m} \pi_k \cdot \{E(R_k(X(t)) - \beta[\mathrm{VaR}_{\alpha_k}(R_k(X(t))) - \mathrm{CVaR}_{\alpha_k}(R_k(X(t)))]\}.$$

The risk control decision problem, which controls the rate and size of shortfalls while optimizing the expected rate of return, is

$$\mathrm{Max}\left\{\sum_{k-1}^{m} \pi_k \cdot \{E(R_k(X(t)) \\ - \beta[\mathrm{VaR}_{\alpha_k}(X(t)) - \mathrm{CVaR}_{\alpha_k}(R_k(X(t)))]\}\right\}$$

$$\text{Subject to } \sum_{K=1}^{m} \pi_k(t) \cdot \Pr[(R_k(X(t))) \leq \ln(b(t))] \leq \alpha.$$

There are important points to consider about this constrained growth rate problem:

1. Without the risk control ($\alpha = \beta = 0$), the problem is the familiar optimal growth rate problem, with the Kelly strategy being optimal.
2. The model assumptions include normality for the within-regime distributions of rates of return on assets. So, the mean vectors and covariance matrices, $\{(\mu_k, \Sigma_k), k = 1, \ldots K\}$, are basic ingredients of the optimal solution.

3. The optimal solution has the format

$$X^* = f\left[\sum_{k=1}^{m} \theta_{2k}\Sigma_k\right]^{-1}\left[\sum_{k=1}^{m} \theta_{1k}(\mu_k - re)\right],$$

   where $0 \leq \theta_{ik} \leq 1, \sum_{i=1}^{m} \theta_{ik} = 1, i = 1, 2$, and f is a real number.
4. So, $X^*(t)$ is determined by $\{f, (\theta_{11}, \ldots, \theta_{1m}, \theta_{21}, \ldots, \theta_{2m})\}$. Typically, the number of regimes will be small, and the optimal investment strategy for the one-period problem, given the target growth b, the penalty parameter β, and the reliability parameter α will be computationally simple.
5. If there is a single regime, $m = 1$, then $\theta_1 = \theta_2 = 1$, and the solution to the benchmarked growth problem is $X^* = f^*[\Sigma^{-1}(\mu - re)]$. This is the fractional Kelly investment formula for the optimal growth problem with downside risk control. X^* is the vector of investment fractions in risky assets and $(1 - f^*)$ is the fraction in the risk-free asset.

Application

We will continue the case on regime switching presented in Chapter 4. The returns on ETFs (exchange-traded funds) were considered for the period December 22, 1998 to November 19, 2019 for a total of 1091 weeks.

The following ETFs are studied:

SPY: S&P 500 INDEX
XLY: CSM.DISCRTNY.SLT. SECT. SPDR FUND
XLP: CONSUMER STAPLES SELECT SECTOR SPDR FUND
XLE: ENERGY SELECT SECTOR SPDR FUND
XLF: FINANCIAL SELECT SECTOR SPDR FUND
XLV: HEALTH CARE SELECT SECTOR SPDR FUND
XLI: SECT.SPDR TST.SBI INTER INDS
XLB: MATERIALS SELECT SECTOR SPDR FUND
XLK: TECHNOLOGY SELECT SECTOR SPDR FUND
XLU: SECTOR SPDR TST.SBI INT-UTILS

The returns for multiple regimes are given in Table 5.7 and without distinct regimes (single regime) are provided in Table 5.8. The single regime is similar to the transition regime, whereas the Bull and Bear regimes are very different. Accounting for the regime in making ETF investment decisions should be important.

Table 5.7. Annualized ETF statistics, by market regime.

ETF	SPY	XLY	XLP	XLE	XLF	XLV	XLI	XLB	XLK	XLU
Bear Market										
Mean	−0.0793	−0.0516	−0.0275	−0.0437	−0.1405	−0.0287	−0.0698	−0.0506	−0.0980	−0.0467
Standard Deviation	0.2470	0.3006	0.1944	0.3146	0.3937	0.2332	0.2800	0.3153	0.3594	0.2407
Correlation	1.0000	0.8595	0.6230	0.6722	0.8317	0.8107	0.9116	0.7632	0.8466	0.6568
		1.0000	0.6076	0.5323	0.7952	0.7063	0.8489	0.7558	0.6479	0.5182
			1.0000	0.4674	0.5381	0.5488	0.5926	0.5345	0.3260	0.5296
				1.0000	0.5206	0.4873	0.6728	0.7419	0.4338	0.5889
					1.0000	0.6071	0.7894	0.6779	0.5771	0.5168
						1.0000	0.7420	0.5985	0.6578	0.5615
							1.0000	0.8340	0.7124	0.6216
								1.0000	0.5220	0.5633
									1.0000	0.4322
Transition Market										
Mean	0.1043	0.0878	0.0823	0.0638	0.0908	0.0690	0.1024	0.0834	0.1567	0.1405
Standard Deviation	0.1215	0.1393	0.1014	0.2195	0.1641	0.1242	0.1443	0.1745	0.1530	0.1259
Correlation	1.0000	0.8971	0.7020	0.6934	0.8658	0.7976	0.8795	0.8305	0.8929	0.3677
		1.0000	0.6425	0.5487	0.7498	0.6763	0.7746	0.7155	0.8294	0.2702
			1.0000	0.3685	0.4904	0.5961	0.5679	0.5388	0.6037	0.5607
				1.0000	0.5907	0.4332	0.6226	0.6780	0.4996	0.2616
					1.0000	0.6779	0.8058	0.7350	0.6830	0.1666
						1.0000	0.6553	0.5956	0.6571	0.3558
							1.0000	0.8253	0.7314	0.2247
								1.0000	0.6972	0.2594
									1.0000	0.2530

(Continued)

Table 5.7. *(Continued)*

ETF	SPY	XLY	XLP	XLE	XLF	XLV	XLI	XLB	XLK	XLU
Bull Market										
Mean	0.1526	0.2096	0.1230	0.1544	0.1565	0.1788	0.1846	0.1702	0.1189	0.1163
Standard Deviation	0.1134	0.1304	0.0975	0.1813	0.1428	0.1227	0.1359	0.1579	0.1641	0.1265
Correlation	1.0000	0.8524	0.7124	0.6526	0.8571	0.7501	0.8932	0.7984	0.8450	0.5551
		1.0000	0.6637	0.4940	0.7128	0.6428	0.7953	0.7178	0.6525	0.4063
			1.0000	0.3722	0.5751	0.5883	0.5952	0.4743	0.4713	0.5110
				1.0000	0.5344	0.3727	0.6233	0.6666	0.4310	0.4034
					1.0000	0.6099	0.7782	0.6620	0.6177	0.4311
						1.0000	0.6485	0.5677	0.5518	0.4021
							1.0000	0.8045	0.6895	0.4827
								1.0000	0.6185	0.4160
									1.0000	0.4145

Table 5.8. Annualized ETF statistics, single regime.

ETF	SPY	XLY	XLP	XLE	XLF	XLV	XLI	XLB	XLK	XLU
Mean	0.0634	0.0859	0.0623	0.0636	0.0411	0.0793	0.0781	0.0732	0.0601	0.0708
Standard Deviation	0.1709	0.2042	0.1377	0.2428	0.2572	0.1675	0.1969	0.2255	0.2433	0.1722
Correlation	1.0000	0.8642	0.6536	0.6665	0.8378	0.7965	0.9034	0.7808	0.8520	0.5922
		1.0000	0.6236	0.5222	0.7766	0.6893	0.8280	0.7414	0.6728	0.4599
			1.0000	0.4263	0.5351	0.5664	0.5909	0.5249	0.3942	0.5324
				1.0000	0.5235	0.4508	0.6488	0.7104	0.4384	0.4812
					1.0000	0.6134	0.7862	0.6791	0.5961	0.4501
						1.0000	0.7100	0.5930	0.6352	0.4951
							1.0000	0.8271	0.7102	0.5306
								1.0000	0.5650	0.4823
									1.0000	0.4046
										1.0000

Investment decisions

There are variations on the investment problem: multiple risky assets (ETFS) versus a composite risky asset (SPY); and alternative financial markets (three regimes versus one regime). In each case, the problem is to optimize penalized growth, with a VaR constraint requiring the growth to exceed a downside target level with high probability. A variety of control problem parameters are considered: $\{(\alpha = 0.01, 0.05, 0.10), (\beta = 0.0, 1.0, 2.0), b(t) = 0.98\}$. The initial wealth is $w_0 = 1$. The control parameter choices are based on common use and some experimentation. The growth target views losses of greater than 2% as undesirable.

With the parameter settings, the one-period problem was solved for each of the periods (weeks). The important feature of the modified Kelly is the reduction of the investment problem to finding optimal weights/probabilities for aggregating the regime means and variances. The average optimal weights are shown in Table 5.9. The weights are very similar for the means $\theta_{1j}, j = 1, 2, 3$ and variances $\theta_{2j}, j = 1, 2, 3$, and strongly support one of the regimes. Of course, the transition matrix was diagonal dominant, and it produced regime probabilities emphasizing one regime.

The strategy for the multiple assets, if you are currently in a regime, is given in Table 5.10. Also shown is the strategy for a single regime. Clearly, the allocation of investment capital to risky assets is quite different depending on the type of regime. It is noteworthy that the risk controls keep the fraction of capital invested in risky assets rather low. So, there is high risk aversion in the parameter settings.

Performance – risk control

The investment decisions are designed to control downside risk. The control was placed on the probability of a shortfall and the average size of shortfalls. The effect of controls by parameter setting is shown in Tables 5.11 and 5.12.

The settings (0.05, 2) are in boldface since they have reasonable risk control with the usual level $\alpha = 0.05$.

Performance – portfolio wealth

The objective with investment in risky assets is to accumulate wealth, with controls on risk. The accumulation of wealth over the weeks for 20 years is provided in Figure 5.9. The contrasts are between multiple

Table 5.9. Optimal parameters (θ) and the Kelly fraction (f).

(α, γ)	Model	θ 11	θ 12	θ 13	θ 21	θ 22	θ 23	f
(0.01, 0)	Multiple Regime	0.7931	0.1754	0.0315	0.8038	0.1442	0.0521	0.1184
		0.0243	0.9489	0.0269	0.0214	0.9400	0.0386	0.0475
		0.0236	0.0213	0.9551	0.0247	0.0232	0.9521	0.0413
	Single Regime		1			1		0.1029
(0.01, 1)	Multiple Regime	0.7781	0.1872	0.0346	0.7876	0.1546	0.0578	0.1153
		0.0265	0.9460	0.0275	0.0275	0.9281	0.0444	0.0493
		0.0242	0.0214	0.9543	0.0274	0.0233	0.9494	0.0417
	Single Regime		1			1		0.1029
(0.01, 2)	Multiple Regime	0.8236	0.1466	0.0298	0.8298	0.1245	0.0457	0.1230
		0.0271	0.9463	0.0266	0.0316	0.9299	0.0385	0.0504
		0.0256	0.0210	0.9534	0.0309	0.0230	0.9461	0.0422
	Single Regime		1			1		0.1029
(0.05, 0)	Multiple Regime	0.7666	0.1921	0.0414	0.7754	0.1551	0.0694	0.1618
		0.0204	0.9542	0.0254	0.0124	0.9578	0.0298	0.0682
		0.0213	0.0222	0.9565	0.0157	0.0240	0.9603	0.0603
	Single Regime		1			1		0.1476
(0.05, 1)	Multiple Regime	0.8257	0.1415	0.0328	0.8372	0.1128	0.0499	0.1429
		0.0233	0.9511	0.0257	0.0212	0.9453	0.0335	0.0709
		0.0226	0.0208	0.9566	0.0208	0.0224	0.9569	0.0608
	Single Regime		1			1		0.1342
(0.05, 2)	Multiple Regime	0.8457	0.1226	0.0317	0.8591	0.0997	0.0411	0.1279
		0.0257	0.9479	0.0263	0.0291	0.9335	0.0374	0.0733
		0.0242	0.0206	0.9552	0.0266	0.0222	0.9512	0.0614
	Single Regime		1			1		0.1121
(0.10, 0)	Multiple Regime	0.8370	0.1271	0.0359	0.8392	0.1093	0.0515	0.2333
		0.0440	0.9152	0.0407	0.0302	0.9099	0.0599	0.0978
		0.0229	0.0237	0.9533	0.0166	0.0282	0.9552	0.0819
	Single Regime		1			1		0.1919
(0.10, 1)	Multiple Regime	0.8412	0.1234	0.0353	0.8514	0.1019	0.0467	0.1466
		0.0318	0.9432	0.0250	0.0227	0.9480	0.0293	0.0906
		0.0239	0.0226	0.9534	0.0229	0.0257	0.9513	0.0819
	Single Regime		1			1		0.1342
(0.10, 2)	Multiple Regime	0.8827	0.0902	0.0271	0.8970	0.0707	0.0324	0.1346
		0.0263	0.9461	0.0276	0.0301	0.9202	0.0403	0.0736
		0.0245	0.0200	0.9555	0.0271	0.0216	0.9513	0.0679
	Single Regime		1			1		0.1121

Note: Optimal parameters are calculated as a weighted average of the parameters by the prior probabilities of the regime for one period ahead. The regime weights are then used to obtain the optimal investment strategy for the risky assets.

assets (SPDRs) and a single asset (S&P500) and between 3 regimes and no regimes (one regime).

The wealth trajectories are very stable, based on the strong risk control. In spite of limited risk, there is considerable growth in

Table 5.10. Average regime-dependent optimal investment weights.

(α, γ)	Model	XLY	XLP	XLE	XLF	XLV	XLI	XLB	XLK	XLU	Total
(0.01, 0)	Multi-Regime	0.1030	−0.0298	0.0186	−0.1528	0.1244	−0.0348	0.0429	−0.1047	−0.0636	−0.0969
		−0.2175	−0.0737	−0.0691	0.0555	−0.1571	0.2381	−0.1581	0.4382	0.4073	0.4636
		0.4197	0.0010	0.0287	−0.1070	0.2631	0.1496	−0.0907	−0.1826	0.0924	0.5742
	Single Regime	0.2088	0.1135	−0.0017	−0.2388	0.1903	0.1595	−0.0431	−0.0799	0.1164	0.4250
(0.01, 1)	Multi-Regime	0.1013	−0.0293	0.0186	−0.1497	0.1223	−0.0350	0.0426	−0.1041	−0.0642	−0.0974
		−0.2105	−0.0585	−0.0698	0.0489	−0.1574	0.2374	−0.1536	0.4273	0.4073	0.4711
		0.4182	0.0032	0.0294	−0.1103	0.2647	0.1513	−0.0909	−0.1825	0.0915	0.5745
	Single Regime	0.2088	0.1135	−0.0017	−0.2388	0.1903	0.1595	−0.0431	−0.0799	0.1164	0.4250
(0.01, 2)	Multi-Regime	0.1045	−0.0303	0.0180	−0.1583	0.1268	−0.0320	0.0421	−0.1027	−0.0593	−0.0912
		−0.2078	−0.0490	−0.0703	0.0459	−0.1596	0.2383	−0.1512	0.4217	0.4085	0.4765
		0.4168	0.0053	0.0301	−0.1137	0.2663	0.1529	−0.0912	−0.1825	0.0906	0.5748
	Single Regime	0.2088	0.1135	−0.0017	−0.2388	0.1903	0.1595	−0.0431	−0.0799	0.1164	0.4250
(0.05, 0)	Multi-Regime	0.1420	−0.0423	0.0261	−0.2094	0.1718	−0.0478	0.0586	−0.1444	−0.0887	−0.1342
		−0.3437	−0.1363	−0.1030	0.0957	−0.2388	0.3607	−0.2462	0.6826	0.6156	0.6867
		0.6338	−0.0047	0.0408	−0.1502	0.3895	0.2196	−0.1354	−0.2736	0.1420	0.8616
	Single Regime	0.2995	0.1628	−0.0025	−0.3426	0.2730	0.2288	−0.0618	−0.1146	0.1670	0.6097

(0.05, 1)	Multi-Regime	0.1193	−0.0376	0.0206	−0.1812	0.1457	−0.0356	0.0469	−0.1151	−0.0659	−0.1029
		−0.3319	−0.1109	−0.1043	0.0862	−0.2404	0.3600	−0.2390	0.6640	0.6160	0.6998
		0.6309	−0.0006	0.0423	−0.1564	0.3926	0.2229	−0.1362	−0.2734	0.1401	0.8624
	Single Regime	0.2724	0.1481	−0.0023	−0.3116	0.2483	0.2081	−0.0562	−0.1042	0.1519	0.5546
(0.05, 2)	Multi-Regime	0.1062	−0.0325	0.0177	−0.1620	0.1293	−0.0290	0.0404	−0.1000	−0.0547	−0.0846
		−0.3191	−0.0852	−0.1049	0.0757	−0.2407	0.3582	−0.2308	0.6429	0.6136	0.7097
		0.6267	0.0041	0.0437	−0.1629	0.3951	0.2261	−0.1365	−0.2727	0.1380	0.8616
	Single Regime	0.2275	0.1237	−0.0019	−0.2602	0.2074	0.1738	−0.0469	−0.0870	0.1269	0.4631
(0.10, 0)	Multi-Regime	0.1958	−0.0587	0.0330	−0.2997	0.2382	−0.0556	0.0766	−0.1875	−0.1046	−0.1624
		−0.4055	−0.1295	−0.1363	0.0922	−0.2928	0.4687	−0.3081	0.8440	0.7995	0.9322
		0.8543	−0.0054	0.0540	−0.2042	0.5251	0.2978	−0.1825	−0.3691	0.1929	1.1630
	Single Regime	0.3895	0.2118	−0.0032	−0.4456	0.3551	0.2976	−0.0803	−0.1491	0.2173	0.7930
(0.10, 1)	Multi-Regime	0.1220	−0.0378	0.0200	−0.1856	0.1482	−0.0311	0.0449	−0.1126	−0.0600	−0.0921
		−0.4483	−0.1516	−0.1392	0.1265	−0.3267	0.4799	−0.3217	0.8905	0.8220	0.9314
		0.8477	0.0011	0.0565	−0.2117	0.5283	0.3021	−0.1837	−0.3671	0.1896	1.1628
	Single Regime	0.2724	0.1481	−0.0023	−0.3116	0.2483	0.2081	−0.0562	−0.1042	0.1519	0.5547
(0.10, 2)	Multi-Regime	0.1094	−0.0347	0.0177	−0.1689	0.1337	−0.0282	0.0407	−0.1007	−0.0533	−0.0842
		−0.3166	−0.0835	−0.1049	0.0743	−0.2393	0.3582	−0.2304	0.6408	0.6135	0.7120
		0.6965	0.0045	0.0487	−0.1806	0.4390	0.2508	−0.1516	−0.3033	0.1529	0.9569
	Single Regime	0.2275	0.1237	−0.0019	−0.2602	0.2074	0.1738	−0.0469	−0.0870	0.1269	0.4631

Table 5.11. Average probabilities of growth deficit by regime.

Model	Risk control parameters (α, γ)								
	(0.01, 0)	**(0.01, 1)**	**(0.01, 2)**	**(0.05, 0)**	**(0.05, 1)**	**(0.05, 2)**	**(0.10, 0)**	**(0.10, 1)**	**(0.10, 2)**
Multi-regime	0.0097	0.0096	0.0092	0.0471	0.0204	**0.0100**	0.0966	0.0213	0.0104
	0.0100	0.0100	0.0100	0.0500	0.0495	**0.0487**	0.0981	0.0982	0.0491
	0.0100	0.0100	0.0100	0.0500	0.0496	**0.0492**	0.0999	0.0986	0.0650
Single-Regime	0.0100	0.0100	0.0100	0.0500	0.0359	**0.0161**	0.1000	0.0359	0.0161

Table 5.12. Average expected annualized growth deficit by regime.

Model	Risk control parameters (α, γ)								
	(0.01, 0)	**(0.01, 1)**	**(0.01, 2)**	**(0.05, 0)**	**(0.05, 1)**	**(0.05, 2)**	**(0.10, 0)**	**(0.10, 1)**	**(0.10, 2)**
Multi-regime	0.0016	0.0015	0.0015	0.0133	0.0042	**0.0018**	0.0401	0.0048	0.0019
	0.0029	0.0029	0.0028	0.0183	0.0179	**0.0175**	0.0493	0.0497	0.0177
	0.0021	0.0021	0.0021	0.0167	0.0166	**0.0164**	0.0494	0.0487	0.0248
Single-Regime	0.0022	0.0022	0.0021	0.0161	0.0130	**0.0120**	0.0464	0.0349	0.0153

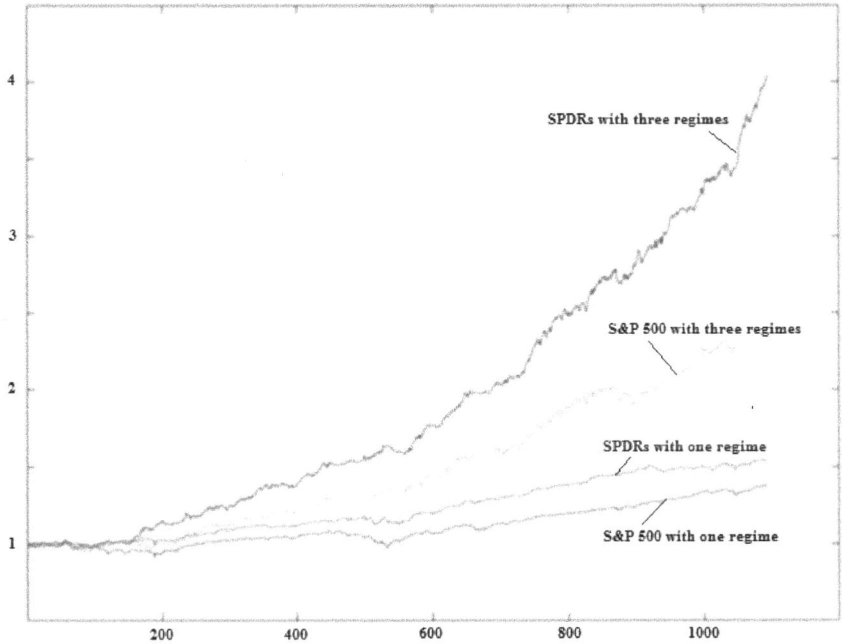

Figure 5.9. Portfolio wealth.

wealth. The observable effects are as follows:

- The single-regime models show little growth. The S&P500 Index shows slight growth over the planning period, and similarly for the SPDRs, although the SPDRs are a bit better.
- The multiple-regime models have much higher growth. The S&P500 doubles and the SPDRs quadruple over the horizon.

Case 5.3: Aircraft operation – downside risk analysis

A risk-focused objective emphasizes the events where the system status falls below a critical level. If a failure is defined as falling below the critical level, then the system trajectory can be considered as a marked point process, where there are failures with specific severities at random points in time. The basic characteristics of risk for the system are the two random quantities: (i) the number of failures and (ii) the consequences of failures (Buhlmann, 1970). The number of failures is analogous to the probability of shortfall, and the consequence of failures is analogous to the size of shortfalls below a threshold.

Although the system status is reduced to a point process, it is important to consider that the system status is a stochastic dynamic process, with the trajectory affected by operating environment factors and operating decisions. So, the failures and severities are also dependent on factors and decisions. We will consider the key decision to be the planned maintenance schedule and specifically the time between scheduled repairs. The maintenance/repair replenishes the system status, returning it to an almost new condition or at least a substantially improved status. After a repair, the status is moved further above the critical level, and thus the chance of failure and the severity of failure are reduced. It is considered that a shorter time between scheduled repairs reduces the number of failures in an observation window if the operating factors are constant. Conversely, differences in operating factors will impact failures when the repair interval is constant.

The description of an operating system is intentionally vague. It encompasses biological systems, mechanical systems, service systems, and financial systems. The health status dynamics, definition of failure, operating factors, and control decisions depend on the system details and are rather complex. However, the classification of system status as failed or not failed would be appropriate for many systems. Even with the financial system, with failure being defined as falling short of a benchmark, the failures would be a marked point process, and VaR and CVaR measure the rate and severity of failures. With the financial system, the objective was to determine the optimal control decision. For the operating system, we will emphasize the ordering of systems based on risk characteristics. That will enable conclusions about best practice without identifying an optimal control. In this case, we will not be considering systems defined by decisions directly, but rather comparing systems with different operations.

Risk process

For a system operating between times 0 and t, there are failures at random times, with $A(t) = \{t_1 < \cdots < t_n < t\}$ = the set of failure times. A depiction of failure times is shown in Figure 5.10.

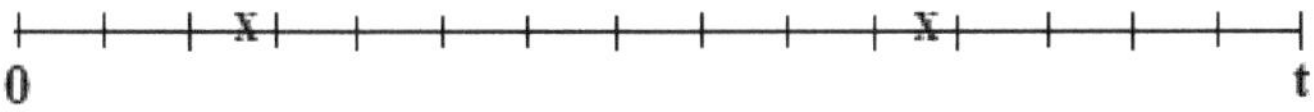

Figure 5.10. Failures – status below threshold.

Time is partitioned into small intervals to connect the failure rate and failure probability. Failure rate tells you how often failures happen, while probability of failure tells you the likelihood of a failure occurring within a certain timeframe. The failure rate is the chance of failure in a very short time interval, so we will consider the concepts equivalent.

Each failure has a random severity defined as $S_{t_i}, t_i \in A(t)$. It will be assumed that severities are real-valued, defined by the cost to the system, and the accumulation of failure severities to time t is the total cost. Consider, then, the accumulated severity to time t:

$$Y(t) = \sum_{t_i \in A(t)} S_{t_i}.$$

The stochastic process $\{Y(t), t > 0\}$ is the accumulated severity process. It is also referred to as the *risk process* (Buhlmann, 1970). $Y(t)$ is random in two respects: It has a random number of terms; each of the terms is a random variable.

Consider an observed trajectory from the risk process to time t, denoted by $y(t) \in Y(t)$. The trajectory is determined by the set $\{(t_i, s_{t_i}), i = 1, \ldots, n(t)\}$, where $n(t)$ is the number of failures, t_i is a failure time, and s_{t_i} is the severity of the failure at time t_i. The value of the risk process at time t for the trajectory is $y(t) = \sum_{i=1}^{n(t)} s_{t_i}$.

If $n(t \cdot s)$ is the number of failures with severity s, then an alternative or *complementary* representation of the observed risk process value is $y(t) = \sum_{s>0} n(t, s) \cdot s$.

In general, for $N(t)$ = number of failures, $N(t, s)$ = number of failures of severity s, and $g(t, s)$ = the distribution of severity in $(0, t)$,

$$Y(t) = \int N(t) g(t, s) ds.$$

The advantage of the complementary representation for $Y(t)$ is the definition of the risk process in terms of (1) the number of failures and (2) the distribution of failure severity.

The Number of System Failures – VaR

Consider $N(t)$ the number of component/system failures up to time t. If $\lambda(\tau)$ is the probability of a system failure at time τ, the counting process $N(t)$ has the following representation (Aven and Jensen, 1999):

$$N(t) = \Lambda(t) + M(t),$$

where $E(M(t)) = 0$, $\Lambda(t) = \int_0^t \lambda(\tau)d\tau$. The predictable process is $\Lambda(t) =$ the expected number of failures, and the unpredictable or innovative process is $M(t)$. There are various models for $\Lambda(t)$, with the Poisson process with constant rate being popular. In that case, the expected number is $\Lambda(t) = \lambda t$. The instantaneous probability or rate of failure is $\lambda = \frac{\Lambda(t)}{t}$. Without specifying the critical threshold, we have

$$\text{VaR}^{-1}(b) = \alpha_b = \lambda.$$

Of course, it is anticipated that the rate is not constant, but rather time-dependent. If time/age is partitioned into intervals, the constant assumption on an interval would be a reasonable approximation, and the increase in rate could be observed as the time interval increases. We will consider this empirical approach in the example.

Severity – CVaR

The failure of a system presents a cost, where costs result from repairs, service disruptions, and liabilities. Severity is a score corresponding to the seriousness of a failure and incorporates the various costs. Consider $S(t) =$ severity of system failures in time interval $(0. t)$. Let the distribution for $S(t)$ on the interval be $G(t, s) = \Pr[S(t) \leq s]$, with density $g(t, s)$. This is the conditional distribution of status given that status is below the threshold. The expected value of severity (status below the threshold) is

$$\text{CVaR}_\lambda(t) = E(S(t)) = \int s \cdot g(t, s)ds.$$

As indicated by the number of failures in the process, time/age can be partitioned into equal-sized intervals. We will assume that the severity distribution of failures is the same within an interval. The distribution of severity on successive age intervals will likely differ.

As the system ages, the number and complexity/severity of failures on an interval will increase.

Risk priority

For the system on a time interval, we have the doublet of risk measures $(\text{VaR}^{-1}(b), \text{CVaR}_{\alpha_b}) = (\lambda, E(S))$. The expression composed of the expected failure rate and expected severity of failures provides a first-order measure of risk, referred to as the Risk Priority Number:

$$\psi(Y(t)) = \lambda(t) \cdot E(S(t)).$$

The risk priority number is consistent with first-order stochastic dominance. It is a standard score for evaluating the risk of system failures. It is desirable in the comparison of systems to order the systems from a risk perspective. The risk process $Y_1(t)$ is considered less risky than $Y_2(t)$ if $\psi(Y_1(t) < \psi(Y_2(t)))$. Systems with the same risk score can be considered equivalent. If the measures are presented on a logarithm scale, the equivalence classes are defined by straight lines, and the classes are $\text{A}(c) = \{Y(t)|\log(\lambda(t)) + \log(E(S(t))) = c\}$. This is illustrated in Figure 5.11. As displayed, the axes are usually partitioned into intervals, and a matrix is created. The regions with low, medium, and high risk are highlighted.

The high-risk region included scenarios where there are frequent low-severity failures and infrequent high-severity failures.

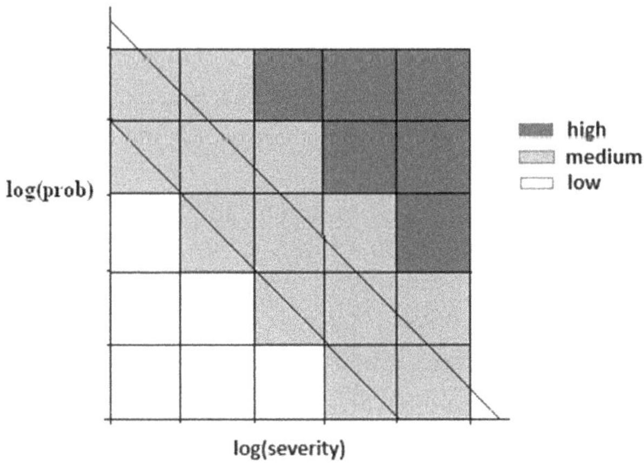

Figure 5.11. Risk graph and matrix.

Table 5.13. Failures by Severity: Model A, built in 2000.

	Year						
Severity	**2001**	**2002**	**2003**	**2004**	**2005**	**2006**	**2007**
<\$2,000	24	63	72	88	120	70	43
\$2,000–\$10,000	6	50	68	69	73	57	55
\$10,000–\$200,000	0	5	3	1	2	0	1
\$200,000–\$1,000,000	1	1	4	5	13	2	5
>\$1,000,000	0	4	3	2	2	1	4
Flying Hours	41717	116063	114674	113782	116731	116106	114813

Example: Aircraft failures

The aggregate risk measures provide a basis for assessing the operation of complex machines, and in particular the mechanical problems encountered. In this example, an application to aircraft operations is considered. The risk measures are computed with the expectation that risk aversion is an important factor in the assessment of operations.

The Federal Aviation Administration requires commercial aircraft operators to report mechanical problems affecting safety, either during operation or at inspection. These Service Difficulty Reports (SDRs) produce a database for comparing aircraft and operators. Alternative risk measures were used to analyze SDRs for two cohorts of comparable regional jets in the USA. The selected jets are similar in size and are used by a range of carriers. As a part of the SDR report, a severity classification of the problem is included. The classification system is defined in the Department of Defense Report MIL-STD-882D (1993).

For the two cohorts of regional jets built in 2000, the number of SDRs for mechanical malfunctions affecting safety in the years 2001–2007 is shown in Tables 5.13 and 5.14. Also, the number of flying hours (use) is displayed. The financial loss from a mishap, as defined in the classification system, is used for the severity categories.

The data on failures were analyzed with the risk scores. The issues of interest are (i) the components of the risk scores; (ii) the variation in the risk components and scores over time; and (iii) the contrast

Table 5.14. Failures by severity: model B, built in 2000.

Severity	Year 2001	2002	2003	2004	2005	2006	2007
<$2,000	22	47	83	134	122	190	179
$2,000–$10,000	7	43	99	60	67	55	93
$10,000–$200,000	0	3	0	1	5	4	5
$200,000–$1,000,000	0	1	0	1	1	4	3
>$1,000,000	1	10	16	9	13	9	17
Flying Hours	76393	161363	163620	173573	172286	170344	172688

Table 5.15. Aggregate risk measures: model A.

Measure	Year 2001	2002	2003	2004	*2005*	2006	2007
$\lambda(t)$	74.31	105.98	130.81	145.01	179.90	111.97	94.07
$E(S(t))$	4458.69	14318.9	13371.4	11193.4	12486.0	8368.43	17899.3
$\log_{10}(\psi(t))$	5.52	6.17	6.24	6.21	6.35	5.97	6.23
$\log_{10}(\psi_B(t))$	5.98	6.73	6.78	6.75	6.88	6.51	6.77

in risk components and scores between aircraft models. The components of the risk measures can be calculated from the table data. The calculations for the components (failure rate, mean severity) were completed for the severity distribution for each of the years from 2001 to 2007. The aggregation occurs within a year. The rate of failures $\lambda(t)$ is per 10,000 flying hours. The expected severity $E(S(t))$ was calculated by fitting a log-logistic distribution to the severity values. The fit was very close to the empirical distribution and provided the advantage of completing the tail of the distribution (severity > 1,000,000).

Obviously, the use as defined by flying hours accumulates for successive years, and degradation with use could result in an increase in the failure rate and a shift in the severity score distribution. That effect will be carried by the failures by severity in each year.

The risk process components and value of the risk indices are displayed in Tables 5.15 and 5.16. The logarithm to the base 10 of

Table 5.16. Aggregate risk measures: model B.

	Year						
Measure	**2001**	**2002**	**2003**	**2004**	**2005**	**2006**	**2007**
$\lambda(t)$	39.2706	64.4510	121.01	118.11	120.73	153.81	171.99
$E(S(t))$	11406.6	22698.1	19747.0	13852.6	17263.5	13143.0	16665.4
$\log_{10}(\psi(t))$	5.65	6.17	6.38	6.21	6.32	6.31	6.46
$\log_{10}(\psi_B(t))$	6.40	6.74	6.96	6.86	6.93	6.97	7.07

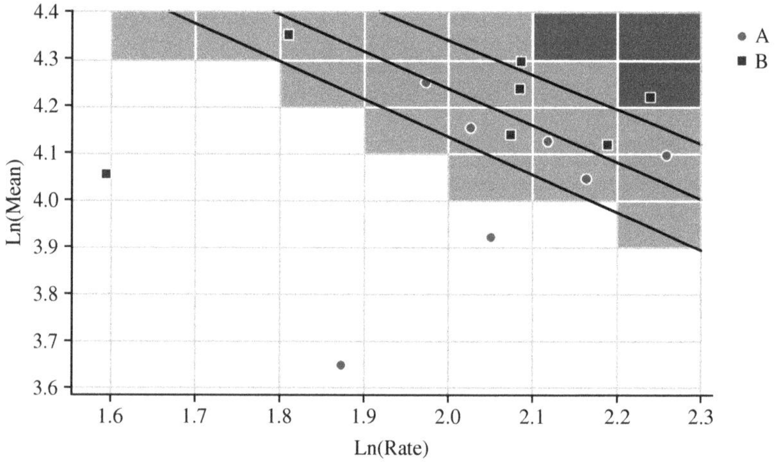

Figure 5.12. Risk graph.

the risk measure is shown since that puts the measure on a linear scale. Also shown are values for the Bohnenbust measure ψ_B, where the severities are inflated by 10%.

The components vary between the models. The rate of failures for Model A is higher than that of Model B, which has a higher expected severity of failures for most years. The combined risk priority number has Model A dominating Model B.

The two-dimensional risk graph for the cohort is given in Figure 5.12. Also plotted are consequence frequency lines for a benchmark.

The benchmark was based on the (rate, mean severity) for all comparable regional jets over the years 2001–2007. The benchmark risk measures $(\lambda, E(S))$ were calculated as well as 95% confidence limits for the benchmark, based on a compound Poisson process model. The consequence frequency lines in the figure are values of $(\log(\lambda), \log(E(S)))$, which give the same value as the benchmark: $\log(\lambda) + \log(E(S)) = \log(\psi) \pm 1.96 \cdot \sigma(\log(\psi))$. This method of defining an indifference region is for illustration, although Virling *et al.* (1998) propose it as a risk aversion adjustment. From the risk graphs, it is possible to identify points that are outside the indifference zone, either too high or too low. Those points depart significantly from the standard defined by the population of all comparable aircraft.

There is an important question over the use of the risk measures to identify extremes. In the risk graphs, the fC lines were equivalence sets defined by the risk measures. Alternatively, each point has a risk measure value, and the trajectory of risk measure values can be considered for extremes. In Figure 5.13, the values for the risk measures are plotted against the year. The benchmark values for the risk measures are also shown.

The high and low points on the risk graph are also picked up by the risk measure. There is a chance the measures will not detect points that are above the benchmark in the risk graph. If the benchmark value is k, then the chance of exceeding the risk measure benchmark is calculated from a joint probability: $\Pr[\log(\lambda) + \log(E(S)) > k]$. In the risk graph, the chance of exceeding the fC line is a conditional probability calculation: $\Pr[\log(E(S)) > k \cdot \log(\lambda_0) | \lambda = \lambda_0]$. With an assumption that λ and S are independent, by taking the marginal over the rate λ, the calculations are the same.

The risk measure is linked to the stochastic dynamic risk process, and the risk measure plot gives the time dynamics of risk. If there is a trend in the risk measure, then that could indicate a degeneration of the system with use (MacLean *et al.*, 2005). The trajectory in Figure 5.13 is similar to a random walk, omitting the initial values in the first time period when the cohort of aircraft was starting operation and use was limited. The volatility of the measures is larger than for the benchmark, but the benchmark values are calculated from many aircraft and failures.

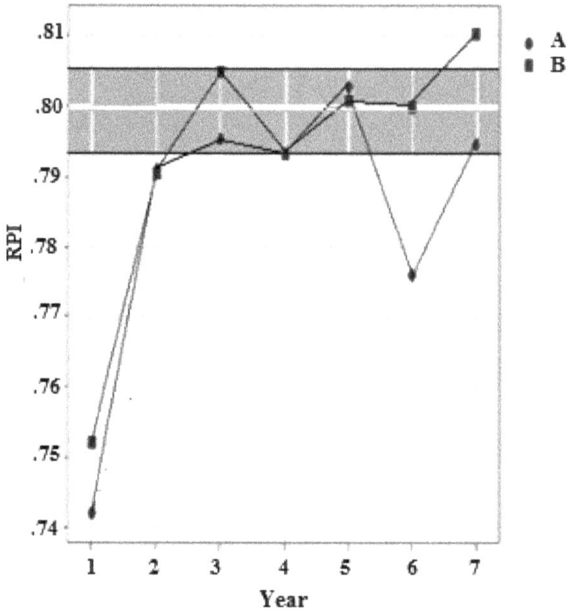

Figure 5.13. Risk priority numbers.

5.6 Conclusion

Risk control is a crucial part of the management of the operations of a system functioning in an uncertain environment. The long-term success and sustainability of a system depend on the techniques undertaken to minimize exposure to unsustainable losses. Risk control is a major topic in the management of business, the environment, health, and society. Risk control is a plan-based strategy that aims to identify, assess, and prepare for any hazardous outcomes that may interfere with a system's operations and objectives. The approaches to risk control are varied, involving a combination of risk control techniques, such as avoidance, loss prevention, loss reduction, separation, duplication, and diversification.

The setting for risk control in our presentation of quantitative risk analysis is the decisions on system operation. The theme is "decisions have consequences," and control implies choosing decisions that manage the probability and consequences of adverse system outcomes. The control decisions in our model are an intrinsic part of the system, with decisions linked to the endogenous components of the system design. We have exogenous risk factors that condition the operating environment by impacting the status of components, and in that way, decisions react to risk factors.

Our system approach has the advantage of facilitating the analysis of decisions given risk factors. Varying the decisions changes the distribution for system outcomes, and decisions can be compared using the stochastic orders for random variables. In the case of investment decisions in financial assets, the stochastic dynamic system approach is well developed, and has provided substantial theoretical and empirical results on the coherence of risk measures, the significance of risk factors, and the efficiency of decisions. The basic foundation of the financial system is stochastic dynamic equations for the status of system components (asset prices). With biological, mechanical, and social systems, the system's architecture is much more complicated. The intrinsic system components may be defined, but the dynamics of component status with use or time are usually not characterized with equations. The performance of the system is learned by a decision changing some component(s) and observing the effect on the outcome.

The quantitative approach to risk control requires a numeric measurement of system output. It does not require the equations for intrinsic components. A comparison of systems whose difference is decision based allows the analyst to contrast the distribution of output with risk measures. The preferred decision is determined from relative risk. The full set of feasible decisions is not involved in the contrast, and an absolute optimal decision is undetermined.

It is worth restating that the management of risk has a behavioral dimension. Qualitative risk analysis emphasizes the human approach to system operation. There are operational principles and practices that mitigate the probability and consequences of failures. Good practice rules have been learned from system operations and clearly have an impact on outcomes. We are focused on quantitative techniques, which complement rules governing operations.

Risk control is a subset of risk management. While risk management is the overarching process of identifying, assessing, and prioritizing risks to a system, risk control focuses specifically on implementing decisions to mitigate the identified risks. Risk management typically involves the development of an overall risk management plan, whereas risk control addresses the techniques and tactics employed to minimize potential losses and protect a system.

Bibliography

Ale, B., Burnap, P., and Slater, D. (2015). On the origin of PCDS – (Probability consequence diagrams). *Safety Science*, 72, 229–239.

Ang, A. and Bekaert, G. (2002). International asset allocation with regime shifts. *Review of Financial Studies*, 15(4), 1137–1187.

Aven and Jensen (1999) *Stochastic Models in Reliability*. Springer Verlag, New York, USA.

Bedford, T. and Cooke, R. (2001). *Probabilistic Risk Analysis: Foundations and Methods*. Cambridge University Press, Cambridge, UK.

Bernoulli, D. (1954). Exposition of a new theory on the measurement of risk. *Econometrica*, 22, 23–36. (Translation of Bernoulli, D. (1738) Specimen theoriae novae de mensura sortis. *Papers of the Imperial Academy of Sciences of St. Petersburg*, 5, 175–192.)

Broadie, M. (1993). Computing efficient frontiers using estimated parameters. *Annals of Operations Research*, 45, 21–58.

Buhlmann, H. (1970) *Mathematical Methods in Risk Theory*. Springer, Berlin.

Chekhlov, A., Uryasev, S., and Zabarankin, M. (2005). A drawdown measure in portfolio optimization. *International Journal of Theoretical and Applied Finance*, 8(1), 13–58.

Cox, L.A. (2008). What's wrong with risk matrices? *Risk Analysis*, 28(2), 497–512.

Costa, G. and Kwon, R.H. (2020). A regime-switching factor model for mean variance optimization. *Journal of Risk*, 22(4), 31–59.

De Santis, G. and Gerard, B. (1997). International asset pricing and portfolio diversification with time-varying risk. *Journal of Finance*, 52(5), 1881–1912.

Dixit, A. and Pindyck, R. (1994). *Investment under Uncertainty*. Princeton University Press, Princeton.

Dybvig, P. and Ross, S. (1982). Portfolio efficient sets. *Econometrica*, 50(6), 1525–1546.

Fama, E.F. and French, K.R. (1993). Common risk factors in the returns on stocks and bonds, *Journal of Financial Economics*, 33(1), 3–56.

Hamilton, J.D. (1989). Analysis of time series subject to changes in regime. *Econometrica*, 45, 39–70.

Hammond, J.S. (1974). Simplifying the choice between uncertain prospects where preference is nonlinear. *Management Science*, 20(7), 1047–1072.

Hanoch, G. and Levy, H. (1969). Efficiency analysis of choices involving risk. *Review of Economic Studies*, 36, 335–346.

Huang, C., Vertinski, I., and Ziemba, W. (1978). On multi-period stochastic dominance. *Journal of Financial and Quantitative Analysis*, XIII, 1–13.

Kaplan, S. and Garrick, B. (1981). On the quantitative definition of risk. *Risk Analysis*, 1, 11–27.

Klein, R.W. and Bawa, V.S. (1976). The effect of estimation risk on portfolio choice. *Journal of Financial Economics*, 3, 215–231.

Levy, H. (1998). *Stochastic Dominance.* Kluwer Academic Publishers, Norwell, MA.

Levy, H. and Paroush, J. (1974). Toward multivariate efficiency criteria. *Journal of Economic Theory*, 7(2), 129–142.

Lorenz, M.O. (1905). Methods of measuring the concentration of wealth. *Publications of the American Statistical Association*, 9(70), 209–219.

Lintner, J. (1965). Security prices, risk, and maximal gains from diversification. *Journal of Finance*, 20(4), 587–615.

Liu, P., Xu, K., and Zhao, Y. (2011). Market regimes, sectorial investments, and time-varying risk premiums. *International Journal of Managerial Finance*, 7(2), 107–133.

Ma, Y., MacLean, L., Xu, K., and Zhao, Y. (2011). A portfolio optimization model with regime-switching risk factors for sector exchange traded funds. *Pacific Journal of Optimization*, 7(2), 281–296.

Maclean, L., MacLean, S., and Richman A. (2019). Failure Event Severity and Risk Assessment. *Safety Science*, 123, 104554.

Maclean, L. and Richman, A. (2012). Aggregate risk measures for dynamic systems from operational data. *International Journal of Reliability, Quality and Safety Engineering*, 19(4), 1250019.

MacLean, L., Richman, A., Richman, V., and Larsson, S. (2005). The dynamics of aircraft degradation and mechanical failure. *Journal of Transportation and Statistics*, 8(1), 1–11.

MacLean, L., Zhao, Y., and Ziemba, W. (2016). Optimal capital growth with convex shortfall penalties. *Quantitative Finance*, 16(1), 101–117.

MacLean, L.C., Thorp, E.O., Zhao, Y., and Ziemba, W.T. (2011). How does the Fortune's Formula – Kelly capital growth model perform? *Journal of Portfolio Management*, 37(4), 96–111.

MacLean, L. and Zhao, Y. (2021). Kelly investing with risk control in a regime-switching market. *Quantitative Finance*, 22(1), 75–94. DOI: 10.1080/14697688.2021.1993617

MacLean, L.C., and Zhao, Y (2021). Kelly investing with downside risk control in a regime-switching market. *Quantitative Finance*, 22(1), 1–20.

MacLean, L. Zhao, Y and Zhang, O (2025). Mean-variance optimization with inferred regimes. *Annals of Operations Research*, 346(1), 341–368.

Markowitz, H. (1952). Portfolio selection. *Journal of Finance*, 7(1), 77–91.

Olabiyi, O. and Annamalai, A. (2012). Invertible exponential-type approximations for the Gaussian probability integral Q(x) with applications. *IEEE Wireless Communications Letters*, 1(5), 544–547.

Schaller, H. and van Norden, S. (1997). Regime switching in stock market returns. *Applied Financial Economics*, 7(2), 177–191.

Schuffham, P., Chambers, D., O'Hare, D., and Wilson, E. (2002). Direct and indirect costs of general aviation crashes. *Aviation, Space and Environmental Medicine*, 73(9), 851–858.

Sortino, F.A. and Satchell, S. (2001). *Managing Downside Risk in Financial Markets*. Butterworth-Heinemann, Oxford.

Virling, J.K., van Hengel W., and Houben, R.J. (1998). Acceptable risk as a basis for design. *Reliability Engineering and System Safety* 59, 141–150.

Vliet, P. and Blitz, D. (2011). Dynamic strategic asset allocation: Risk return across economic regimes. *Journal of Asset Management*, 12, 360–375.

Zucchini, W. and MacDonald, I. (2009). *Hidden Markov Models for Time Series: An Introduction Using R*. CRC Press, Taylor & Francis Group, Oxfordshire, UK.

Chapter 6

Volatility

6.1 Introduction

Risk measurement at its core concerns itself with volatility measurement. Volatility of outcomes is necessary for risk, although other features of the outcome distribution are relevant. There are systematic and idiosyncratic terms in volatility, and our models have typically separated those terms. We considered factors which contribute to systematic variation, and initially modeled the idiosyncratic variance as independent of system factors. A consequence of that assumption is the independent and identically distributed error. An expanded model which included hidden regimes was proposed to capture cyclical patterns in returns. In the regime model, the factors impacted the expected returns and also the volatility of returns. So, the variance of returns is time varying in the regime model.

The concept of time-varying volatility warrants further consideration. In this chapter, we will consider some alternative models for volatility that incorporate aspects of time dependence. We know that decisions to control a stochastic dynamic system require projections on the future status of system components. It seems reasonable to propose that the current state and possibly the trajectory leading to the current state will affect the variation in the next time period, whether that variation is explainable by factors or is unexplained. We will take a closer look at the unexplained variation.

6.2 Unit Root Tests

Consider the series of errors $\{\varepsilon_t\}$ in the linear model: $R_t = BF_t + \varepsilon_t,\ t = 1, \ldots$. We have usually assumed that $\varepsilon_t \sim N(0, \sigma^2)$ That is, the errors are stationary. A simple generalization is to assume the error process follows an autoregressive model. Consider the first-order autoregressive model for error (AR(1) model):

$$\varepsilon_t = \rho\varepsilon_{t-1} + \epsilon_t, \epsilon_t \sim N(0, \sigma^2).$$

This is the same as $\Delta\varepsilon_t = (\rho - 1)\varepsilon_{t-1} + \epsilon_t$. If $\rho \neq 1$, then changes in error will depend on the preceding level of error. If $\rho = 1$, then changes will occur with a probability not depending on the current level, as in a random walk. We can see that repeated substitutions in $\varepsilon_t = \varepsilon_{t-1} + \epsilon_t$ will $\varepsilon_t = \sum_{s=1}^{t} \epsilon_s$. So, the variance of ε_t is $t\sigma^2$ and the series $\{\varepsilon_t\}$ is non-stationary. The property $\rho = 1$ is called a unit root. If it is known that a series has a unit root, the series can be differenced to render it stationary. The important point is to check for a unit root in the time series of residuals/errors.

A standard test for a unit root is the Dickey–Fuller test. Since the change in error is the emphasis, it is convenient to write $\delta = \rho - 1$ and test for $H_0 : \delta = 0$. Considering the numerous alternatives to stationarity, there are versions of the Dickey–Fuller test:

1. Test for $H_0 : \delta = 0$ in the model $\Delta\varepsilon_t = \delta\varepsilon_{t-1} + \epsilon_t$. So, the variance of ε_t depends on time.
2. Test for $H_0 : \delta = 0$ in the model $\Delta\varepsilon_t = a_0 + \delta\varepsilon_{t-1} + \epsilon_t$. The mean and variance of ε_t depend on time.
3. Test for $H_0 : \delta = 0$ in the model $\Delta\varepsilon_t = a + a_1 t + \delta\varepsilon_{t-1} + \epsilon_t$. The mean and variance of ε_t depend on time.

The decision about which of the three main versions of the test should be used needs testing. Exclusion of the intercept or deterministic time trend term may lead to *bias* in the coefficient estimate for δ. The bottom line is that when the observations from the stochastic system are a time series of random variables, the error terms in the linear factor model may have time-varying volatility. If we consider that the risk measures for the linear model depend on the variance, then the estimate for variance at a time trial for the system is very important. We will consider some established models in the case of time-varying volatility of error.

6.3 Modeling Error Variance

For the series of errors $\{\varepsilon,\ t = 1, \ldots T\}$ in the model for system output, the possible heteroscedasticity of error variance is a concern. We will consider autoregressive models for the conditional variance. An autoregressive (AR) model assumes that the current value of a series is a function of its previous values.

6.3.1 *ARCH model*

The autoregressive conditional heteroscedasticity (ARCH) model is a statistical model for time series data that model the variance of the current error as a function of the actual sizes of the previous time periods' errors. ARCH models were introduced by Engle (1982) and generalized as GARCH (Generalized ARCH) by Bollerslev (1986) and Taylor (1986).

To formulate the ARCH model, consider the conditional variance of ε_t, denoted by σ_t^2. We have $\sigma_t^2 = E[(\varepsilon_t - E(\varepsilon_t))^2 | \varepsilon_{t-1}, \varepsilon_{t-2}, \ldots]$. It is usually assumed that $E(\varepsilon_t) = 0$, so

$$\sigma_t^2 = E[\varepsilon_t^2 | \varepsilon_{t-1}, \varepsilon_{t-2}, \ldots].$$

For the simplest ARCH model, the conditional variance of the error term σ_t^2 depends on the immediately previous value of the squared error

$$\sigma_t^2 = E[\varepsilon_t^2 | \varepsilon_{t-1}] = \alpha_0 + \alpha\varepsilon_{t-1}^2.$$

The above-mentioned model is known as an ARCH(1), since the conditional variance depends on only one lagged squared error. If we consider the conditional error model together with the linear factor model, we have

$$\begin{aligned} R_t &= \beta_0 + \beta_1 F_{t1} + \cdots + \beta_m F_{tm} + \epsilon_t, \varepsilon_t \sim N(0, \sigma_t^2) \\ \sigma_t^2 &= \alpha_0 + \alpha_1 \varepsilon_{t-1}^2. \end{aligned}$$

The model can easily be extended to the general case where the error variance depends on q lags of squared errors, which would be known as an ARCH(q) model:

$$\sigma_t^2 = \alpha_0 + \alpha_1 \varepsilon_{t-1}^2 + \cdots + \alpha_q \varepsilon_{t-q}^2.$$

To complete the specification of the ARCH model, note that variance, by definition, is always positive. Therefore, a non-negativity constraint is imposed on the coefficients $\{\alpha_j,\ j = 1, \ldots, q\}$.

Testing for ARCH effects

A test for determining whether "ARCH effects" are present in the residuals of an estimated model may be conducted using the steps outlined in the following:

1. Run the postulated linear regression: $R_t = \beta_0 + \beta_1 F_{t1} + \cdots + \beta_m F_{tm} + \varepsilon_t$, storing the residuals $\{e_t,\ t = 1, \ldots, T\}$.
2. Calculate the squared residuals e_t^2, and run the ARCH(q) regression $e_t^2 = \alpha_0 + \alpha_1 e_{t-1}^2 + \cdots + \alpha_q e_{t-q}^2 + u_t$. R_q^2 is the coefficient of determination from this regression.
3. With T observations, compute the test statistic TR_q^2, which is distributed as a χ_q^2.
4. If $P_0 = Pr[\chi_q^2 > TR_q^2] < 0.05$, then reject $H_0 : \alpha_1 = \alpha_2 = \cdots = \alpha_q = 0$ and conclude $\alpha_j \neq 0$ for at least on j.

If the null hypothesis is rejected, then we conclude there is time-varying volatility. The significance of that conclusion is that the conditional variance of error in the next period is predicted by the ARCH model, and would be a theoretical and practical improvement on the mean squared error from regression.

6.3.2 *GARCH models*

The GARCH model is a generalization of the ARCH model. The GARCH model allows the conditional variance to be dependent upon its own previous lags. The simplest GARCH specification is GARCH (1, 1):

$$R_t = \beta_0 + \beta_1 F_{t1} + \cdots + \beta_m F_{tm} + \epsilon_t, \varepsilon_t \sim N(0, \sigma_t^2)$$

$$\sigma_t^2 = \gamma_0 + \gamma_1 \varepsilon_{t-1}^2 + \gamma_2 \sigma_{t-1}^2.$$

The (1, 1) in GARCH (1, 1) refers to the presence of a first-order autoregressive GARCH term, $\gamma_2 \sigma_{t-1}^2$, and a first-order moving average ARCH term, $\gamma_1 \varepsilon_{t-1}^2$. An ordinary ARCH model is a special case of a GARCH specification in which there are no lagged forecast variances in the condition variance equation, i.e., a GARCH (0,1).

If we recursively substitute for the lagged variance on the right-hand side of the equation, we can express the conditional variance as a weighted average of all of the lagged squared residuals to get $\sigma_t^2 = \frac{\gamma_0}{(1-\gamma_2)} + \gamma_1 \sum_{j=1}^{t-1} \gamma_2^{j-1} \varepsilon_{t-j}^2$. We see that the GARCH (1,1) variance specification is analogous to the mean squared error, $\hat{\sigma}^2 = \frac{1}{T-m} \sum_{i=1}^{T} e_i^2$, but that down-weights more distant lagged squared errors.

The GARCH $(p.q)$ model is the general formulation with longer lags:

$$\sigma_t^2 = \gamma_0 + \sum_{j=1}^{p} \gamma_{1j} \varepsilon_{t-j}^2 + \sum_{j=1}^{q} \gamma_{2j} \sigma_{t-j}^2.$$

The equation may be extended further by including exogenous volatility factors. These would be factors in addition to those risk factors F affecting the conditional mean in the linear factor model. Consider the volatility factors V_j, $j = 1, \ldots, H$, then the extended GARCH model is

$$\sigma_t^2 = \gamma_0 + \sum_{j=1}^{p} \gamma_{1j} \varepsilon_{t-j}^2 + \sum_{j=1}^{q} \gamma_{2j} \sigma_{t-j}^2 + \sum_{j=1}^{H} \gamma_{3j} V_j.$$

The GARCH models are attractive to analysts. Empirical evidence suggests that volatility reverts to the mean in the long run. The GARCH model exhibits this property under stationarity assumptions. In general, a GARCH (1,1) model will be sufficient to capture the volatility clustering in the data, and rarely is any higher-order model estimated in the academic finance literature.

Model estimation

The analysis of error variance with the ARCH/GARCH model follows standard statistical methods. Parameters are estimated by maximum likelihood. The regression model minimizes the residual sum of squares: $\sum(e_i - \hat{e}_i)^2$. The ARCH/GARCH specification includes a variance equation, hence estimation involves both the sum of squares and the variance of residuals. This minimization of the simultaneous equations is best estimated by maximum likelihood techniques. The EViews software provides the maximum likelihood estimates.

Model validation

Model validation follows the usual procedures. Individual coefficients are tested using z-statistics with the null hypothesis that coefficient values are zero. Hypotheses on the existence of ARCH and GARCH effects are based on model fittings with and without the ARCH and GARCH terms.

After estimation, it is important to revisit the residuals to ensure they appear to be white noise, indicating that the model is capturing the volatility dynamics and the model error is normal. Residual tests include the Histogram–Normality Tests. The Jarque–Bera statistic tests whether the standardized residuals are normally distributed.

The ARCH LM Test carries out Lagrange multiplier tests to test whether the standardized residuals exhibit additional ARCH. If the variance equation is correctly specified, there should be no ARCH left in the standardized residuals.

Prediction

Once the model is estimated and tested, it can be used to forecast future volatility. The forecast would be a theoretical and practical improvement on the mean squared error from regression.

Model alternatives

In addition to the standard GARCH specification, EViews has the ability to estimate other variance models. These include IGARCH, TARCH, EGARCH, PARCH, and component GARCH. The variations on the standard GARCH model are provided in Table 6.1.

6.4 Risk Measures

The linear factor model for conditional mean and the ARCH/GARCH model for conditional variance are applicable to risk analysis based on the estimated mean and variance of system output. The models are appropriate for evaluating the risk of past periods and especially for forecasting the risk from decisions in future periods. That is, with forecasts for period $t + 1$,

$$\hat{R}_{t+1}(X) = \hat{\beta}_0(X) + \hat{\beta}_1(X)f_{t,1} + \cdots + \hat{\beta}_m(X)f_{t,m}$$

Table 6.1. Alternative GARCH models.

GARCH model	Equation	Comment
IGARCH	$\sigma_t^2 = \sum_{j=1}^q \beta_j \sigma_{t-j}^2 + \sum_{i=1}^p \alpha_i \varepsilon_{t-i}^2$ $\sum_{j=1}^q \beta_j + \sum_{i=1}^p \alpha_i = 1$	It restricts the parameters of the GARCH model to sum to one and drops the constant term.
TARCH	$\sigma_t^2 = \varpi + \sum_{j=1}^q \beta_j \sigma_{t-j}^2 + \sum_{i=1}^p \alpha_i \varepsilon_{t-i}^2 + \sum_{k=1}^r \gamma_k \varepsilon_{t-k}^2 I_{t-k}$ $\mathrm{I}_t = 1$ if $\varepsilon_t < 0$ and 0 otherwise	In this model, good news, $\varepsilon_{t-i} > 0$, and bad news, $\varepsilon_{t-i} < 0$, have differential effects on the conditional variance.
EGARCH	$\log(\sigma_t^2) = \varpi + \sum_{j=1}^q \beta_j \log(\sigma_{t-j}^2) + \sum_{i=1}^p \alpha_i \left\lvert \frac{\varepsilon_{t-i}}{\sigma_{t-i}} \right\rvert + \sum_{k=1}^r \gamma_k \frac{\varepsilon_{t-k}}{\sigma_{t-k}}$	The log implies that the leverage effect is exponential, rather than quadratic, and that forecasts of the conditional variance are guaranteed to be non-negative.
PARCH	$\sigma_t^\delta = \varpi + \sum_{j=1}^q \beta_j \sigma_{t-j}^\delta + \sum_{i=1}^p \alpha_i (\lvert\varepsilon_{t-i}\rvert - \gamma_i \varepsilon_{t-i})^\delta$ where $\delta > 0, \lvert\gamma_i\rvert \leq 1$ for $i = 1, \ldots, r, \gamma_i = 0$ for all $i > r$, and $r \leq$ p.	The power parameter δ of the standard deviation can be estimated rather than imposed.
CGARCH	$\sigma_t^2 - m_t = \alpha(\varepsilon_{t-1}^2 - m_{t-1}) + \beta(\sigma_{t-1}^2 - m_{t-1})$ $m_t = \varpi + p(m_{t-1} - \varpi) + \phi(\varepsilon_{t-1}^2 - \sigma_{t-1}^2)$	The component model allows mean revision to a varying level m_t.

and

$$\hat{\sigma}_{t+1}^2(X) = \hat{\gamma}_0 + \hat{\gamma}_1 \varepsilon_t^2(X) + \hat{\gamma}_2 \hat{\sigma}_t^2(X).$$

The forecast outcome from decision X in period t is

$$R_{t+1}(X) \sim N(\hat{R}_{t+1}(X), \hat{\sigma}_{t+1}^2(X)).$$

The values of various risk measures can be calculated using formulas in Chapter 2 for the normal distribution.

Finally, Value at Risk can be computed based solely on the estimation of the quantile of the forecast distribution. This has been proposed by Engle and Manganelli (2000), adapting the quantile regression methods of Koenker and Basset (1978).

6.5 Multivariate Models: MGARCH

The models for time-varying volatility have been univariate. That is consistent with the approach in Chapter 3. The linear factor model postulates that the system output at trial t was generated from the model $R_t(X) = [\tilde{\beta}_0(X) + \tilde{\beta}_1(X)f_{t1} + \cdots + \tilde{\beta}_m(X)f_{tm}] + \varepsilon_t(X)$, where the decision X on investment weights on components is considered part of the system being assessed. Underlying the system output are the dynamics of components, which are interrelated. As discussed in Chapter 5, the co-movements of components are of great practical importance. It is therefore important to extend the considerations to multivariate GARCH (MGARCH) models. For example, asset pricing depends on the covariance of the assets in a portfolio, and risk management and asset allocation decisions relate, for instance, to finding and updating optimal hedging positions.

Recall the linear model for components, in matrix form,

$$\begin{bmatrix} R_{t1} \\ \vdots \\ R_{tn} \end{bmatrix} = \begin{bmatrix} \beta_{10} & \cdots & \beta_{1m} \\ \vdots & \ddots & \vdots \\ \beta_{n0} & \cdots & \beta_{nm} \end{bmatrix} \begin{bmatrix} F_{t0} \\ \vdots \\ F_{tm} \end{bmatrix} + \begin{bmatrix} \varepsilon_{t1} \\ \vdots \\ \varepsilon_{tn} \end{bmatrix},$$

where $F_{t0} = 1$. The error term $\boldsymbol{\varepsilon_t}' = (\varepsilon_{t1}, \ldots, \varepsilon_{tn})$ is multivariate normal: $\varepsilon \sim MN(0, \Sigma)$. The covariance matrix Σ is generalized to a time-varying matrix in a similar form to the univariate variance. We have the vector ε_t, with $E(\varepsilon_t) = 0$. Then, every conditional variance and covariance is a function of all lagged conditional variances and covariances, as well as lagged cross-products of errors. The equation is

$$\Sigma_t = \Gamma_0 + \sum_{j=1}^{p} \Gamma_{1j}(\varepsilon_{t-j} \cdot \varepsilon'_{t-1}) + \sum_{j=1}^{q} \Gamma_{2j}\Sigma_{t-j}.$$

In an application, the residual vectors $\{e'_t = (e_{t1}, \ldots, e_{tn}),\ t = 1, \ldots, T\}$ replace the theoretical errors and the matrices $(\Gamma_0, \Gamma_{1j}, \Gamma_{2j})$ are estimated. Usually, $p = q = 1$, so the number of parameters is manageable. Estimation of the MGARCH model is an option in the EViews software. The time-varying conditional means and conditional covariances can be the basis for optimal decisions for controlling the distribution of random returns over time.

The multivariate approach to time-varying volatility with MGARCH is complicated but has advantages:

- **Time-varying correlations:**

  MGARCH models can capture how correlations between assets change over time, which is crucial for understanding and managing risk.

- **Volatility spillover effects:**

  MGARCH models can analyze how volatility from one asset can spread to others, helping to identify and understand contagion effects.

- **Portfolio optimization:**

  By modeling the joint distribution of asset returns, MGARCH models can be used to optimize portfolio weights for desired levels of risk and return.

We introduce the multivariate model as an extension and a consideration for further analysis. The univariate GARCH will be illustrated with the following cases.

6.6 Cases Studies

Case 6.1: Inflation rates

The Consumer Price Index (CPI) is a numerical representation of the average change in prices of a specific basket of goods and services purchased by households. It is a way to track changes in the cost of living over time. Statistics Canada publishes the CPI data on daily, monthly, and annual bases.

Inflation is the rate at which the general price level of goods and services is increasing. It is essentially the overall increase in prices. The CPI is used to calculate the inflation rate. The percentage rate of change in the CPI is used as a measure of inflation. We will look at monthly CPI change in an analysis of Canadian inflation rates, with data from January 1981 to January 2024.

We are focused on time-varying volatility. Consider the Canadian monthly inflation rate $R_t, t = 1, \ldots, T$. The model specification for estimation is the GARCH(1,1):

$$R_t = \beta_0 + \epsilon_t, \quad \varepsilon_t \sim N(0, \sigma_t^2),$$
$$\sigma_t^2 = \gamma_0 + \gamma_1 \varepsilon_{t-1}^2 + \gamma_2 \sigma_{t-1}^2.$$

The parameters are estimated using EViews. In the main menu toolbar, select Quick/Estimate Equation. In the Equation Estimation/Method, select ARCH. The dialog box appears.

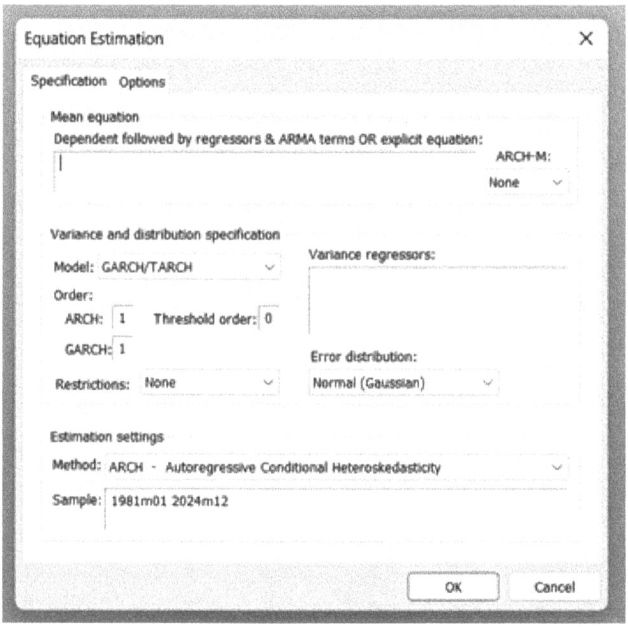

We will have to provide the mean equation, variance equation, the error distribution, and sample. For the GARCH(1, 1), assuming a normal distribution, we have the following:

- Fill in the Mean Equation Specification edit box.
- Enter 1 for the number of ARCH terms, and 1 for the number of GARCH terms, and select GARCH/TARCH.

- Select None for the ARCH-M term.
- Leave the Variance Regressors edit box blank.

The output results are shown in the following.

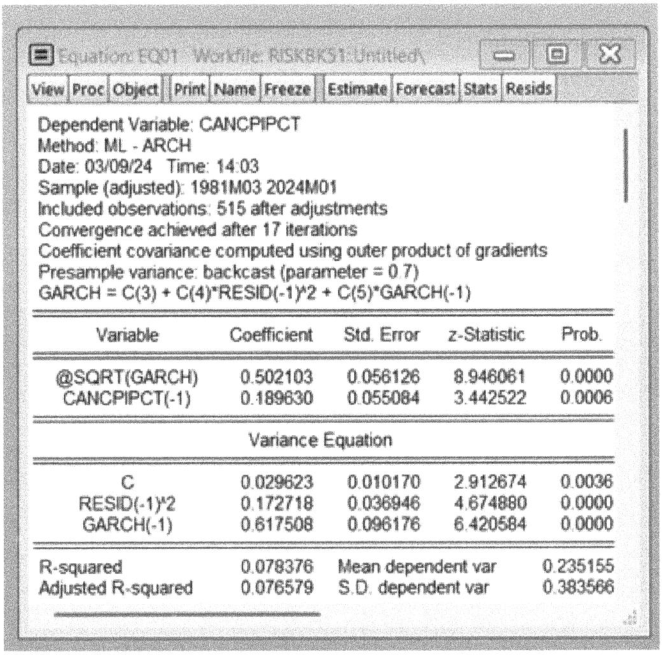
Equation: EQ01 Workfile: RISKBK51::Untitled\

View | Proc | Object | Print | Name | Freeze | Estimate | Forecast | Stats | Resids

Dependent Variable: CANCPIPCT
Method: ML - ARCH
Date: 03/09/24 Time: 14:03
Sample (adjusted): 1981M03 2024M01
Included observations: 515 after adjustments
Convergence achieved after 17 iterations
Coefficient covariance computed using outer product of gradients
Presample variance: backcast (parameter = 0.7)
GARCH = C(3) + C(4)*RESID(-1)^2 + C(5)*GARCH(-1)

Variable	Coefficient	Std. Error	z-Statistic	Prob.
@SQRT(GARCH)	0.502103	0.056126	8.946061	0.0000
CANCPIPCT(-1)	0.189630	0.055084	3.442522	0.0006
	Variance Equation			
C	0.029623	0.010170	2.912674	0.0036
RESID(-1)^2	0.172718	0.036946	4.674880	0.0000
GARCH(-1)	0.617508	0.096176	6.420584	0.0000
R-squared	0.078376	Mean dependent var		0.235155
Adjusted R-squared	0.076579	S.D. dependent var		0.383566

The estimated GARCH model is reproduced in Table 6.2. The evidence for time-varying volatility in inflation rates is clear. All coefficients are statistically significant at a p value level of significance of 0.01. All coefficients are statistically significant at a p value level of significance of 0.01.

Table 6.2. Estimates for GARCH(1,1) model.

Variable	Coef	SE	Z	P
Constant	0.029623	0.010170	2.912674	0.0036
ARCH: ε_{t-1}^2	0.172716	0.036946	4.674880	0.0000
GARCH: σ_{t-1}^2	0.617508	0.096176	6.420584	0.0000

Applying the ARCH-LM test, we do not reject the null hypothesis of no heteroscedasticity given the F statistic and the chi-square statistic.

Case 6.2: Portfolio value at risk

The numbers in this case were based on a paper by Robert Engle (2001). The GARCH model is contrasted with the historical distribution of portfolio returns in the estimation of return volatility.

A portfolio is constructed from indices, with 50 percent in the Nasdaq, 30 percent in the Dow Jones, and 20 percent in long bonds. Data on the indices and the portfolio are the daily rates of return from March 26, 1990 to March 23, 2000. Summary statistics on the returns for the assets and the portfolio are provided in Table 6.3.

The portfolio is an intuitive combination of assets. The investment fractions are not determined from the optimization of an objective. However, it illustrates the benefits of diversification since it is less volatile than the equity indices. The skewness and kurtosis statistics indicate that returns are not normal.

We are concerned with estimating the 1% VaR for a portfolio investment of $1,000,000 on March 23, 2000. It was a time of high volatility and investment anxiety.

The basic GARCH(1,1) results are given in Table 6.4.

Table 6.3. Summary statistics for portfolio.

Statistic	Nasdaq	Dow Jones	Bond	Portfolio
Mean	0.0009	0.0005	0.0001	0.0007
St Dev	0.0115	0.0090	0.0073	0.0083
Skewness	−0.5310	−0.3593	−0.2031	−0.4738
Kurtosis	7.4936	8.3288	4.9579	7.0026

Table 6.4. Estimates for ARCH and GARCH models.

Variable	Coef	SE	Z	P
Constant	1.40E-06	4.48E-07	3.1210	0.0018
ARCH	0.0772	0.0179	4.3046	0.0000
GARCH	0.9046	0.0196	46.1474	0.0000

The three coefficients in the variance equation are listed as C, the intercept, ARCH(1), the first lag of the squared return, and GARCH(1), the first lag of the conditional variance. The ARCH and GARCH effects are very significant.

The forecast standard deviation for the next day from the model is 0.0146.

The estimated standard deviation from the data is 0.0083, which is based on a constant volatility over the observed period. The normal Value at Risk =\$33,977.

As it turns out, the residuals are not very close to a normal. With the GARCH model volatility estimate for the next period, the estimated 1% VaR is \$39,996. Notice how much this Value at Risk has risen to reflect the increased risk in 2000.

The GARCH analysis is statistical and is intended to illustrate the importance of estimation methods in determining planning values for model parameters. The risk analyst will make decisions to control risk. The decisions and their consequences are very dependent on the quality of parameter estimates.

6.7 Conclusion

The ARCH/GARCH models can be viewed in the context of the linear factor (LF) model. The significant parameters in the outcome from a stochastic dynamic system are the mean and variance. The LF model defines the conditional mean, and the GARCH model defines the conditional variance of the distribution of output. The idea that the (mean, variance) parameters depend on current and past conditions is totally reasonable, and improving the estimates of parameters will result in better decisions to control risk and generate growth.

Bibliography

Bollerslev, T. (1986). Generalized autoregressive conditional heteroskedasticity. *Journal of Econometrics*, 31, 307–327.

Bollerslev, T. and Wooldridge, J.M. (1992). Quasi-maximum likelihood estimation and inference in dynamic models with time-varying covariances. *Econometric Reviews*, 11(2), 143–172.

Dickey, D.A. and Fuller, W.A. (1979). Distribution of the estimators for autoregressive time series with a unit root. *Journal of the American Statistical Association*, 74, 427–432.

Engle, R. (2001). GARCH 101: An introduction to the use of ARCH/GARCH models in applied econometrics. *Journal of Economic Perspectives*, 15(4), 157–168.

Engle, R.F. (1982). Autoregressive conditional heteroscedasticity with estimates of the variance of United Kingdom inflation. *Econometrica*, 50(4), 987–1007.

Engle, R.F. and Manganelli, S. (2000). CAViaR: Conditional autoregressive value at risk by regression quantiles. Econometric Society World Congress 2000 Contributed Papers 0841, Econometric Society.

Engle, R.F. and Ng, V. (1993). Measuring and testing the impact of news on volatility. *Journal of Finance*, 48, 1749–1778.

Glosten, L.R., Jagannathan, R., and Runkle, D.E. (1993). On the relation between the expected value and the volatility of the nominal excess returns on stocks. *Journal of Finance*, 48(5), 1779–1801.

Koenker, R. and Bassett, G. (1978). Regression quantiles. *Econometrica*, 46(1), 33–50.

Nelson, D.B. (1991). Conditional heteroscedasticity in asset returns: A new approach. *Econometrica*, 59(2), 347–370.

Taylor, S.J. (1986). *Modelling Financial Time Series*. John Wiley: Chichester.

Appendices

The chapters in this book include many models and equations. The formal definition of a stochastic dynamic system is important for the analysis of the system and in particular for the risk assessment. The requirements for reading and understanding equations involve some basic mathematics. The calculations of estimates for parameters used in defining expressions are performed with statistical software. An introduction to the statistical software EViews is presented in Appendix A. Then, the notation and operations with matrices are outlined in Appendix B. Finally, some principles of probability are defined in Appendix C. The intention of the appendices is to provide a refresher. A more detailed treatment is provided in the reference texts as follows.

Bibliography

Freund, J. (1993). *Introduction to Probability.* Dover, New York.

Lang, S. (1988). *Basic Mathematics*, Springer, New York.

Strang, G. (2023). *Introduction to Linear Algebra.* Wellesley-Cambridge Press, Wellesley, MA.

Appendix A

Introduction to EViews

The number of packages available for econometric modeling is large, and over time, all packages have improved in the breadth of available techniques and have also converged in terms of what is available in each package. EViews is a menu-driven package that is based on a standard Microsoft Windows graphical user interface. EViews has a command-based programming language as well as a click-and-point interface that offers flexibility as well as user-friendliness. The following section gives an introduction to this software and outlines the key features and how basic tasks are executed.

1. Accomplishing Simple Tasks Using EViews

EViews is built around the concept of objects, with each object having its own window, its own menu, its own procedure, and its own view of the data. Using menus, it is easy to change between displays of a spreadsheet, line and bar graphs, regression results, etc. One of the most important features of EViews that makes it useful for model-building is a wealth of diagnostic (misspecification) tests that are automatically computed, making it possible to test whether the model is econometrically valid or not. You work your way through EViews using a combination of windows, buttons, menus, and submenus.

This section assumes that readers have obtained a licensed copy of EViews and have successfully loaded it onto an available computer. We will present a description of the EViews package, together with instructions to achieve standard tasks and sample output. Any instructions that must be entered or icons to be clicked are illustrated by bold-faced type. The object of the treatment in this appendix is not to demonstrate the full functionality of the package but rather to get readers started quickly and to explain how the techniques are implemented and how the results may be interpreted. For further details, readers should consult the software manuals, which are now available electronically with the software as well as in hard copy. Note that EViews is not case sensitive, so it does not matter whether commands are entered as lowercase or capital letters.

(1) Opening the software

To load EViews from Windows, click the Start button, then All Programs, EViews8, and finally EViews8 again.

(2) Reading in data

EViews provides support to read from or write to various file types, including "ASCII" (text) files, Microsoft Excel ".XLS" and "XLSX" files (reading from any named sheet in the Excel workbook), and Lotus ".WKS1" and ".WKS3" files. It is usually easiest to work directly with Excel files.

(3) Creating a workfile and importing data

The first step when the EViews software is opened is to create a workfile that will hold the data. To do this, select **New** from the **File** menu. Then, choose **Workfile**. The "Workfile Create" window in screenshot 1.1 will be displayed.

We are going to use as an example a time series of UK average house price data obtained from Nationwide, which comprises 269 monthly observations from January 1991 to May 2013.

Under "Workfile structure type," keep the default option, **Dated – regular frequency**. Then, under "Date specification," choose **Monthly**. Note the format of data entry for monthly and quarterly data: YYYY:M and YYYY:Q, respectively. For daily data, a US date format must usually be used, depending on how EViews has been set up: MM/DD/YYYY (e.g., 03/01/1999 would be 1 March 1999, not 3 January). Caution, therefore, needs to be exercised here to ensure that the date format used is the correct one. Type the start and end dates for the sample into the boxes: **1991:01** and

2013:05, respectively. Then, click **OK**. The workfile will now have been created. Note that two pairs of dates are displayed "Range" and "Sample": The first one is the range of dates contained in the workfile and the second one (which is the same as above in this case) is the current workfile sample. Two objects are also displayed: C (which is a vector that will eventually contain the parameters of any estimated models) and RESID (a residuals series, which will currently be empty). All EViews workfiles will contain these two objects, which are created automatically.

Now that the workfile has been set up, we can import the data from the Excel file UKHP.XLS. So, from the File menu, select **Import** and **Import from File**. You will then be prompted to select the directory and file name. Once you have found the directory where the file is stored, enter **UK.LS** in the file name box and click **Open**. You are then faced with a series of three screens where it is possible to modify the way that the data are imported. Most of the time, it is not necessary to change any of the default options as EViews peeks inside the data file and identifies the structure of the data, whether there is a header row containing the names of the series, etc. The three screens are shown in screens 1 to 3 of screenshot 1.2. In the third screen, click **Rename Series** and in the box that appears, type AVERAGE_HOUSE_PRICE HP, and this will change the name of the series to "HP," which is a bit easier to deal with!

Click **Finish**, and the series will be imported. The series will appear as a new icon in the workfile window, as in screenshot 1.3. Note that EViews has sensibly not imported the column of data as if it were an additional variable.

(4) Verifying the data

Double-click on the new hp icon that has appeared, and this will open a spreadsheet window within EViews containing the monthly house price values. Make sure that the data file has been correctly imported by checking a few observations at random.

The next step is to save the workfile: Click on the **Save As** button from the **File** menu and select **Save Active Workfile** and **OK**. A save dialog box will open, prompting you for a workfile name and location. You should enter XX (where XX is your chosen name for the file), then click **OK**. EViews will save the workfile in the specified directory with the name XX.wf1. I have called my file "ukhp.wf1."

You will also be prompted to select whether the date in the file should be saved in "single precision" or "double precision." The latter is preferable for obvious reasons, unless the file is likely to be very large because of the quantity of variables and observations it contains (single precision will require less space), so just click **OK**.

The saved workfile can be opened later by selecting File/Open/ EViews Workfile ... from the menu bar.

(5) Transformations

Variables of interest can be created in EViews by selecting the *Genr* button from the workfile toolbar and typing in the relevant formula. Suppose, for example, we have a time series called Z. The latter can be modified in the following ways so as to create variables A, B, C, etc. The mathematical background and simple explanation of these transformations, including powers, logarithms, and exponents, will be discussed in detail in the following section. Some common transformations are as follows:

A=Z/2	Dividing
B=Z*2	Multiplication
C=Z^2	Squaring
D=LOG(Z)	Taking the logarithm
E=EXP(Z)	Taking the exponential
F=Z(-1)	Lagging the data
F=LOG(Z/Z(-1))	Creating the log-returns

Other functions that can be used in the formula include abs, sin, and cos. Notice that no special instructions are necessary; simply type "new variables = function of old variable(s)." The variables will be displayed in the same workfile window as the original (imported) series.

In this case, it is of interest to calculate simple percentage changes in the series. Click **Genr** and type **DHP=100*(HP-HP(-1))/ HP(-1)**. It is important to note that this new series **DHP** will be a series of monthly percentage changes and will not be annualized.

(6) Computing summary statistics

Descriptive summary statistics of a series can be obtained by selecting **Quick/SeriesStatistics/Histogram and Stats** and typing in the name of the variable (**DHP**). The view in screenshot 1.4 will be displayed in the window.

As can be seen, the histogram suggests that the series has a slightly longer upper tail than lower tail (note the x-axis scale) and is centered slightly above zero. Summary statistics, including the mean, maximum and minimum, standard deviation, higher moments, and a test for whether the series is normally distributed, are all presented. Interpreting those will be discussed in subsequent sections. Other useful statistics and transformations can be obtained by selecting the command Quick/Series Statistics, but these are also covered later in the book.

(7) Plots

EViews supports a wide range of graph types including line graphs, bar graphs, pie charts, mixed line-bar graphs, high-low graphs, and scatterplots. A variety of options permit the user to select the line types, color, border characteristics, headings, shading, and scaling, including logarithmic scale and dual-scale graphs. Legends are automatically created (although they can be removed if desired), and customized graphs can be incorporated into other Windows applications using copy to paste or by exporting as Windows metafiles.

From the main menu, select **Quick/Graph** and type in the name of the series that you want to plot (**HP** to plot the level of housing prices) and click **OK**. You will be prompted with the "Graph Options" window, where you choose the type of graph that you want (line, bar, scatter, or pie charts) and also control the layout and style of the graph (e.g., whether you want a legend, or axis labels) Choosing a line and symbol graph would produce screenshot 1.5.

It is always useful to plot any series you are working with to get a feel for the basic features of the data. It is clear that in this case house prices appreciated quickly to reach a peak in October 2007 before falling sharply until early 2009, after which a partial recovery began. It is possible to identify any value on the chart and its timing by simply hovering the mouse over it. Double-clicking on the graph will revert to the Graph Options menu.

As an exercise, try **plotting the DHP** series – you will see that the volatility of the percentage change series makes their graphs much harder to interpret, even though they are usually the form of the data that we work with in econometrics.

(8) Printing results

Results can be printed at any point by selecting the Print button on the object window toolbar. The whole current window contents will be printed. Graphs can be copied to the clipboard if desired by right-clicking on the graph and choosing Copy to clipboard.

(9) Saving data, results, and workfile

Data generation in EViews can be exported to other Windows applications, e.g., Microsoft Excel. From the Main menu, select File/Export/Write Text-Lotus-Excel. You will then be asked to provide a name for the exported file and to select the appropriate directory. The next window will ask you to select all the series that you want to export, together with the sample period.

Assuming that the workfile has been saved after the importation of the dataset (as mentioned earlier), additional work can be saved by just selecting Save from the File menu. The workfile will be saved, including all objects in it – data, graphs, equations, etc., so long as they have been given a title. Any untitled objects will be lost upon exiting the program.

(10) Econometric tools available in EViews

Box 1.5 describes the features available in EViews, following the format of the user guides for version 8, with material discussed in this book indicated by italics.

Appendix B

Matrices

1. Definitions

(1) Matrix

A matrix is a rectangular array of numbers arranged in rows and columns. More precisely, a matrix of order, or dimension, $m \times n$ is a set of numbers arranged in m rows and n columns. Thus, a $m \times n$ matrix A is written as

$$A = [a_{ij}] = \begin{bmatrix} a_{11} & \cdots & a_{1n} \\ \vdots & \ddots & \vdots \\ a_{m1} & \cdots & a_{mn} \end{bmatrix},$$

where a_{ij} is the element appearing in the ith row and the jth column of A and where $[a_{ij}]$ is a shorthand expression for the matrix A. The order, or dimension, of the matrix – that is, the number of rows and columns – is often written underneath the matrix for easy reference:

$$\underset{2x3}{A} = \begin{bmatrix} 2 & 6 & 5 \\ 6 & 2 & 3 \end{bmatrix} \quad \underset{3x3}{B} = \begin{bmatrix} 1 & 5 & 7 \\ -1 & 0 & 4 \\ 8 & 9 & 11 \end{bmatrix}.$$

(2) Scalar

A scalar is a single (real) number. Alternatively, a scalar is a 1×1 matrix.

(3) Column vector

A matrix consisting of m rows and only one column is called a column vector. An example of a column vector is

$$x = \begin{bmatrix} 3 \\ 5 \\ 9 \end{bmatrix}.$$

(4) Row Vector

A matrix consisting of only one row and n columns is called a row vector. For example,

$$y = \begin{bmatrix} 1 & 2 & 5 \end{bmatrix}.$$

(5) Transpose

The transpose of an $m \times n$ matrix A, denoted by A', is an $n \times m$ matrix obtained by interchanging the rows and columns of A. That is, the ith row of A becomes the ith column of A'. For example,

$$\underset{3x2}{A} = \begin{bmatrix} 4 & 5 \\ 3 & 1 \\ 5 & 0 \end{bmatrix} \quad \underset{2x3}{A'} = \begin{bmatrix} 4 & 3 & 5 \\ 5 & 1 & 0 \end{bmatrix}.$$

Since a vector is a special type of matrix, the transpose of a row vector is a column vector and the transpose of a column vector is a row vector. Thus,

$$x = \begin{bmatrix} 4 \\ 5 \\ 6 \end{bmatrix} \quad \text{and} \quad x' = \begin{bmatrix} 4 & 5 & 6 \end{bmatrix}.$$

We shall follow the convention of indicating the row vectors by primes.

(6) Submatrix

Given an $m \times n$ matrix A, if all but **r** rows and **s** columns of **A** are deleted, the resulting matrix of order $r \times s$ is called a submatrix of A.

Thus, if

$$\underset{3x3}{A} = \begin{bmatrix} 3 & 5 & 7 \\ 8 & 2 & 1 \\ 3 & 2 & 1 \end{bmatrix}$$

and we delete the third row and the third column of A, we obtain the submatrix

$$\underset{2x2}{B} = \begin{bmatrix} 3 & 5 \\ 8 & 2 \end{bmatrix}.$$

2. Types of Matrices

(1) Square matrix

A matrix that has the same number of rows and columns is called a square matrix. For example,

$$A = \begin{bmatrix} 3 & 5 & 8 \\ 7 & 3 & 1 \\ 4 & 5 & 0 \end{bmatrix}.$$

(2) Diagonal matrix

A square matrix with at least one non-zero element on the main diagonal (running from the upper-left-hand corner to the lower-right-hand corner) and zeros elsewhere is called a diagonal matrix:

$$A = \begin{bmatrix} 3 & 0 & 0 \\ 0 & 5 & 0 \\ 0 & 0 & 1 \end{bmatrix}.$$

(3) Scalar matrix

A diagonal matrix whose elements are all equal is called a scalar matrix. An example is the variance–covariance matrix of the population disturbance of the classical linear regression model,

$$\Sigma = \begin{bmatrix} \sigma^2 & 0 & 0 \\ 0 & \sigma^2 & 0 \\ 0 & 0 & \sigma^2 \end{bmatrix}.$$

(4) Identity matrix

A diagonal matrix whose diagonal elements are all 1 is called an identity, or unit, matrix, and is denoted by I. It is a special kind of scalar matrix:

$$I = \begin{bmatrix} 1 & 0 & 0 \\ 0 & 1 & 0 \\ 0 & 0 & 1 \end{bmatrix}.$$

(5) Symmetric matrix

A square matrix whose elements above the main diagonal are mirror images of the elements below the main diagonal is called a symmetric matrix. Alternatively, a symmetric matrix is such that its transpose is equal to itself; that is, $\boldsymbol{A} = \boldsymbol{A}'$. An example is the general variance–covariance matrix

$$\Sigma = \begin{bmatrix} \sigma^2 & \sigma_{12} & \sigma_{13} \\ \sigma_{12} & \sigma^2 & \sigma_{23} \\ \sigma_{13} & \sigma_{23} & \sigma^2 \end{bmatrix}.$$

(6) Null matrix

A matrix whose elements are all zero is called a null matrix and is denoted by **0**.

(7) Null vector

A row or column vector whose elements are all zero is called a null vector and is also denoted by **0**.

(8) Equal matrices

Two matrices A and B are said to be equal if they are of the same order and their corresponding elements are equal. For example, the matrices

$$\underset{3x3}{A} = \begin{bmatrix} 3 & 4 & 5 \\ 0 & -1 & 2 \\ 5 & 1 & 3 \end{bmatrix} \quad \text{and} \quad \underset{3x3}{B} = \begin{bmatrix} 3 & 4 & 5 \\ 0 & -1 & 2 \\ 5 & 1 & 3 \end{bmatrix}$$

are equal, that is, $A = B$.

3. Matrix Operations

(1) Matrix addition

Let $A = [a_{ij}]$ and $B = [b_{ij}]$. If A and B are of the same order (dimension), we define matrix addition as

$$A + B = C,$$

where $\boldsymbol{C}$ is of the same order as $\boldsymbol{A}$ and $\boldsymbol{B}$ and is obtained as $c_{ij} = a_{ij} + b_{ij}$ for all $\boldsymbol{i}$ and $\boldsymbol{j}$. C is obtained by adding the corresponding elements of A and B. If such an addition can be effected, A and B are said to be conformable for addition. For example, if

$$A = \begin{bmatrix} 2 & 3 & 4 & 5 \\ 6 & 7 & 8 & 9 \end{bmatrix} \quad \text{and} \quad B = \begin{bmatrix} 1 & 0 & -1 & 3 \\ -2 & 0 & 1 & 5 \end{bmatrix}$$

and $C = A + B$, then

$$C = \begin{bmatrix} 3 & 3 & 3 & 8 \\ 4 & 7 & 9 & 14 \end{bmatrix}.$$

Matrix subtraction follows the same principle as matrix addition, except that $C = A - B$; that is, we subtract the elements of B from the corresponding elements of A to obtain C, provided A and B are of the same order.

(2) Scalar multiplication

To multiply a matrix A by a scalar λ (a real number), we multiply each element of the matrix by λ:

$$\lambda A = [\lambda a_{ij}].$$

For example, if $\lambda = 2$ and

$$A = \begin{bmatrix} -3 & 5 \\ 8 & 7 \end{bmatrix},$$

then

$$\lambda A = \begin{bmatrix} -6 & 10 \\ 16 & 14 \end{bmatrix}.$$

(3) Matrix multiplication

Let A be $m \times n$ and B be $n \times p$. Then, the product AB (in that order) is defined to be a new matrix C of order $m \times p$, $C = [c_{ij}]$, such that

$$c_{ij} = \sum_{k=1}^{n} a_{ik} b_{kj}, i = 1, \ldots, m; \quad j = 1, \ldots, p.$$

That is, the element in the ith row and the jth column of C is obtained by multiplying the elements of the ith row of A by the corresponding elements of the jth column of B and summing over all terms; this is known as the row-by-column rule of multiplication. Thus, to obtain c_{11}, the element in the first row and the first column of C, we multiply the elements in the first row of A by the corresponding elements in the first column B and sum over all terms.

Note that for multiplication to exist, matrices A and B must be conformable with respect to multiplication; that is, the number of columns in A must be equal to the number of rows in B. If, for example,

$$\underset{2x3}{A} = \begin{bmatrix} 3 & 4 & 7 \\ 5 & 6 & 1 \end{bmatrix} \quad \text{and} \quad \underset{3x2}{B} = \begin{bmatrix} 2 & 1 \\ 3 & 5 \\ 6 & 2 \end{bmatrix},$$

$$AB = \underset{2x2}{C} = \begin{bmatrix} (3x2) + (4x3) + (7x6)(3x1) + (4x5) + (7x2) \\ (5x2) + (6x3) + (1x6)(5x1) + (6x5) + (1x2) \end{bmatrix}$$

$$= \begin{bmatrix} 60 & 37 \\ 34 & 37 \end{bmatrix}.$$

But if

$$\underset{2x3}{A} = \begin{bmatrix} 3 & 4 & 7 \\ 5 & 6 & 1 \end{bmatrix} \quad \text{and} \quad \underset{2x2}{B} = \begin{bmatrix} 2 & 3 \\ 5 & 6 \end{bmatrix},$$

the product AB is not defined since A and B are not conformable with respect to multiplication.

Properties of matrix multiplication

1. Matrix multiplication is not necessarily commutative; that is, in general $AB \neq BA$. Therefore, the order in which the matrices are multiplied is very important. AB implies that A is post-multiplied by B or B is pre-multiplied by A.
2. Even if AB and BA exist, the resulting matrices may not be of the same order. Thus, if A is $m \times n$ and B is $n \times m$, AB is $m \times m$, whereas BA is $n \times n$, hence of different order.
3. Even if A and B are both square matrices, so that AB and BA are both defined, the resulting matrices will not necessarily be equal. For example, if

$$A = \begin{bmatrix} 4 & 7 \\ 3 & 2 \end{bmatrix} \quad \text{and} \quad B = \begin{bmatrix} 1 & 5 \\ 6 & 8 \end{bmatrix}$$

then

$$AB = \begin{bmatrix} 46 & 76 \\ 15 & 31 \end{bmatrix} \quad \text{and} \quad BA = \begin{bmatrix} 19 & 17 \\ 48 & 58 \end{bmatrix}$$

and $AB \neq BA$.
4. A row vector post-multiplied by a column vector is a scalar. Thus, consider the ordinary least squares residuals $e' = [e_1, e_2, \ldots, e_n]$. We have $e'e = \sum_{i=1}^{n} e_i^2$, which is a scalar.
5. A column vector post-multiplied by a row vector is a matrix. As an example, consider the residuals $e' = [e_1, e_2, \ldots, e_n]$. Then,

$$ee' = \begin{bmatrix} e_1 \\ \vdots \\ e_n \end{bmatrix} [e_1 \cdots e_n = [e_i e_j]], \text{ which is a matrix of order } n \times n.$$

Note that the preceding matrix is symmetrical.
6. A matrix post-multiplied by a column vector is a column vector.
7. A row vector post-multiplied by a matrix is a row vector.
8. Matrix multiplication is associative; that is, $(AB)C = A(BC)$, assuming the matrices are conformable.
9. Matrix multiplication is distributive with respect to addition; that is, $A(B + C) = AB + AC$ and $(B + C)A = BA + CA$, assuming the matrices are conformable.

Matrix transposition properties

We have already defined the process of matrix transposition as interchanging the rows and columns of a matrix (or a vector). We now state some of the properties of transposition:

1. The transpose of a transposed matrix is the original matrix itself. Thus, $(A') = A$.
2. If A and B are conformable for addition and $C = A + B$, then $C' = (A + B)' = A' + B'$. That is, the transpose of the sum of two matrices is the sum of their transposes.
3. If AB is defined, then $(AB)' = B'A'$. That is, the transpose of the product of two matrices is the product of their transposes in the reverse order. This can be generalized: $(ABCD)' = D'C'B'A'$.
4. The transpose of an identity matrix I is the identity matrix itself.
5. The transpose of a scalar is the scalar itself.
6. The transpose of $(\lambda A)'$ is $\lambda A'$ where λ is a scalar.
7. If A is a square matrix such that $A = A'$, then A is a symmetric matrix.

(4) Matrix inversion

An inverse of a square matrix A, denoted by A^{-1} (read A inverse), if it exists, is a unique square matrix such that $AA^{-1} = A^{-1}A = I$, where I is an identity matrix whose order is the same as that of A. For example,

$$A = \begin{bmatrix} 2 & 4 \\ 6 & 8 \end{bmatrix} \quad A^{-1} = \begin{bmatrix} -1 & \frac{1}{2} \\ \frac{6}{8} & -\frac{1}{4} \end{bmatrix} \quad AA^{-1} = \begin{bmatrix} 1 & 0 \\ 0 & 1 \end{bmatrix} = I$$

Properties of the inverse:

1. $(AB)^{-1} = B^{-1}A^{-1}$. That is, the inverse of the product of two matrices is the product of their inverses in the reverse order.
2. $(A^{-1})' - (A')^{-1}$. That is, the transpose of A inverse is the inverse of A transpose.

4. Determinants

To every square matrix, A, there corresponds a number (scalar) known as the determinant of the matrix, which is denoted by $\det(A)$ or by the symbol $|A|$. The determinant of a matrix is a real number.

The process of finding the value of a determinant is done by manipulating the entries of the matrix in a well-defined manner. The Laplace expansion expresses the determinant of an $n \times n$ matrix A recursively in terms of determinants of smaller matrices, known as its minors. The minor M_{ij} is defined to be the determinant of the $(n-1) \times (n-1)$ matrix that results from removing the ith row and the jth column. For every row i, one has the equality

$$\det(A) = \sum_{j=1}^{n} (-1)^{i+j} a_{ij} M_{ij},$$

which is called the Laplace expansion along the ith row.

Evaluation of a 2×2 Determinant

$$A = \begin{bmatrix} a_{11} & a_{12} \\ a_{21} & a_{22} \end{bmatrix}$$

is

$$|A| = \begin{vmatrix} a_{11} & a_{12} \\ a_{21} & a_{22} \end{vmatrix} = a_{11}a_{22} - a_{12}a_{21}.$$

The Laplace expansion is complicated, with many terms, since the minors M_{ij} successively expanded in terms of reduced matrices until arriving at a 2×2 matrix. Fortunately, the determinant function is included in the toolkit of statistical software.

Properties of determinants

1. A matrix whose determinant value is zero is called a singular matrix, whereas a matrix with a non-zero determinant is called a non-singular matrix. The inverse of a matrix as defined earlier does not exist for a singular matrix.
2. If all the elements of any row of A are zero, its determinant is zero. Thus,

$$|A| = \begin{vmatrix} 0 & 0 & 0 \\ 3 & 4 & 5 \\ 6 & 7 & 9 = 8 \end{vmatrix} = 0.$$

3. $|A| = |A'|$; that is, the determinants of A and A transpose are the same.
4. Interchanging any two rows or any two columns of a matrix A changes the sign of |A|.
5. If every element of a row or a column of A is multiplied by a scalar λ, then |A| is multiplied by λ.
6. If two rows or columns of a matrix are identical, its determinant is zero.
7. If one row or a column of a matrix is a multiple of another row or column of that matrix, its determinant is zero. More generally, if any row (column) of a matrix is a linear combination of other rows (columns), its determinant is zero.
8. $|AB| = |A||B|$; that is, the determinant of the product of two matrices is the product of their (individual) determinants.

Rank of a matrix

The rank of a matrix is the order of the largest square submatrix whose determinant is not zero.

Cofactor

The cofactor of the element a_{ij} of a $n \times n$ matrix A, denoted by c_{ij} c_{ij}, is defined as

$$c_{ij} = (-1)^{i+j}|M_{ij}|$$

$$c_{ij} = (-1)^{i+j}|M_{ij}|.$$

Cofactor Matrix

Replacing the elements a_{ij} of an $n \times n$ matrix A, by cofactors c_{ij}, we obtain a matrix known as the cofactor matrix of A, denoted by $(cof\,A)$.

Adjoint Matrix

The adjoint matrix, written as $(adj\ A)$, is the transpose of the cofactor matrix; that is, $(adj\ A) = (cof\ A)'$.

5. Finding the Inverse of a Square Matrix

If A is square and non-singular (that is, $|A| \neq 0$), its inverse A^{-1} can be found as follows:

$$A^{-1} = \frac{1}{|A|}(adj\ A).$$

The steps involved in the computation are as follows:

1. Find the determinant of A. If it is a non-zero, proceed to step 2.
2. Replace each element of A by its cofactor to obtain the cofactor matrix.
3. Transpose the cofactor matrix to obtain the adjoint matrix.
4. Divide each element of the adjoint matrix by |A|.

Appendix C

Probability

1. Probability Density Function

Let X be a discrete random variable taking the distinct values $\{x_1, x_2, \ldots, x_n\}$. Then, the function

$$f(x_i) = P(X = x_i) > 0 \text{ for } i = 1, \ldots, n,$$

$$f(x) = 0 \text{ for } x \neq x_i,$$

$$\sum_{i=1}^{n} f(x_i) = 1,$$

is called the discrete probability density function (PDF) of X

Let X be a continuous random variable. Then, f is said to be the PDF of X if the following conditions are satisfied:

$$f(x) \geq 0$$

$$\int_{\infty}^{\infty} f(x)dx = 1$$

$$\int_{a}^{b} f(x)dx = P(a \leq x \leq b).$$

$f(x)dx$ is known as the probability element (the probability associated with a small interval of a continuous variable) and $P(a \leq X \leq b)$ means the probability that X lies in the interval a to b.

Joint probability distribution

Discrete Joint PDF

Let X and Y be two random variables. Then, the function

$$f(x, y) = P(X = x \text{ and } Y = y)$$

is known as the joint probability density function and gives the (joint) probability that X takes the value of x and Y takes the value of y.

Marginal probability distribution

Let X and Y be two random variables with variable joint probability density function $f(x, y)$. In relation to $f(x, y)$, the marginal probability density functions are $f(x)$ and $f(y)$, where

$$f(x) = \sum_y f(x, y) \text{ or } f(x) = \int_{-\infty}^{\infty} f(x, y)dy,$$

$$f(y) = \sum_x f(x, y) \text{ or } f(y) = \int_{-\infty}^{\infty} f(x, y)dx.$$

Conditional distribution

As noted in Chapter 2, in regression analysis, we are often interested in studying the behavior of one variable conditional upon the value(s) of another variable(s). This can be done by considering the conditional PDF. The function

$$f(x|y) = P(X = x|Y = y)$$

is known as the conditional PDF of X given that $Y = y$. It gives the probability that X takes on the value of x given that Y has assumed the value y. Similarly,

$$f(y|x) = P(Y = y|X = x),$$

which gives the conditional PDF of Y given $X = x$.

The conditional PDFs satisfy the relations

$$f(x|y) = \frac{f(x, y)}{f(y)} \quad \text{conditional PDF of } X$$

$$f(y|x) = \frac{f(x, y)}{f(x)} \quad \text{conditional PDF of } Y.$$

Independence

Two random variables X and Y are independent if and only if

$$f(x, y) = f(x)f(y),$$

that is, if the joint PDF can be expressed as the product of the marginal PDFs.

2. Characteristics of Probability Distributions

A probability distribution can often be summarized in terms of a few of its characteristics, known as the moments of the distribution. Two of the most widely used moments are the mean, or expected value, and the variance.

Expected value

The expected value of a random variable X, denoted by $E(X)$, is defined as follows:

$$E(X) = \sum_x xf(x) \text{ for discrete rv,}$$

$$E(X) = \int_{-\infty}^{\infty} xf(x)dx \text{ for continuous rv.}$$

Properties of expected value

1. The expected value of a constant is the constant itself. Thus, if b is a constant, E(b)= b.
2. If a and b are constants,

$$E(aX + b) = aE(X) + b.$$

This can be generalized. If $X_1, \ldots, X_N$ are N random variables and $a_1, \ldots, a_N, b$ are constants, then

$$E(a_1X_1 + a_2X_2 + \cdots + a_NX_N + b) = a_1E(X_1) + a_2E(X_2) + \cdots + a_NE(X_N) + b.$$

3. If X and Y are independent random variables, then

$$E(XY) = E(X)E(Y).$$

That is, the expectation of the product XY is the product of the (individual) expectations if X and Y are independent.
4. If X is a random variable with PDF $f(x)$ and if $g(X)$ is any function of X, then

$E[g(X)] = \sum_x g(X)f(x)$ if X is discrete,
$= \int_{-\infty}^{\infty} g(X)f(x)dx$ if X is continuous.
Thus, if g(X)=X^{2},
$E(X^2) = \sum_x x^2 f(X)$ if X is discrete,
$= \int_{-\infty}^{\infty} x^2 f(X)dx$ if X is continuous.

Variance

Let X be a random variable and let $E(X) = \mu$. The spread of the X values around the expected value can be measured by the variance, which is defined as

$$\text{var}(X) = \sigma_x^2 = E(X - \mu)^2.$$

The positive square root of σ_x^2, σ_x, is defined as the standard deviation of X. The variance or standard deviation gives an indication of how closely or widely the individual X values are spread around their mean value.

For computational convenience, the variance formula given earlier can also be expressed as

$$\begin{aligned}\text{var}(X) = \sigma_x^2 &= E(X - \mu)^2 \\ &= E(X^2) - \mu^2 \\ &= E(X^2) - [E(X)]^2.\end{aligned}$$

Properties of variance

1. $E(X - \mu)^2 = E(X^2) - \mu^2$, as noted before.
2. The variance of a constant is zero.
3. If a and b are constants, then

$$\text{var}(aX + b) = a^2\text{var}(X).$$

4. If X and Y are independent random variables, then

$$\text{var}(X+Y) = \text{var}(X) + \text{var}(Y)$$
$$\text{var}(X-Y) = \text{var}(X) + \text{var}(Y).$$

This can be generalized to more than two independent variables.
5. If X and Y are independent rvs and a and b are constants, then

$$\text{var}(aX+bY) = a^2\text{var}(X) + b^2\text{var}(Y).$$

Covariance

Let X and Y be two rvs with means μ_X and μ_Y, respectively. Then, the covariance between the two variables is defined as

$$\text{cov}(X,Y) = \sigma_{XY} = E[(X-\mu_X)(Y-\mu_Y)].$$

It can be readily seen that the variance of a variable is the covariance of that variable with itself. The covariance is computed as follows:

$$\text{cov}(X,Y) = \sum_y \sum_x (x-\mu_X)(y-\mu_Y) \times f(x.y) \ if \ X \ and \ Y \ are \ discrete,$$
$$\text{cov}(X,Y) = \int_{-\infty}^{\infty}\int_{-\infty}^{\infty} (x-\mu_X)(y-\mu_Y) \times f(x.y) \ if \ X \ and \ Y \ are \ continuous.$$

Properties of covariance

1. If X and Y are independent, their covariance is zero,

$$\text{Cov}(X,Y) = E(XY) - \mu_X\mu_Y = 0.$$

2. For constants a, b,

$$\text{cov}(aX+bY) = ab \cdot \text{cov}(X,Y).$$

Correlation coefficient

The (population) correlation coefficient ρ is defined as

$$\rho_{XY} = \frac{\text{cov}(X, Y)}{\sigma_X \sigma_Y}.$$

Thus defined, p is a measure of linear association between two variables and lies between -1 and $+1$, -1 indicating perfect negative association and $+1$ indicating perfect positive association.

Variances of correlated variables

Let X and Y be two rvs. Then,

$$\begin{aligned}
\text{var}(X+Y) &= \text{var}(X) + \text{var}(Y) + 2\text{cov}(X, Y) \\
&= \text{var}(X) + \text{var}(Y) + 2p\sigma_x\sigma_y \\
\text{var}(X-Y) &= \text{var}(X) + \text{var}(Y) - 2\text{cov}(X, Y) \\
&= \text{var}(X) + \text{var}(Y) - 2p\sigma_x\sigma_y.
\end{aligned}$$

The preceding result can be generalized as follows:

Let $\sum_{i=1}^{n} X_i = X_1 + X_2 + \cdots + X_n$, then the variance of the sum is

$$\begin{aligned}
\text{var}\left(\sum_{i=1}^{n} X_i\right) &= \sum_{i=1}^{n} \text{var}(X_i) + 2\sum_{i,j:i<j} \text{cov}(X_i, X_j) = \sum_{i=1}^{n} \text{var}(X_i) \\
&\quad + 2\sum_{i,j:i<j} \rho_{X_i X_j} \sigma_{X_i} \sigma_{X_j}.
\end{aligned}$$

This formula is the basis of diversification in an investment portfolio, since assets with negatively correlated returns reduce the portfolio variance.

Conditional expectation

Let $f(x, y)$ be the joint PDF of random variables X and Y. The conditional expectation of X, given $Y = y$, is defined as

$$\begin{aligned}
E(X|Y=y) &= \sum_x x f(x|Y=y) \quad &&\text{if X is discrete} \\
&= \int_{-\infty}^{\infty} x f(x|Y=y)dx &&\text{if X is continuous,}
\end{aligned}$$

where $E(X|Y = y)$ means the conditional expectation of X given $Y = y$ and where $f(x|Y = y)$ is the conditional PDF of X.

Conditional variance

The conditional variance of X given $Y = y$ is defined as

$$\begin{aligned}\text{var}(X|Y = y) &= E\{[X - E(X|Y = y)]^2|Y = y\}\\ &= \sum_x [X - E(X|Y = y)]^2 f(x|Y = y) \quad \text{if X is discrete}\\ &= \int_{-\infty}^{\infty} [x - E(X|Y = y)]^2 f(x|Y = y)dx \quad \text{if X is continuous.}\end{aligned}$$

Properties of conditional expectation and variance

1. If $f(X)$ is a function of X, then $E(f(X)|X) = f(X)$, that is, the function of X behaves as a constant in computation of its expectation, conditional on X.
2. If X and Y are independent, $E(Y|X) = E(Y)$. That is, if X and Y are independent random variables, then the conditional expectation of Y, given X, is the same as the unconditional expectation of Y.
3. The law of iterated expectations:

$$E(Y) = E_X[E(Y|X)].$$

   This is known as the law of iterated expectations, which in the present context states that the marginal, or unconditional, expectation of Y is equal to the expectation of its conditional expectation, the symbol E_X denoting that the expectation is taken over the values of X. Put simply, this law states that if we first obtain $E(Y|X)$ as a function of X and take its expected value over the distribution of X values, you wind up with $E(Y)$, the unconditional expectations of Y.
4. If X and Y are independent, then $\text{var}(Y|X) = \text{var}(Y)$.
5. $\text{var}(Y) = E[\text{var}(Y|X)] + \text{var}[E(Y|X)]$; that is, the (unconditional) variance of Y is equal to expectation of the conditional variance of Y plus the variance of the conditional expectation of Y.

Higher moments

Although mean, variance, and covariance are the most frequently used summary measures of univariate and multivariate PDFs, we occasionally need to consider higher moments of the PDFs, such as the third and fourth moments. The third and fourth moments of a univariate PDF $f(x)$ around its mean value μ are defined as

$$\text{Third moment:} \quad E(X-\mu)^3.$$
$$\text{Fourth moment:} \quad E(X-\mu)^4.$$

The third and fourth moments of a distribution are often used in studying the "shape" of a probability distribution, in particular, its skewness, S (i.e., lack of symmetry), and kurtosis, K (i.e., tallness or flatness).

One measure of skewness is defined as

$$\begin{aligned} S &= \frac{E(X-\mu)^3}{\sigma^3}, \\ &= \frac{\text{third moment about the mean}}{\text{cube of the standard deviation}}. \end{aligned}$$

A commonly used measure of kurtosis is given by

$$\begin{aligned} K &= \frac{E(X-\mu)^4}{[E(X-\mu)^2]^2}, \\ &= \frac{\text{fourth moment about the mean}}{\text{square of the second moment}}. \end{aligned}$$

PDFs with values of K less than 3 are called platykurtic (far or short-tailed), and those with values greater than 3 are called leptokurtic (slim or long-tailed). A PDF with a kurtosis value of 3 is known as mesokurtic, of which the normal distribution is the prime example.

The measures of skewness and kurtosis can be combined to determine whether a random variable follows a normal distribution. Recall that our hypothesis-testing procedure, as in the t and F tests, is based on the assumption (at least in small or finite samples) that the underlying distribution of the variable (or sample statistic) is normal. It is therefore very important to find out in concrete applications whether this assumption is fulfilled.

Appendix D

Important Probability Distributions

1. Normal Distribution

The best known of all the theoretical probability distributions is the normal distribution, whose bell-shaped picture is familiar to anyone with a modicum of statistical knowledge.

A (continuous) random variable X is said to be normally distributed if its PDF has the following form:

$$f(x) = \frac{1}{\sigma\sqrt{2\pi}} \exp\left(-\frac{1}{2}\frac{(x-\mu)^2}{\sigma^2}\right) - \infty < x < \infty,$$

where μ and $\sigma 2$, known as the parameters of the distribution, are, respectively, the mean and the variance of the distribution. Figure D.1 displays the normal pdf.

The properties of this distribution are as follows:

1. It is symmetrical around its mean value.
2. Approximately 68 percent of the area under the normal curve lies between the values $(\mu - \sigma)$ and $(\mu + \sigma)$, about 95 percent of the area lies between the values $(\mu - 2\sigma)$ and $(\mu + 2\sigma)$, and about 99.7 percent of the area lies between the values $(\mu - 3\sigma)$ and $(\mu + 3\sigma)$.

   The normal distribution depends on the two parameters μ and σ^2, so once these are specified, one can find the probability that X will lie within a certain interval by using the PDF of the normal distribution. By convention, we denote a normally distributed variable as

$$X \sim N(\mu, \sigma^2).$$

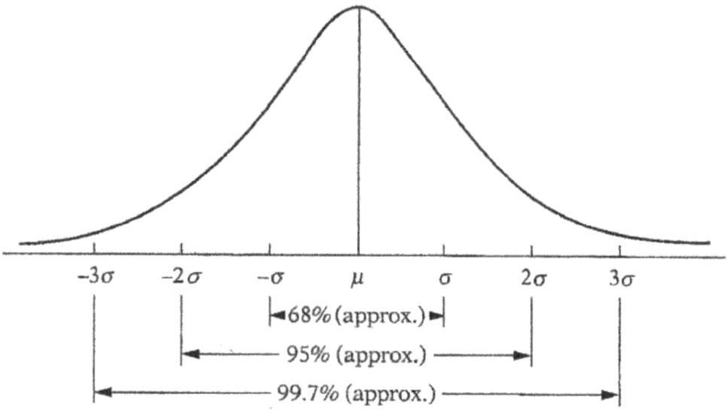

Figure D.1. Normal pdf.

3. We convert the given normally distributed variable X with mean μ and σ^2 into a standardized normal variable Z by the following transformation:

$$Z = \frac{X - \mu}{\sigma}.$$

An important property of any standardized variable is that its mean value is zero and its variance is unity. Thus, Z has zero mean and unit variance. Substituting z into the normal PDF given previously, we obtain

$$f(z) = \frac{1}{\sqrt{2\pi}} e^{-\frac{z^2}{2\sigma^2}}$$

which is the PDF of the standardized normal variable. So,

$$Z \sim N(0, 1).$$

For the normal variable X, we have

$$P[X \leq x] = P\left[Z \leq \frac{x - \mu}{\sigma}\right].$$

So, tables for Z are used to find probabilities for X.

4. Let $X_1 \sim N(\mu_1, \sigma_1^2)$ and $X_2 \sim N(\mu_2, \sigma_2^2)$ and assume that they are independent. Now, consider the linear combination

$$Y = aX_1 + bX_2,$$

where a and b are constants. Then, it can be shown that

$$Y \sim N(a\mu_1 + b\mu_2, a^2\sigma_1^2 + b^2\sigma_2^2).$$

This result, which states that a linear combination of normally distributed variables is itself normally distributed, can be easily generalized to a linear combination of more than two normally distributed variables.

5. Central limit theorem.
   Let $\{X_1, \ldots, X_n\}$ denote n independent random variables, all of which have the same PDF with mean $= \mu$ and variance $= \sigma^2$. Let $\bar{X} = \sum X_i/n$ (i.e., the sample mean). Then, as n increases indefinitely (i.e., $n \to \infty$),

$$\bar{X}_{n\to\infty} \sim N\left(\mu, \frac{\sigma^2}{n}\right).$$

   That is, $\bar{X}$ approaches the normal distribution with mean μ and variance $\frac{\sigma^2}{n}$. Notice that this result holds true regardless of the form of the PDF. As a result, it follows that

$$Z = \frac{\bar{X} - \mu}{\sigma\sqrt{n}} \sim N(0, 1).$$

   That is, Z is a standardized normal variable.
6. The third and fourth moments of the normal distribution around the mean value are as follows:

$$\text{Third moment:} \quad E(X - \mu)^3 = 0,$$
$$\text{Fourth moment:} \quad E(X - \mu)^4 = 3\sigma^4.$$

   Note: All odd-powered moments about the mean value of a normally distributed variable are zero.
7. As a result, and following the measures of skewness and kurtosis discussed earlier, for a normal PDF skewness $= 0$ and Kurtosis $= 3$; that is, a normal distribution is symmetric and mesokurtic. Therefore, a simple test of normality is to find out whether the computed values of skewness and kurtosis depart from the norms of 0 and 3. This is in fact the logic underlying the Jarque–Bera (JB) test of normality:

$$JB = n\left[\frac{S^2}{6} + \frac{(K-3)^2}{24}\right],$$

   where S stands for skewness and K for Kurtosis. Under the null hypothesis of normality, JB is distributed as a chi-square variable with 2 df.

8. The mean and the variance of a normally distributed random variable are independent in that one is not a function of the other.
9. If X and Y are jointly normally distributed, then they are independent if, and only if, the covariance between them [i.e., $\text{cov}\,(X, Y)$] is zero.

2. The χ^2 (Chi-square) Distribution

Let $(Z_1, \ldots, Z_k)$ be independent standardized normal variables (i.e., normal variables with zero mean and unit variance). Then, the random variable

$$Z = \sum_{i=1}^{k} Z_i^2$$

is said to possess the chi-square distribution with k degrees of freedom (df), where the term df means the number of independent quantities in the previous sum. A chi-square-distributed variable is denoted by χ_k^2, where the subscript k indicates the df. Geometrically, the chi-square distribution appears in Figure D.2.

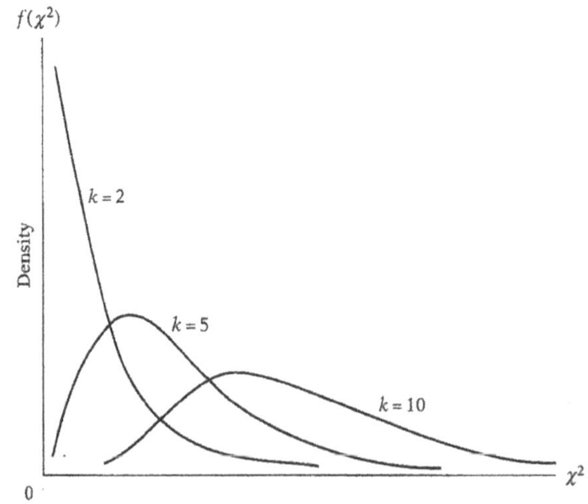

Figure D.2. Chi-square distribution.

Properties of the χ^2_k distribution

1. As Figure D.2 shows, the χ^2_k distribution is a skewed distribution, the degree of skewness depending on the df. For comparatively few dfs, the distribution is highly skewed to the right; but as the number of dfs increases, the distribution becomes increasingly symmetrical. As a matter of fact, for dfs in excess of 100, the variable

$$\sqrt{2\chi^2_k} - \sqrt{2k-1}$$

can be treated as a standardized normal variable, where k is the df.
2. The mean of the chi-square distribution is k, and its variance is $2k$, where k is the df.
3. If Z_1 and Z_2 are two independent chi-square variables with k_1 and k_2 df, then the sum $Z_1 + Z_2$ is also a chi-square variable with df $= k_1 + k_2$.

3. Student's t Distribution

If Z_1 is a standardized normal variable [that is, $Z_1 \sim N(0,1)$] and the variable Z_2 follows a chi-square distribution with k df and is distributed independently of Z_1, then the variable is defined as

$$t = \frac{Z_1}{\sqrt{(Z_2/k)}} = \frac{Z_1\sqrt{k}}{\sqrt{Z_2}}.$$

Follows a Student's t distribution with k df. A t-distributed variable is often designated as t_k, where the subscript k denotes the df. Geometrically, the t distribution is shown in Figure D.3.

Properties of the Student's t distribution

1. As Figure D.3 shows, the t distribution, like the normal distribution, is symmetrical, but it is flatter than the normal distribution. But as the df increases, the t distribution approximates the normal distribution.
2. The mean of the t distribution is zero, and its variance is $k/(k-2)$.

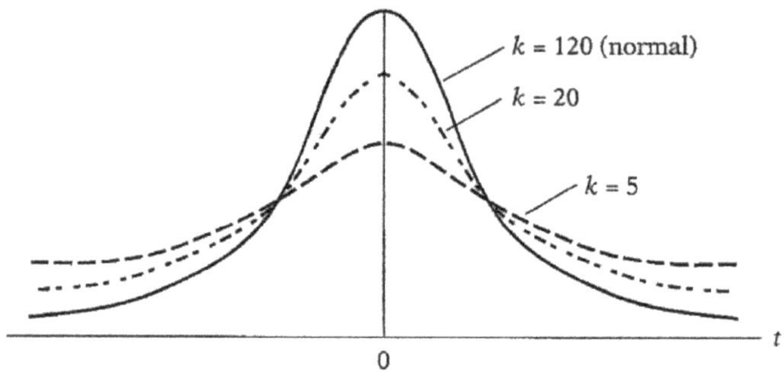

Figure D.3. Student's t distribution.

4. The F Distribution

If Z_1 and Z_2 are independently distribution chi-square variables with k_1 and k_2 df, respectively, the variable

$$F = \frac{Z_1/k_1}{Z_2/k_2}$$

follows (Fisher's) F distribution with k_1 and k_2 df. An F-distributed variable is denoted by F_{k_1,k_2} where the subscripts indicate the df associated with the two Z variables, k_1 being called the numerator df and k_2 the denominator df. The F distribution is shown in Figure D.4.

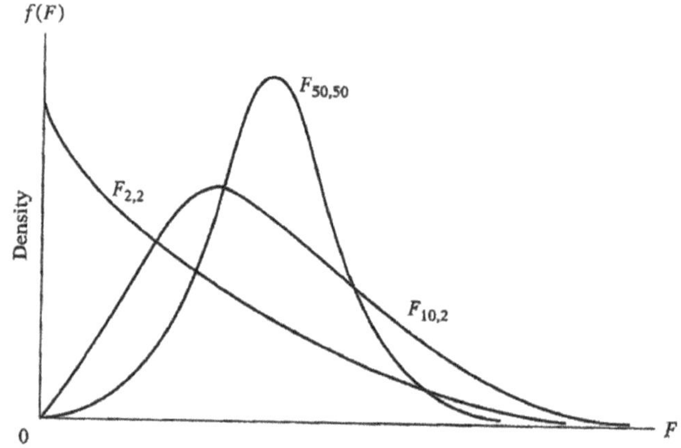

Figure D.4. F distribution.

The F distribution properties:

1. Like the chi-square distribution, the F distribution is skewed to the right. But it can be shown that as k_1 and k_2 become large, the F distribution approaches the normal distribution.
2. The mean value of an F-distributed variable is $k_1/(k_2-2)$, which is defined for $k_2 > 2$, and its variance is

$$\frac{2k_2^2(k_1+k_2-2)}{k_1(k_2-2)^2(k_2-4)},$$

which is defined as $k_2 > 4$.
3. The square of a t-distributed random variable with k df has an F distribution with 1 and k df. Symbolically,

$$t_k^2 = F_{1,k}.$$

4. If the denominator df, k_2, is fairly large, the following relationship holds between the F and the chi-square distributions $k_1 F = \chi^2_{k_1}$.
   That is, for fairly large denominator df, the numerator df times the F value is approximately the same as a chi-square value with numerator df.

5. Binomial Distribution

The random variable X is said to follow a Bernoulli distribution if its probability density (PDF) is

$$P(X = 0) = 1 - p,$$
$$P(X = 1) = p,$$

where $p, 0 \leq p \leq 1$, is the probability that some event is a "success," such as the probability of obtaining a head in a toss of a coin. For such a variable,

$$E(X) = p,$$
$$\mathrm{Var}(X) = pq,$$

where $q = (1 - p)$, that is, the probability of a "failure."

The binomial distribution is the generalization of the Bernoulli distribution. Let n denote the number of independent trials, each of which results in a "success" with probability p and a "failure" with a probability $q = (1 - p)$. If X represents the number of successes in the n trials, then X has the binomial distribution whose PDF is

$$f(X) = \binom{n}{x} p^x (1-p)^{n-x},$$

where x represents the number of successes in n trials and where

$$\binom{n}{x} = \frac{n!}{x!(n-x)!},$$

where $n!$, read as n factorial, means $n(n-1)(n-2)\ldots 1$.

The binomial is a two-parameter distribution, n and p. For this distribution,

$$E(X) = np,$$
$$\text{var}(X) = np(1-p).$$

6. Poisson Distribution

A random X variable is said to have the Poisson distribution if its PDF is

$$f(x) = \frac{e^{\lambda}\lambda^x}{x!}, \quad \text{for } x = 0, 1, 2, \ldots, \lambda > 0.$$

The Poisson distribution depends on a single parameter, λ. A distinguishing feature of the Poisson distribution is that its variance is equal to its expected value, which is λ. That is,

$$E(X) = \text{var}(X) = \lambda.$$

The Poisson model is used to model rare or infrequent phenomena, such as the number of phone calls received in a span of, say, 5 minutes, or the number of speeding tickets received in a span of an hour, or the number of patents received by a firm, say, in a year.

Index

E

F

G

H

I

J

K

L

www.ingramcontent.com/pod-product-compliance
Lightning Source LLC
LaVergne TN
LVHW051056210926
848486LV00002B/125